Jesus and Addiction to Origins

NAASR Working Papers

Series Editor: Brad Stoddard, McDaniel College in Westminster, Maryland.

NAASR Working Papers provides a venue for publishing the latest research carried out by scholars who understand religion to be an historical element of human cognition, practice, and organization. Whether monographs or multi-authored collections, the volumes published in this series all reflect timely, cutting edge work that takes seriously both the need for developing bold theories as well as rigorous testing and debate concerning the scope of our tools and the implications of our studies. NAASR Working Papers therefore assess the current state-of-the-art while charting new ways forward in the academic study of religion.

Published

Constructing "Data" in Religious Studies: Examining the Architecture of the Academy
Edited by Leslie Dorrough Smith

Hijacked: A Critical Treatment of the Public Rhetoric of Good and Bad Religion
Edited by Leslie Dorrough Smith, Steffen Führding, and Adrian Hermann

Method Today: Redescribing Approaches to the Study of Religion
Edited by Brad Stoddard

"Religion" in Theory and Practice: Demystifying the Field for Burgeoning Academics
Russell T. McCutcheon

Remembering J. Z. Smith: A Career and its Consequence
Edited by Emily D. Crews and Russell T. McCutcheon

Forthcoming

Imagining Smith: Mapping Methods in the Study of Religion
Barbara Krawcowicz

Key Categories in the Study of Religion: Contexts and Critiques
Edited by Rebekka King

Jesus and Addiction to Origins

Toward an Anthropocentric Study of Religion

Willi Braun

Edited by Russell T. McCutcheon

SHEFFIELD UK   BRISTOL CT

Published by Equinox Publishing Ltd.

UK: Office 415, The Workstation, 15 Paternoster Row, Sheffield, South Yorkshire S1 2BX

USA: ISD, 70 Enterprise Drive, Bristol, CT 06010

www.equinoxpub.com

First published 2020

Preface © Willi Braun 2020
Selection, editorial apparatus and Foreword © Russell McCutcheon 2020
Chapters 1–10 © Willi Braun, reproduced with permission of original publishers as listed under "Sources" on pages xiii–xv
Afterword © William E. Arnal 2020

All rights reserved. No part of this publication may be reproduced or transmitted in any form or by any means, electronic or mechanical, including photocopying, recording or any information storage or retrieval system, without prior permission in writing from the publishers.

ISBN-13 978 1 78179 942 0 (hardback)
         978 1 78179 943 7 (paperback)
         978 1 78179 944 4 (ePDF)

British Library Cataloguing-in-Publication Data

A catalogue record for this book is available from the British Library.

Library of Congress Cataloging-in-Publication Data

Names: Braun, Willi, 1954- author. | McCutcheon, Russell T., 1961- editor.
Title: Jesus and addiction to origins : toward an anthropocentric study of religion / Willi Braun ; edited by Russell T McCutcheon.
Description: Bristol : Equinox Publishing Ltd., 2020. | Series: NAASR working papers | Includes bibliographical references and index. | Summary: "This collection of essays constitute an extended argument for an anthropocentric, human-focused, study of religious practices"-- Provided by publisher.
Identifiers: LCCN 2020010245 (print) | LCCN 2020010246 (ebook) | ISBN 9781781799420 (hardback) | ISBN 9781781799437 (paperback) | ISBN 9781781799444 (ebook)
Subjects: LCSH: Church history--Primitive and early church, ca. 30-600. | Rites and ceremonies. | Religion--Philosophy.
Classification: LCC BR162.3 .B73 2020 (print) | LCC BR162.3 (ebook) | DDC 200.7--dc23
LC record available at https://lccn.loc.gov/2020010245
LC ebook record available at https://lccn.loc.gov/2020010246

Typeset by JS Typesetting Ltd, Porthcawl, Mid Glamorgan

Contents

	Editor's Foreword—Russell T. McCutcheon	vii
	Preface	xi
	Sources	xiii
	Part I: Generalities	
1	Religion: A Guide	3
2	The Irony of Religion	17
3	Introducing Religion	26
	Part II: Particularities	
4	Jesus and Addiction to Origins	41
5	Christian Origins and the Gospel of Mark: Fragments of a Story	59
6	The Sayings Gospel Q and the Making of an Early Jesus Group	76
7	In the Beginning Was Not the Word	98
8	Sex, Gender and Empire: Virgins and Eunuchs in the Ancient Mediterranean World	121
9	Physiotherapy of Femininity in Early Christianity: Ideology and Practice	141
10	"Our Religion Compels Us to Make a Distinction": Prolegomena on Meals and Social Formation	165
	Part III: Afterword	
	Reification, Religion, and the Relics of the Past—*William E. Arnal*	181
	Index	189

Editor's Foreword

Russell T. McCutcheon

I don't recall the first time that I met Willi Braun; it was likely around 1987 or 1988, when I was an M.A. student at what was called the Centre for Religious Studies, the cross-disciplinary graduate unit at the University of Toronto, then up on the fourteenth floor of Robarts Library; Willi was already enrolled in his doctoral degree and I was to earn my own Ph.D. there as well, two years behind him. (Eventually, the Centre was moved, renamed, and finally collapsed into what had been the undergraduate Department of Religious Studies, a lamentable devolution, at least from some of our points of view, but that's a story for another preface.) I remember him always looking like he was fresh from biking around the city and, over time, getting to know him in the library cafeteria, bumping into each other and having a coffee. We eventually joined the editorial team of *Method & Theory in the Study of Religion* at the same time, in 1990, just as issue 2(2) was being published, which was the beginning of what became our career-long collaboration—one that has resulted in a variety of publications but which also, behind the scenes, meant that he read and commented on much of what I've written over the years, before anyone else ever saw it.

His dissertation, defended in 1993, was entitled "The Use of Mediterranean Banquet Traditions in Luke 14:1-14" and it became his first book, *Feasting and Social Rhetoric in Luke 14*, published as volume 85 in the Society for New Testament Studies Monograph Series (Cambridge University Press, 1995). Like the essays collected here, his specialty in Christian origins is obvious, perhaps making both our collaboration and my role as editor of this volume all the more curious to some. But given the shift that a few of us experimented with, early on, in our Toronto days (and which has defined much of the work that this small group has produced since then), it makes sense to me. For only if you think that the things that we study as scholars of religion are somehow set apart and special would you conclude that someone interested in the politics of the modern field would not have something in common with a person studying, among other things, feasting in antiquity.

On other occasions I've reflected on another friendship in grad school, with a history doctoral student then studying late-nineteenth-century Englishness— someone with whom I obviously had nothing in common, at least at the level of data, but with whom I had much in common at the level of theory; for after all, both of us were interested in how group identities formed and were reproduced.

At the time I just happened to be using as an example the formation of a mid to late-twentieth century scholarly discipline. So too with Willi, someone with whom I shared questions of theory about this thing that many of us call religion. In fact, I would credit my ability to write that preceding sentence, which considers something that we might study as an example—an e.g., as we sometimes say it— thanks to him. For, as I've also noted in print before, it was Willi who (in that same library, as I recall) recommended that I read this J. Z. Smith fellow (from whom we eventually picked up that habit of talking about e.g.s, by the way), someone often working on Christian origins materials, sure, but who was invariably doing so in the service of a larger and more general point, ultimately making a claim about how we, as scholars, all ought to be going about our work, regardless the region, group, or historical period that we happened to study. That too was sometime in the late 1980s, or maybe when Smith's *Drudgery Divine* was first published in 1990. It's a piece of advice that I followed (as I've tried to do with all advice he offered) and one that has not just changed my thinking of a host of topics but also defined much of my own career.

And that's the sort of influence that, I would argue, Willi has had on the whole field for the past thirty years—subtle yet significant and long-lasting. The subtle part is just his style; if you've met him, sat in a class or a meeting with him, or maybe heard him deliver a paper at a conference, you'd already know that he's understated and quiet, thinking a fair bit about what he'll say, long before saying it. But that affords him the opportunity to zero in on something of consequence— something that, if addressed the right way, with precision and care, might ripple through much of the topic under consideration, perhaps shifting how we saw the problem we were first interested in examining. Given the number of scholars whom I know to have also benefited from their friendship and collaboration with him, I think it fair to say that they would likely agree that his impact on the field, while being tremendous, has largely been unsung, precisely because of its strategic subtlety, often happening one-on-one, in conversations or via email threads. For though he has held executive offices in some of our field's professional leading associations (both his presidency of the North American Association for the Study of Religion [2008–2011] and the Canadian Society of Biblical Studies [2016–2017] come to mind), played leadership roles in two Departments (Bishop's University, in Quebec, and then the University of Alberta in Edmonton), long participated in the Society of Biblical Literature's ground-break project redescribing the origins of Christianity, and sat on national grants committees as well as presented his work at international congresses, I think that it's his always collegial and gentle nudging of the field, usually carried out behind-the-scenes, that deserves public notice.

And so we come to this collection of his essays (one was co-written with Bill Arnal, another Toronto grad from those days, also a longtime friend and collaborator of Willis's, and who has also authored the Afterword that closes this volume), most of which are on topics in the study of early Christianity but, come to think of it, none of which are solely or even mainly on that topic; instead, at least as I read them, each invites the reader to consider an e.g., sometimes in depth and in detail, as a way to think through a problem that we also see elsewhere in the field, usually a problem in method or a problem in theory—*how* we do what we do and *why* we do it in the first place. For nothing considered here is self-evidently important; rather, its importance always derives from the relationships in which we place whatever it is that we're studying, the specific questions that it helps us to answer, and the general things that we learn that can be applied elsewhere. Much like Willi's advice that I read Smith, despite not working on the same material, my advice is that readers who have no working knowledge of the data of early Christianity consider tackling the following chapters; for while you'll certainly learn a thing or two about this sub-field you'll also see links to analogous issues in your own domain, just as with reading Smith. (Those already working in Christian origins will undoubtedly benefit from the following chapters as well, given that Willi's uncompromising anthropocentric approach, as he calls it, may even strike some of them as challenging a few long-held assumptions.) For, just as with J. Z., Willi's work gets us thinking about issues of definition and description, issues of comparison and explanation, using the area in which he has most historical and linguistic familiarity as an opportunity to mull over what it is that we as scholars do when we say that we study religion in a way different from how its own participants may already be talking and writing about it.

If this is how readers approach the following essays, then past experience tells me that they'll come away with new insights into their own work, focused as it is either on the things people do or what they left behind after they were gone, finding it in places and at times that are probably drastically different from the ancient world of the earliest Christians. And if that happens, as I'm guessing it will, then they'll come to appreciate what some of us have long known about just how effective Willi's subtle provocations can be.

Preface

The essays in the first part of this volume are offered in the service of a plea for an anthropocentric, human-focused study of religious practices. By no means am I the first, much less the only to make this plea, but it deserves to be made again—and again—in the theoretically timid, sometimes confused field of the study of religion. The basic premise of the argument that the essays make in concert is that all human performances that present themselves as religious are human productions. There is no more-than-human substance or kernel in these products, no divine inspiration or revelation, no connection to superhuman knowledge or authority, although such connection is usually claimed by these products or by humans who treasure and revere them. That is all to say, as Maurice Bloch, Bruce Lincoln and many others have argued, there is nothing special, nothing extraordinary about human behaviors and constructs that claim religious status and authority. They are fundamentally human and so the scholar is engaged in nothing more or less than studying humans across time and place and all their complex existence that includes creating more-than-human beings and realities.

The second part contains essays that address practices, rhetoric and other data in early Christianities within Greco-Roman cultures and religions. The underlying aim is to insert studies of the New Testament and non-canonical texts, most often presented as "biblical studies," into the anthropocentric study of religion. A general reading of biblical scholarship, unabatedly prolific in the form of commentaries, monographs and articles in the field's many scholarly journals, not to speak of the hundreds of papers read at the annual Society of Biblical Literature meetings, requires the impression that the predominant and enduring scholarly practices in the field are what the late J. Z. Smith called "an affair of native exegesis," though highly learned, complexly technical and often arcane. Of course, there are many and profound exceptions, but the exceptions underscore the field's presumption that the Christian bible is a sacred text whose principal *raison d'être* is to stand, fetish-like, as the foundational and highest authority in matters moral, ritual or theological. All in all, the tactics of interpreting the texts are "preservationist," as Smith also noted, implicitly in the service of the faith communities that claim these texts as their sacred authorities. It is true that in the last several decades we have seen numerous "external" literary or social theories and methods enter the circle of biblical studies, but they too have been coopted for the preservationist exegetical agenda of the field. Ward Blanton and Yvonne Sherwood are very much on the mark when they claim, in engagement with J. Z. Smith, that "'[a]dapted' and softened versions of literary and social theories seem specifically designed to allow biblical scholars to steal the cache of theory and yet escape the 'cost'"

("Bible/Religion/Critique," in Richard King, ed., *Religion, Theory, Critique: Classic and Contemporary Approaches and Methodologies*, New York: Columbia University Press, 2017, 44). I trust that the essays in the second part of this volume avoid the preservationist, even when apparently innovative, tendencies of biblical studies. Whether I have been successful—well, may the reader decide.

This volume would not have come to be except for the work of my long-time friend and intellectual comrade, Russell McCutcheon, who first persuaded me to compile these essays, then insisted on taking on the chore of editing them—with the assistance of Sierra Lawson, now a doctoral student at the University of North Carolina. I could not be more grateful to Russell and Sierra. The fact that another long-time friend and comrade in thought, Bill Arnal, agreed to write an afterword completes the volume in a way that both cheers me and instructs me on my own work. Thank you. This book appears in the North American Association for the study of Religion Working Papers. I am very proud of that and grateful to Brad Stoddard for including it in the series, published by the fearless and innovative Janet Joyce of Equinox Publishing.

Willi Braun
September 2020

Sources

Chapter 1

"Religion: A Guide" is a version of "Religion," in *Guide to the Study of Religion*, 3–18 (ed. Willi Braun and Russell T. McCutcheon; London: Cassell, 2000). Material in this chapter is used by the kind permission of Bloomsbury Publishing Plc.

Chapter 2

"The Irony of Religion," co-authored with William Arnal, was published in *Failure and Nerve in the Academic Study of Religion*, 230–238 (ed. William Arnal, Willi Braun and Russell T. McCutcheon; Sheffield: Equinox, 2012). Material in this chapter is used by the kind permission of Routledge, part of the Taylor and Francis group.

Chapter 3

"Introducing Religion" appeared in *Introducing Religion: Essays in Honor of Jonathan Z. Smith*, 480–495 (ed. Willi Braun and Russell T. McCutcheon; London: Equinox, 2008); portions were first presented to the symposium "The Study of Religion as a Discipline," Finnish Society for the Study of Religion, University of Turku, Finland; March 26, 2007, then published in *Temenos* 43 (2007): 223–242. Material in this chapter is used by the kind permission of Routledge, part of the Taylor and Francis group.

Chapter 4

"Jesus and Addiction to Origins" is a revised and combined version of "The Past as Simulacrum in the Canonical Narratives of Christian Origin," *Religion & Theology: A Journal of Contemporary Religious Discourse* 8(3/4) (2001): 213–228; and "'Wir haben doch den amerikanischen Jesus'. Das amerikanische Jesus Seminar: Eine Standortbestimmung," *Zeitschrift für Neues Testament* 16(8) (2005): 30–40. Material in this chapter is used by permission of Koninklijke Brill NV of the Netherlands.

Chapter 5

"Christian Origins and the Gospel of Mark: Fragments of a Story" was given as the presidential address to the Canadian Society of Biblical Studies, 2017, then published in *Bulletin of the Canadian Society of Biblical Studies* 77 (2017/2018): 1–25; an earlier, briefer version was published as "Mark and Christian Origins," in *Method and Theory in the Study of Religion: Working Papers from Hannover*, 153–175 (ed. Steffen Führding; Leiden: Brill, 2007); some material also is found in "The First Shall Be Last: The Gospel of Mark After the First Century," in *Chasing Down Religion in the Sights of History and the Cognitive Sciences: Essays in Honor of Luther H. Martin*, 41–57 (ed. Panayotis Pachis and Donald Wiebe; Thessaloniki: Barbounakis, 2010). Material in this chapter is used by permission of: Koninklijke Brill NV of the Netherlands; the Canadian Society of Biblical Studies; and Barbounakis Publications of Thessaloniki, Greece.

Chapter 6

"The Sayings Gospel Q and the Making of an Early Jesus Group" is a moderately revised version of "The Schooling of a Galilean Jesus Association (The Sayings Gospel Q)," in *Redescribing Christian Origins*, 43–66 (ed. Ron Cameron and Merrill Miller; SBL Symposium Series; Atlanta, GA: Scholars Press; Leiden: Brill, 2004). The revision does not include erasing traces that signal the original purpose and audience of this essay, as will be seen in references to the "redescription project" and "us" and "we," referring in the first instance to members of the SBL Redescription seminar, but not restricted to them. A briefer version was first published as "Socio-Mythic Invention, Graeco-Roman Schools, and the Sayings Gospel Q," *Method & Theory in the Study of Religion* 11 (1999): 210–235. Material in this chapter is used by permission of Koninklijke Brill NV of the Netherlands.

Chapter 7

"In the Beginning Was Not the Word" is a version of "Modes of Religiosity and Theories of Persuasion—To Early Christianities" in *Imagistic Traditions in the Roman World: A Cognitive Modeling of History of Religions Research* (ed. Luther H. Martin and Panayotis Pachis; Thessaloniki: Vanias, 2007). Material in this chapter is used by the kind permission of Vanias Publishers of Thessaloniki, Greece.

Chapter 8

"Sex, Gender and Empire: Virgins and Eunuchs in the Ancient Mediterranean World" was published as "Virgins, Eunuchs, Empire," *Acta Patristica et Byzantina* 21 (2010): 19–38; a briefer version appeared as "Celibacy in the Greco-Roman World," in *Celibacy and Religious Traditions*, 21–40 (ed. Carl Olson; Oxford: Oxford University Press, 2008). Material in this chapter is reproduced by permission of Oxford University Press.

Chapter 9

"Physiotherapy of Femininity in Early Christianity: Ideology and Practice" was more briefly presented at a "Body and Religion" seminar at the University of South Africa (UNISA) in the summer of 2000, and at the meeting of the Association for Research in Religious Studies and Theology at the University of Alberta in the spring of 2002. A portion of this paper appeared as "Body, Character, and the Problem of Femaleness in Early Christian Discourse" in *Religion & Theology: A*

Journal of Contemporary Religious Discourse 9(1/2) (2002), 108–117; portions of this essay are also found in "Fugitives from Femininity: Greco-Roman Gender Ideology and the Limits of Early Christian Women's Emancipation," in *Fabrics of Discourse: Essays in Honor of Vernon K. Robbins*, 317–332 (ed. David B. Gowler, Gregory L. Bloomquist and Duane Watson; Harrisburg, PA: Trinity Press International, 2003); and in *Text and Artifact in the Religions of Mediterranean Antiquity: Essays in Honour of Peter Richardson*, 209–230 (ed. Stephen G. Wilson; Studies in Christianity and Judaism/Études sur le christianisme et le judaïsme, 9; Waterloo, Ontario: Wilfrid Laurier University Press, 2000). Material in this chapter is used by permission of: Koninklijke Brill NV of the Netherlands; Bloomsbury Publishing Plc; and Wilfrid Laurier University Press.

Chapter 10

"'Our Religion Compels Us to Make a Distinction': Prolegomena on Meals and Social Formation" was published in *Identity and Interaction in the Ancient Mediterranean: Jews Christians and Others, Essays in Honour of Stephen G. Wilson*, 41–55 (ed. Zeba A. Crook and Philip A. Harland; Sheffield: Sheffield Phoenix Press, 2007). Material in this chapter is used by kind permission of Sheffield Phoenix Press.

Part I

Generalities

1

Religion: A Guide

> When the most basic concepts—the concepts from which we begin—are suddenly seen to be not concepts but problems ... there is no sense in listening to their sonorous summons or their resounding clashes. (Williams 1977: 11)

Aristotle, legendary for his relentless insistence on classifying the terms, categories, and objects of knowledge, once remarked that the beginning of wisdom is the definition of terms. And why not? Some initial, even if imprecise demarcation of something we want to know or explain, or of something we set out to discover, is in the order of common sense. If, for example, I want to study the craft of pottery making, about which I know nothing, I should know that the object of my interest is not the evolution of reptiles. Or, although I know next to nothing about linear algebra, I would know that I was not in a linear algebra tutorial if the tutor's talk was about plot variations in detective fiction. These examples may be uninteresting, but they do serve to indicate that researching the world we live in, including comparatively across time (worlds of past societies) and space (worlds other than our own), is always a complex exercise of selecting, inventing and fiddling with categories in order to render—to force—the natural world and the range of human doings as intelligible, differentiated, ours to respond to, to make and remake.

"Religion" as Specter

What, then, about "religion"? As is the case with many other common words in the large domain of cultural studies—think of "culture" itself, or of "society," "ideology," "experience," "history," "tradition" (and many more in Williams 1976)—the term "religion" is as familiar as it is difficult to contain within a cogent, agreed-upon, manageable frame of reference. Like the apparition of ghosts that often are a feature of religious talk and behavior, "religion" is a phantom-like category, a specter (on the idea of specter see Derrida 1994; Žižek 1994), a free floating Something. As a specter, "religion" presents us with the dual problem of being flamboyantly real, meeting us in all forms of speech and in material representations, on the one hand, and frustratingly apt to turn coy or disintegrate altogether when put under inquisition, on the other.

As a linguistic denomination "religion" is robustly real, evidently one of those "experience-near" categories (Geertz 1993: 56–59) used by millions of Western people as routinely as they use the words "politics" or "sex," and with an apparently effortless sense of its self-evident meaning. If a class of fifty undergraduate students in an introductory course on the study religion may stand as a sample of popular knowledge, it demonstrates that people, whether they describe themselves as religious or not, do not need to have studied religion in order to think they know what it is. A general, if fuzzy, knowledge of "religion" seems to be a precipitate of formally untaught learning, whereby people simply absorb elements of their cultural marinade—à la the lines from rock singer John Mellencamp's song "Small Town": "I was educated in a small town / taught to fear Jesus in a small town." As a culturally induced mental representation (on which see Shore 1996; Sperber 1996) "religion" is articulatable either as something-in-itself or, by a process of ostentation, usable as a descriptor of different sets of phenomena: religious ideas, religious experiences, religious rituals, religious art, religious traditions, religious fanatics and the like.

In my tabulary of student definitions "religious" seems to have no domain limits and therefore no discriminatory utility when it is the adjective of choice to describe the state one feels when writing poetry, or the rush that comes from riding a motorcycle, or spending quality time with one's pet. Just as pop singer Paul Simon knows of "fifty ways to leave your lover," so students in my classroom have no trouble counting at least "fifty ways to meet your religion," confirming Jonathan Z. Smith's response to some professional thinkers' lament over the impossibility of defining religion. From James Leuba's (1912) list of fifty definitions, Smith draws the lesson not that religion cannot be defined, "but that it can be defined, with greater or lesser success, more than fifty ways" (1998: 281). So, the problem of "religion" in popular speech is the problem of excess and spectrality: there are too many meanings and the meanings are too indeterminate (or, perhaps, too over-determined) to be of value for sustained thought and public discourse. To this we might add that the indeterminacy of meanings tends to be prized and protected with appeals to the immediacy and inscrutability of "private" experience and opinion, effectively setting up taboo-like barriers to a bit of rough critical handling of the ubiquitous popular "religion" talk, lest, one suspects, "the mystery that appears to surround ["religion"] is entirely superficial and fades upon closer scrutiny" (Durkheim 1995: 431). (I have been at more than one dinner party where "religion" has been ceremoniously declared off-limits as a subject of discussion!)

If we add to the popular understandings of "religion" the definitional offerings of scholars, the inordinate strength of "religion" as an uncontrollable, wind-driven reference is underscored. As surveys of the career of the category "religion" indicate (Bossy 1982; Smith 1998), the word is a "floating signifier" capable of attaching itself to a dizzying range of objects—many of them remarkably obscure—to countless blurry ideas, and a host of often imprecise definitional propositions. Little wonder that in the history of theorizing "religion" the term has tended to fidget nervously in its own opaqueness and that it therefore has not infrequently transvested itself to play peek-a-boo behind substitute terms such as "the holy" (the spectral legacy of Rudolf Otto 1969 [1917]) or "the sacred" (the conjuring influence of Mircea Eliade 1959). Both of these substitute terms, however, are equally mysterious, making their use conducive to explaining *obscurium per obscurius*, to account for one mystery by means of other mysteries. Readers may wish to consider the counsel of Marvin Harris (1979: 315–341), whose exposition of obscurantism in the social sciences applies, *mutatis mutandis*, to a dominant discourse in the academic study of religion. Little wonder, too, that the history of the category "religion" is at the same time in part a history of the category's vanishing act in the folds of confessional (theological, apologetic) discourses of religious communities or, more generally, in what Jacques Derrida calls discourses of "hauntology" (Derrida 1994: 51): discourses such as theology, even global theology of world religions that emerged under the influence of Wilfrid Cantwell Smith and finds expression in the work of Frank Whaling (1986), and ontology (talk about the Being of being) that are spent on discussing the realities and presences of absences (ghosts are and are not!). Without denying their noble aims, necessity and appropriateness for confessional locales, these hauntologies are obscurantist in that they subvert a research strategy whose aim is to enlist the study of religion as a contributing partner in the pursuit of a science of human social life, an exercise that is credible within the family of human and social sciences in the modern university. In the effort to counter obscurantist strategies in the study of religion, other approaches have divested "religion" of utility altogether, claiming that it has no independent, proper-to-itself substance; such approaches prefer to collapse "religion" into other classes of social life and to talk about it in terms of the vocabularies drawn from the social sciences or comparative "cultural studies" (Fitzgerald 1997, 1999).

The spectrality of the category "religion" and the fact that divergent, conflictual, even contradictory incantations of "religion" are not only possible but vigorously alive side-by-side in hundreds of university religion departments whose knowledge is relayed for scholarly and popular consumption by an astonishing volume of publications, is enough reason for a *Guide to the Study of Religion* (Braun and McCutcheon 2000). The field of religious studies is a bewildering jungle. If one wants to slash one's way into it and come out the other end with an increase of critical judgment and theorizing potential about what "religion" is or does, especially what it is not, and what ought usefully to be entailed (or not entailed) in calling some aspect of human doing "religious," then a direction-whispering companion is something to take along. This *Guide* aims to be just such a companion. Intended for students from undergraduate to professional levels, the collection of substantial articles presented there are a concert of critical expositions of the ways that "religion" and "religious" are used by scholars intent on defining, describing, classifying and explaining sets of human activities as well as social and cultural processes. Just to be sure that readers are not misled, a cartographical metaphor may help to sharpen the identity of this volume: think of the *Guide* as an atlas of maps to the field of the study of religion. It is therefore not another encyclopedia that catalogues descriptions of religious artifacts, practices, heroes and saints, authoritative texts, myths, and rituals—in short, it is not a compendium of the phenomena central to a religious tradition or commonly shared by religious traditions. Nor is it a dictionary that gives thumbnail descriptions of predominantly native (i.e., a community's own) religious terms and facts compiled on the model of language dictionaries. These kinds of deposits of knowledge are abundant in every academic library and there is no need to add to this crowd.

Rather, the *Guide* takes as its focus of interest precisely those intellectual processes and choices in the study of religion that few encyclopedias and dictionaries of religion put up for inspection—namely scholars' conceptual key-terms and their theory-loaded methods of explanation, their translations of religious insider terms into the language of scientific social and cultural studies, their practices of comparison and their attempts to set boundaries between what counts as religious and what does not. Most simply put, the *Guide* is a multi-faceted asking and replying to two basic questions that students of religion must, sooner or later, take up with some degree of seriousness as a matter of remaining transparent and cogent about what they are up to when they study religion: What is religion? How is it successfully investigated within the shared aims of the family of human and social sciences in the modern university? If readers need an analogy, the relationship of the *Guide* to actual fieldwork in religion—whether that fieldwork consists of students' research in the archives and encyclopedias of religions, of specialists' expositions of the properties of religious communities, or of ethnographers' documentaries of the religious life of group X or Y—is like a guide to historiography (i.e., theory of history) is to the fieldwork of historians, or like a handbook on the theories of lexicography stands as a second-order reflection in relation to the work of compiling actual dictionaries. In the turbulent intellectual storms of late modernity, whose swirls are buffeting us well into the third millennium, the *Guide* presents an attempt at second-order reflection so as to retain, perhaps regain or gain for the first time, some handles on the core concepts in the study of religion.

"Religion" in Concept

The *Guide* does not make an argument for a single grand theory of religion, nor does it offer an exhaustive set of unified methods for studying religion, but the essays in the *Guide* do participate, more or less, in a common stance on matters of theory and method. It will quickly become evident to readers that the *Guide* is not neutral on what makes for "greater or lesser success" (Smith 1998: 281) in positioning the study of religion as a viable and sustainable academic pursuit within the terms of knowledge-production that distinguishes the modern academy. The *Guide* thus comes with a bit of "attitude" and the articulation and rationalization, quite explicitly in some essays and more tacitly in others, of this attitude is a second major reason for the labors contained in it. The elements of this attitude need to be explicated for the benefit of general readers—even if they never read the *Guide*.

(1) Gifts from the Past

The critical study of religion—a creation of European cultures—has historically developed simultaneously as a negative process of disaffiliation from Christian theology and as a positive process of affiliation with the values of scientific rationality associated with the European Enlightenment (see Preus 1987, 1998; Capps 1995). Out of this struggle of estrangement and affinity emerged the possibility of a research stance outside the indigenous perspectives and knowledge frameworks of religious structures, one that was driven by uncensored curiosity rather than by the confessional and apologetic requirements of religious bodies. It became possible to become an observer of religion without being a participant in religion; it was now conceivable to distinguish the *study* of religion from the *practice* of religion; it was now reasonable to separate caring, either positively or negatively, for religion from analyzing, comparing and explaining religion; it was now justifiable to use nonreligious epistemologies (i.e., theories of knowing) to generate knowledge about religious phenomena. What is astonishing is not that these possibilities emerged, but that the research activity (*Wissenschaft*) which formed itself around these possibilities was specifically called religion-science (*Religionswissenschaft*), in polemical opposition to the study of the (Christian) "faith in faith for faith" (*Glaubenslehre*). "Religion" thus had its modern (re)birth as a signifier of difference from theological inquiry where the difference was, in the first place, "a sort of absence" (Preus 1998: 3), a way of saying "not this." This emptiness of "religion" would not last, of course, and "not this" had to be changed to "not this, but that." Binaries—A/not A—rarely are helpful, however. Just to say that the study of religion (A) is not theology (not A) follows a logic that inevitably allows almost anything to be included in/as the study of religion (A). It is precisely when the study of religion was defined in such binary terms—the study of religion is not theology—that a legacy was created that we have inherited today, with our over fifty ways to define religion. This problem would need to be addressed and I will return to the "that" of the study of religion below.

It is worth noting in the past of "religion" a second moment when the word was employed as a category of comparison to signify some difference between "us" and "them." As David Chidester demonstrates in his essay in the *Guide*, "religion" was used in the management of "the natives" on colonial frontiers:

> European explorers, travellers, missionaries, settlers and colonial administrators recorded their findings on indigenous religions all over the world. With remarkable consistency over a period of five hundred years, these European observers reported that they had found people in the Americas, Africa and the Pacific Islands who *lacked any trace of religion*. (Chidester 2000: 427; my emphasis; see also Chidester 1996)

"Religion," filled with some generic (but nevertheless Christian-informed) essence distilled by the emerging science of comparative religion (Sharpe 1986), could be used as a mark on the colonial periphery, one that differentiated the civilized, properly religious European *homo urbanus* from the uncivilized "savage" who was thought to have no religion or, at best, whose religion did not measure up and whose practices therefore had to be called something else. "Superstition" was, and for some it still is, the age-old handy term for flawed, futile, or false religion—as judged from the powerful defining centers of normative religion.

The lesson to be drawn from this brief look at the recent past of "religion" is that the term has had a more consistently successful career as a marker of difference and separation than as a container and carrier of an irreducible, stable, empirical and thus inspectable knowledge. Or, more precisely, the substance supposedly contained in "religion" seems to be utterly variable and that variation is dependent on the term's classifying function as determined by the interests of the classifiers. The editorial attitude in the *Guide* is to seize with appreciation one gift of our field's past and regard "religion" as essentially empty, of use only as a marking device. It should go without saying that in accepting this gift from our past we do not also have to take over the classifying interests and social values of the past, those that constructed such oppositions as *their* conjuration versus *our* knowledge, *their* superstition versus *our* religion. These polarities are not useful in the study of religion and ought to be regarded as conceptual relics in the museum of our discipline's past.

(2) From Substance to Concept

If "religion" is substantively empty—or infinitely fillable with vague qualities, as we have noted—let us abandon the hope, so tenaciously persistent in our field, that by some brilliant hermeneutical can-do we will spook the true genie out of the bottle of "religion." If "religion" is substantively empty, then there is no genie in the bottle! In more genteel terms, the problem with using "religion" as a nominal for a substance with its own inherent characteristics is that it conjures definitions that are "*ad hoc* and/or taken-for-granted (and ultimately incoherent)." Moreover, such incoherence is generally unnoticed by scholars who, instead, "tend to take the *significance* of [any] definition for granted" (Arnal 2000: 28), as if it was sheltered from critique. To be sure, it is possible for faith-generated premises to secure for those who believe in them credibility-supports by means of intellectual crafts. But the attitude embraced in the *Guide* is to forsake the ethereal and exalted "It" of religion and, instead, to use "religion" to retrieve something on the ground, something on the hard surface of social life in time and space, something that counts as data according to the generally shared, scientific evidentiary principles of the modern academy. That is, the editorial attitude in the *Guide reverses* the well-known interdict offered by one of the grandfathers of religious studies, Rudolf Otto (1869–1937), in the opening pages of his *The Idea of the Holy*; contrary to Otto, the *Guide* advises that whoever has an "intimate personal knowledge" of the *ontos* (Greek, "being") of religion "is requested to read no further" (Otto 1969 [1917]: 8). Accordingly, the contributors to the *Guide* make no claim to privileged, intuitive knowledge about "religion"; instead, they set out to develop taxonomies and theories to assist them in answering questions about the nature, origin, and functions of that part of the social world that have been and are labeled "religion."

This means that we must regard religion as a *concept* and not as a *substance* that floats "out there," a something that might invade and enlighten us if we should only be so fortunate as to have the right kind of receiving apparatus. Concepts are ideas used to allocate the stuff of the real world into a class of objects so as to position these objects for thought that is aimed toward explanation of their causes, functions, attractiveness to individuals and societies, relationships to other concepts, and so on. Norwood R. Hanson's conceptual distinction between two kinds of terms might help us to think about this. He differentiates, albeit on a line of continuum, "sense-datum" words or "data-words" from more or less "theory-loaded" words, using as his illustration of their difference the data-word "hole," a spatial concavity, and the concept "crater": "To speak of a concavity as a crater is to commit oneself as to its origin, to say that its creation was quick, violent, explosive" (Hanson 1958: 56–60). Simply, for our purpose, concepts are precipitates of scholars' cognitive operations to be put to work in the service of scholars' theoretical interest in the objects of their research; concepts are not given off by the objects of our interests. They neither descend from the sky nor sprout out of the ground for our plucking. Claiming that "religion" is a concept is to say something like what Hanson suggests and to subscribe to what Erik Olin Wright states with reference to the concept of "class":

> Concepts are produced. The categories that are used in social theories, whether they be the relatively simple descriptive categories employed in making observations, or the very complex and abstract concepts used in the construction of "grand theory," are all produced by human beings. ... They are never simply given by the real world as such but are always produced through some sort of intellectual process of concept formation. (Wright 1985: 20)

(3) Owning Our Concepts

Concept formation, which is never a once-for-all-time process, in the service of a successful research strategy, is not just the prerogative of the scholar, *but it is indeed her or his primary obligation as a scholar.* In the study of religion no one has recognized this obligation for self-conscious concept formation more clearly and stated it more sharply than Jonathan Z. Smith. Though often cited, it is worth intoning once again his words from the introductory paragraphs of his influential book, *Imagining Religion*:

> *there is no data for religion.* Religion is solely the creation of the scholar's study. It is created for the scholar's analytic purposes by his imaginative acts of comparison and generalization. Religion has no independent existence apart from the academy. For this reason, the student of religion, and most particularly the historian of religion, must be relentlessly self-conscious. Indeed, this self-consciousness constitutes his primary expertise, his foremost object of study. (Smith 1982: xi; emphasis original)

Let us then regard "religion" as a concept, as a semantic marker in a specific sense of the Greek word *sēma*: a boundary indicator around particular and conspicuous things in the observable, real world, analogous to the markers that designate places for playing football or burying the dead. Or, better put, let us understand "religion" as analogous to the manner in which the Library of Congress or the

British Library divides published material quite artificially among "classes of conceptual and topical relations in the service of data retrieval" (Smith 2000).

(4) Defining the "Religion" Concept

But what kind of marker is "religion"? What conspicuous things does it pick out and bring into relations for our inspection? Here is a proposal that expresses the orientation of this volume. Tinkering just a bit with Bruce Lincoln's definitional thesis (Lincoln 1996: 225), let's think of "religion" (a) as ordinary and mundane (i.e., in this world) discourses or *arts de faire* (Certeau 1984) that are characterized (b) by an orientation to speak of matters transcendent (i.e., beyond the limited spaces of this material world) and eternal (i.e., beyond the limits of time) and (c) by a desire to speak of these matters "with an authority equally transcendent and eternal" (Lincoln 1996: 225). Or, very plainly, "religion" is a kind of human talk that can be differentiated from other human talk by its topical content and its rhetorical propensity (see Spiro 1966: 98).

"Religion" in Theory

Readers will no doubt detect that defining "religion" in this way is to push it well into the domain of Hanson's theory-loaded terms. Perhaps "theory-redolent" is preferable, indicating that the concept gives off some theoretical odors, in that it is dependent on some moves of theoretical proposition-making in the formulation of the concept itself. But it is also theory-suggestive, indicating that the term "religion" is subject to further intellectual maneuvers in the direction of generating more fecund explanations of those things contained and entailed in the definitional concept.

As to indications of the first kind, notice first that the concept implicitly locates the origin (not to be thought of in primordial absolute terms but in terms of ongoing beginnings) and explicitly the "life" of religion within the complex fabric of active interests of people in the real world. The "transcendent" beyond-human-beings, such as gods, spirits, ancestors, or whatever else one would name to this class, have their lives not in some ontic selfhood, but as discursive entities (see Murphy 2000). To phrase it another way, Lincoln's definition implies that, insofar as the gods or ancestors "live," it is contemporary people who give them life by talking about, to, and with them. This, in turn, suggests that the object of the scholar's study is not the gods but the complex social operations by which, and the conditions under which, people discursively bring the gods to life. This orientation opens new lines of inquiry: What human interests are served in keeping the gods alive? What is the variety of ramifications for self, society and culture in the cultivation and preservation of the gods and their authority?

Second, the proposed religion concept is redolent of an act of general classification for the purpose of delimiting the objects of our inquiry. It retrieves not invisible things, but conspicuous *arts de faire* or what we can simply term discourses—a term used most capaciously to include "not only verbal, but also the symbolic discourses of spectacle, gesture, costume, edifice, icon, musical performance, and the like" (Lincoln 1989: 4). From these proliferations of socially cultivated discourses, our concept "religion" selects not all, not just any, but specifically some, those marked by an orientation to certain topics (the transcendent) that are then handled within a rhetorical framework of self-authorizing credibility structures. That is, there is enough discriminating power in our concept to distinguish specifically religious discourses from other ideological discourses with which they may share enough similarities in rhetorical orientation so as to allow us to regard religious discourses as but one type of ideological discourse, but without holding the converse, i.e., that all ideological discourses are also religious (see Lease 2000).

It is important to observe that the formula, though theory-loaded, does not *explain* religious discourses; more is needed. Lincoln's concept gives no indication, for example, that it contains an explanation of the *arts de faire* that his definition selects and retrieves for us. By what networks of operations and dynamics, we might ask for example, do religious discourses maintain (or lose) their credibility in the lives of people and societies who live in them? What are their intended goals and their unintended consequences? Supposing, for the moment, that religion is among the hundreds of human universals (Brown 1991)—meaning that religious discourses are cultivated in all societies across time and place (Burkert 1996)—how do we account for them as both ubiquitous and resiliently persistent? How do we explain the peculiar nature of the authority of, and the authority-orientation in, religious discourses (see Lincoln 1994)? And so on. That Lincoln's definitional thesis does not contain answers to these and many other questions is not, however, a mark of its weakness. Concepts, after all, are not full-fledged theories, but somewhat elastic, provisional set-ups for theories; they axiomatically delimit the focus and types of theorizing that are possible. Concepts thus select theories appropriate to the concept, which also means, obviously, that they exclude some types of theorizing as *not* apropos. For example, a concept that defines religion as a human discourse is not hospitable to explaining religion in terms of propositions that postulate it as a *sui generis*, one of a kind substance set apart from human discourses, an explanatory option that Weston La Barre characterizes as explaining religion "in the terms provided by religion" (La Barre 1970: xi). Concepts simply are jealously discriminating romancers and lovers of explanatory stratagems that are commensurate with (i.e., faithful to) the core sensibilities of the concept. The mark of a strong religion concept for our research purposes it its ability to initiate, direct, and sustain a rich historical, this-worldly oriented, social "science" (*Wissenschaft*) of religious *arts de faire*. At the very least, this means that a religion concept ought to make possible a critical inquiry whose theories, methods and results are not esoteric, private, and intelligible only within the terms of a special-to-religion epistemology and credibility structure.

Third, the specific expertise that is the aim of religion scholars is made apparent when we notice that the classificatory act expressed in the definitional concept relativizes "religion" taxonomically. "Religion" is not a *summum genus* (Smith 1998: 281), but is a sub-class of human *arts de faire* or discourses. Hence, the specificness of the scholar's expertise in various religious discourses is similarly subordinated to an overarching, more general critical purpose of which the core problem, always to be theorized itself, concerns the complex and multiple interrelated processes of cultural production, structuration and representation (e.g., Giddens 1984; Goodman 1997). The religion scholar is thus a social theorist whose distinction from other social theorists is marked by the data-focus of her or his labors, i.e., that part of the observable world named religion.

This, I should point out, is not really a novel plea for the rectification of religious studies as a species of social studies. It is, rather, a reminder and recuperation of a generative orientation in the modern study of religion's past. Recall that the study of religion (*Religionswissenschaft*) emerged in post-Enlightenment, science-oriented Europe. Out of the processes of shaping the emergent sense of what religion is, and how to investigate it scientifically arose a general commitment to explain religion as a natural phenomenon, as opposed to a divine phenomenon—to regard the religious practices of societies as discursive devices generated by human beings to make sense of their world and to authorize their values and practices. Let's regard Ludwig Feuerbach's famous reduction of theology to anthropology as an example of the general orientation of this period toward secular theories of religion: "Theology is anthropology, that is, in the object of religion which we call *Theos* in Greek and *Gott* in German, nothing but the essence of man is expressed" (Feuerbach 1967 [1851]: 10). Of interest to us here is not Feuerbach's *particular* psycho-philosophy of human consciousness and cognition, but the fact that he, along with many others of his time, sought to explain religion and its postulated superhuman objects as the precipitates of entirely human doings. To understand religion thus inescapably entailed as the investigative starting and ending point the very anthropological and social questions of the what, how and why of human "religious" being and doing in historical, material and social situatedness.

It is hardly coincidental that this turn to natural, anthropological explanations of religion roughly coincided with the modern beginnings of the disciplines known as anthropology, psychology and sociology. Most of the so-called founders of these social-scientific disciplines formed the fundamentals of these sciences more or less in their effort to explain religion. This can be said of W. Robertson Smith, Edmund B. Tylor and James G. Frazer, David Hume (anthropology), Ludwig Feuerbach, Sigmund Freud and Carl G. Jung (psychology) and Auguste Comte, Émile Durkheim, Karl Marx and Max Weber (sociology), to call the roll of merely the most famous. What all these scholars had in common was their effort to answer the what, how and why of religion without appealing to a divine being, a god, or any other nonhuman transcendent "other" reality. All of them basically agreed that it is not the gods that make people revere and fear them, but, on the contrary, that people make their gods whom they then revere and fear.

Now, this brief rehearsal of the anthropological foundations of modern religious studies' beginnings is not meant as an exhortation that religion scholars ought restrictively to become Durkheimians, Freudians or Marxians. The point is more general and it concerns the religion scholar's theoretical orientation: when it comes to theorizing religion and explaining religious *arts de faire*, let us not abandon, but rather continue to explore, the naturalistic, anthropological and sociological turn that marked *Religionswissenschaft* from its beginning.

"Religion" and Disciplinarity

What about the disciplinarity of religious studies? Readers may well take what has been said so far as an implicit subversion of the specialized technologies and disciplines that have been developed around religious studies and that have garnered for the study of religion an officially sanctioned place in the university. There is, however, neither subversive intent nor any suggestion that religion scholars should rename themselves and reappear as generic social theorists or ethnographers. On the contrary—and here I have in mind the recent trend in some North American universities to see religion departments as unrationalizable in these economically stringent times (documented early on by Lease 1995)—a wide collaborative expertise-coalition (see Capps 1995: 336–337), intentionally gathered around religious *arts de faire* for the purpose of compiling an "archive" of these *arts* from near and far in time and space, which then manages that archive with self-consciously critical practices of concept formation, theory construction, classificatory and interpretive operations, all for the larger purpose of generating and disseminating an academically credible public knowledge about religion, is undoubtedly best pursued in an institutionally designated and legitimated place. Thick knowledge, unlike revelations, about highly complex social practices comes neither by *ad hoc* pursuit nor without costly investment in disciplinary props.

It is also to be acknowledged that the data-domain "religion" is extensive and almost limitlessly varied across time and locale, from one culture to another, on the large scale, and within bounded cultural domains, on a more restricted scale. Even descriptive mastery of mere subsets of the facts of religion will require a range of technical knowledges such as archaeology, art history, demography, linguistics, philology, and so on, none learnt or taught overnight. In the real world of academic practice the mastery, use, and teaching of these technologies will undoubtedly take up the bulk of the religion scholar's day and days.

But at the end of the day there remain the conceptual and theoretical problems posed by "religion" that the specialized, empirical technologies of "field work" in religion will not solve. In the final analysis, then, the *sine qua non* of the religion scholar's contribution to a general science of culture and society lies less in disciplined employment of this or that *technē*, though this is not unimportant by any means, than in the theoretical imagination that can translate the merely curious or puzzling data of religion or the self-evidently significant but spectral objects of religious discourses into categories that can help us as scholars of religion—and the various publics who value (or merely tolerate) our labors—to understand the human interests and social arrangements in which religious discourses play their various generative and representational roles. Thought of in this way, the study of religion is more like an organized, specific-purpose field trip into the general study of social and cultural processes than it is a fenced-in disciplinary or departmental acre with its own, non-shared, special-to-religion methods.

Postscript

All of the articles in the present volume were written with this anthropocentric disposition in mind. The next two essays further elaborate general theoretical and pedagogical issues in the anthropocentric study of religion. All the remaining essays attempt to exemplify, by various probes into specific texts and topics of the period of emergent Christianity (the subset within the broader field where I have carried out most of my own work) what can be gained in our understanding of one particular site, early Christianities, when we refuse to reduce their texts to elusive metaphysical meanings, and when, instead, we presume that the religiosity of these texts, which are filled with gods, spirits, demons and ancestors, is itself a human production. Once this attitudinal shift is made, and we commit ourselves to read religious texts non-religiously (see Lincoln 2012), we might more clearly see the human interests and agencies involved in the production, reproduction, and use of these texts (then as well as now). Most of them are transparently argumentative; they aim to persuade. But who and whom? Of what? And why? Although some of the following essays, especially those that treat topical issues—such as power, persuasion, gender and morality, and the specter of origins—are directed more at the intellectual practices that are dominant in the field of New Testament and early Christian studies, they all put these practices under critical scrutiny, exemplifying the attitudinal shift recommended and outlined here.

References

Arnal, William E. (2000). "Definition." In Willi Braun and Russell T. McCutcheon (eds.), *Guide to the Study of Religion*, 23–34. London: Cassell.

Bossy, John (1982). "Some Elementary Forms of Durkheim," *Past & Present* 95: 3–18. https://doi.org/10.1093/past/95.1.3

Braun, Willi and Russell T. McCutcheon (eds.) (2000). *Guide to the Study of Religion*. London: Cassell.

Brown, Donald E. (1991). *Human Universals*. Philadelphia, PA: Temple University Press.

Burkert, Walter (1996). *Creation of the Sacred: Tracks of Biology in Early Religions*. Cambridge, MA: Harvard University Press.

Capps, Walter H. (1995). *Religious Studies: The Making of a Discipline*. Minneapolis, MN: Fortress.

Certeau, Michel de (1984). *The Practice of Everyday Life*. Steven Rendall (trans). Berkeley, CA: University of California Press.

Chidester, David (1996). *Savage Systems: Colonialism and Comparative Religion in Southern Africa*. Studies in Religion and Culture. Charlottesville, VA: University Press of Virginia.

—— (2000). "Colonialism." In Willi Braun and Russell T. McCutcheon (eds.), *Guide to the Study of Religion*, 423–437. London: Cassell.

Derrida, Jacques (1994). *Specters of Marx, the State of the Debt, the Work of Mourning, & the New International*. Peggy Kamuf (trans.). New York: Routledge.

Durkheim, Émile (1995) [1912]. *The Elementary Forms of Religious Life*. Karen E. Fields (trans. and intro.). New York: Free Press.

Eliade, Mircea (1959). *The Sacred and the Profane: The Nature of Religion*. Willard R. Trask (trans.). New York: Harcourt, Brace Jovanovich.

Feuerbach, Ludwig (1967) [1851]. *Lectures on the Essence of Religion*. Ralph Mannheim (trans.). New York: Harper & Row.
Fitzgerald, Timothy (1997). "A Critique of 'Religion' as a Cross-Cultural Category," *Method & Theory in the Study of Religion* 9: 91–110. https://doi.org/10.1163/157006897X00070
―― (1999). *The Ideology of Religious Studies*. New York: Oxford University Press.
Geertz, Clifford (1993). *The Interpretation of Cultures: Selected Essays*. New York: Basic Books.
Giddens, Anthony (1984). *The Constitution of Society: Outline of the Theory of Structuration*. Berkeley, CA: University of California Press.
Goodman, Jordan (1997). "History and Anthropology." In Michael Bentley (ed.), *Companion to Historiography*, 783–804. London: Routledge.
Hanson, Norwood R. (1958). *Patterns of Discovery: An Inquiry into the Conceptual Foundations of Science*. Cambridge: Cambridge University Press.
Harris, Marvin (1979). *Cultural Materialism: The Struggle for a Science of Culture*. New York: Random House.
La Barre, Weston (1970). *The Ghost Dance: The Origins of Religion*. New York: Dell.
Lease, Gary (guest ed.) (1995). *Pathologies in the Academic Study of Religion: North American Institutional Cases*. Special Issue of *Method & Theory in the Study of Religion* 7(4): 295–416. https://doi.org/10.1163/157006895X00487
―― (2000). "Ideology." In Willi Braun and Russell T. McCutcheon (eds.), *Guide to the Study of Religion*, 438–447. London: Cassell.
Leuba, James H. (1912). *The Psychological Study of Religion: Its Origin, Function, and Future*. New York: Macmillan.
Lincoln, Bruce (1989). *Discourse and the Construction of Society: Comparative Studies of Myth, Ritual, and Classification*. Oxford: Oxford University Press.
―― (1994). *Authority: Construction and Erosion*. Chicago, IL: University of Chicago Press.
―― (1996). "Theses on Method," *Method & Theory in the Study of Religion* 8: 225–227. https://doi.org/10.1163/157006896X00323
―― (2012). "How to Read a Religious Text." In *Gods and Demons, Priests and Scholars: Critical Explorations in the History of Religions*, 5–15. Chicago, IL: University of Chicago Press.
Murphy, Tim (2000). "Discourse." In Willi Braun and Russell T. McCutcheon (eds.), *Guide to the Study of Religion*, 396–408. London: Cassell.
Otto, Rudolf (1969) [1917]. *The Idea of the Holy: An Inquiry Into the Non-Rational Factor in the Idea of the Divine and Its Relation to the Rational*. John W. Harvey (trans.). London: Oxford University Press.
Preus, J. Samuel (1987). *Explaining Religion: Criticism and Theory from Bodin to Freud*. New Haven, CT: Yale University Press.
―― (1998). "The Bible and Religion in the Century of Genius," *Religion* 28: 3–27, 111–138. https://doi.org/10.1006/reli.1997.0116
Sharp, Eric J. (1986). *Comparative Religion: A History*. 2nd ed. La Salle, IL: Open Court.
Shore, Bradd (1996). *Culture in Mind: Cognition, Culture, and the Problem of Meaning*. Oxford: Oxford University Press.
Smith, Jonathan Z. (1982). *Imagining Religion: From Babylon to Jonestown*. Chicago, IL: University of Chicago Press.
―― (1998). "Religion, Religions, Religious." In Mark C. Taylor (ed.), *Critical Terms for Religious Studies*, 269–284. Chicago, IL: University of Chicago Press.
―― (2000). "Classification." In Willi Braun and Russell T. McCutcheon (eds.), *Guide to the Study of Religion*, 35–44. London: Cassell.
Sperber, Dan (1996). *Explaining Culture: A Naturalistic Approach*. Oxford: Blackwell.

Spiro, Melford E. (1966). "Religion: Problems of Definition and Explanation." In Michael Banton (ed.), *Anthropological Approaches to the Study of Religion*, 85–126. London: Tavistock.

Whaling, Frank (1986). *Christian Theology and World Religions: A Global Approach*. Basingstoke: Marshall Pickering.

Williams, Raymond (1976). *Keywords: A Vocabulary of Culture and Society*. London: Fontana.

—— (1977). *Marxism and Literature*. Oxford: Oxford University Press.

Wright, Erik Olin (1985). *Classes*. London: Verso.

Žižek, Slavoj (1994). "Introduction: The Spectre of Ideology." In Slavoj Žižek (ed.), *Mapping Ideology*, 1–33. London: Verso.

2

The Irony of Religion[1]

> Know then thyself, presume not God to scan;
> The proper study of mankind is Man.
> —Alexander Pope, *An Essay on Man* (1733)

The proper object of Religious Studies is *Religion*, ostensibly a set of human expressions and performances that merit a humanistic or social-scientific analysis in accord with our academic approach to other types of human behaviors. The distinction between Theology, which presumes and addresses supernatural or divine realities, and Religious Studies, which does not, is predicated on this identification of the subject matter of a secular, or humanistic, or scientific approach to the study of Religion, one which is not required to bow to the dictates of Theology, confessional or otherwise, nor address Theology's subject matter, nor be bound by Theology's methods.

Yet the contemporary practice and conceptualization of Religious Studies as a field not only distinct from Theology, but a worthy endeavor in its own right and on its own terms is predicated on a further assumption: that "Religion" is a coherent category in humanistic, social-scientific, or generally non-theological academic terms, that is, an empirical category or a descriptively nominal one. Such a claim is critically necessary for any assertion of Religious Studies *as a discipline*. Disciplinary identity assumes a distinctive approach to a taxonomically coherent entity. The coherence of such entities as "literature," "society," "culture," and "psychology," for example, dictates a distinctive set of tools and approaches that respect the fundamental character of the phenomena that constitute the entity. These distinctive analytic methods ensure that literature is treated *as* literature, society *as* society, and so on, and that the rigorous techniques developed for studying these entities are learned and properly applied by the discipline's trained practitioners. Thus one would expect something similar if Religious Studies is conceived, as it normally and normatively is, as a discipline distinct from Theology.[2]

Here, however, we encounter the monumental *irony* of Religious Studies as a field and as a discipline.[3] "Religion" itself as a framework, a category, and thus as a demarcation for a non-theological discipline (Religious Studies) is defined precisely by its theological content.[4] And hence the futility of its perpetual efforts to distinguish itself from the very discipline—Theology—on which its existence is predicated. Various data that are grouped together by the concept or taxon "Religion" are linked, not by the analytic frameworks specified by humanistic or social-scientific interests, but by the assertions of various theologians and other religious practitioners that the objects in question have a claim to ultimacy or transcendence. The difference between Macbeth, which is a *literary* datum, and the Gospel of Matthew, which is a *religious* datum, is simply that the former is assumed to be *merely* literature, while the latter is taken by Christians to be somehow *more than* or *other than* literature. The creation of a field devoted to a set or class of sacred objects that are defined by their *extra* quality (*extra*-social, *extra*-anthropological, *extra*-empirical, *extra*-historical, *extra*-ordinary) is simply a restatement of their sacrality—i.e., their difference from other objects and their incommensurability with ordinary objects—and thus represents a religious or theological *practice*.[5] It does not matter whether we in Religious Studies orient ourselves to "scientific" *explanation* of religion, or to a more interpretative goal of *understanding* religion; it does not matter whether we accede to the specific dogmatic claims made for religious objects. In explaining or interpreting or describing religion, we are drawing a circle around a class of objects that devotees have identified as sacred, and we are asserting that they are indeed a distinct class, and, hence, that they *are* sacred.[6] This is why the most robust effort to date to establish a *discipline* of religious studies—that of Mircea Eliade—is so justly accused of participating in theological discourse in orienting our study to "the Sacred" (see McCutcheon 1997, 2003: 54–82). Even the constitution of "religions" or "religious traditions" as our field's primary constituent data sets, and the comparison thereof in the mode of "world religions," has its roots in theology, as Tomoko Masuzawa has shown. And no wonder: "it seems obvious enough that the discourse of world religions takes for granted the idea of 'religion itself' as a 'unique sphere of life,' and that it presumes that this sphere is prevalent throughout the world and its history" (Masuzawa 2005: 313).[7]

The irony is embedded in the very category of Religion itself. This is the problem. If we wish to study Religion, we are studying an object that is as theologically constituted as the gods themselves. Religion—and the study thereof—requires Theology for its cogency, just as the field or discipline of Religious Studies continues to require the existence of Theology as an amorphous Other against which to establish our otherwise indeterminate identity. This of course reinforces a deep intimacy between Theology and Religious Studies, an intimacy whose perpetuation has been the only real product of the fruitless "debate" over theological versus non-theological approaches to Religion,[8] a debate that takes place in various registers of key terms.[9] Scholars of Religion fuel and justify their own institutional identity by constantly invoking and then exorcizing the specter of their very condition of possibility: Theology. It is as impossible to end or dismiss the "debate" as it is to resolve it. The issue here is no mere "postmodern" dismissal or dissolution of categories, nor is it, conversely, an effort to reify disciplinary boundaries, or to rule out interdisciplinary analysis of synthetic objects. Rather, the problem is that this *particular* category, this *particular* manner of classifying things, is intrinsically theological and therefore cannot provide any basis for a discussion or analysis of religious objects or data that is genuinely *non*-theological.[10] The question, therefore, of Religious Studies *versus* Theology or Theology *in* Religious Studies is moot. The objects of the classification "Religion"—this canonical text, that ritual, these gods—are, as we contend below, perfectly amenable to humanistic or social-scientific analysis outside the confines of Religion as such, i.e., as independent non-religious objects of various disciplinary investigations. But the *class* of objects so designated is not.[11]

So, let us then in all honesty hand over Religion to them that know what it is, to them that are sure which human productions, performances, affectations and the like are religious and why "religious" must be *the* descriptive or classifying adjective for a given, or any, human datum. Let us transfer the deed of ownership of Religion to its legitimate disciplinary proprietors, to its epistemological and analytic virtuosi, the religiologists or theologians, be they confessional theologians, world religiologists, aficionados of the universal Sacred, or analysts of a natural *homo religiosus* or *religio eo ipso*. Let them, we say with utter seriousness and with an assist from Ernest Gellner and a sympathetic nod to Charles Davis, "succumb with ecstasy ... [to] the difficulty of explicating the Other [Religion] ... [and] let them content themselves with elaborating the theme of its inaccessibility, offering a kind of initiation into a Cloud of Unknowing, a Privileged Non-Access ... a mystery on its own" (Gellner 1992: 56; cf. Davis 1984). Rudolf Otto and Mircea Eliade and their numerous descendants had and continue to have it right. They did and do in fact own Religion in substance, as a category, and as a discipline. That discipline is Theology. Pleas for place of Theology in Religious Studies thus are redundant. Since Theology is probably best or at least most productively undertaken in a confessional context, it makes little sense to promote a generalized Theology (= Religion) in secular institutional settings. Dispensing with the study of Religion *qua* Religion in secular universities would block the covert inroads that confessional Theology has made into these secular institutions, most frequently in the form of Religious Studies departments and—for the greatest numbers of students—by means of the Religious Studies introductory course. In principle and in theory the entire designation "Religion" can be and should be left to theologians, obviating any need or justification for Religious Studies departments or courses that introduce students to Religion *qua* Religion in secular academies.

This, however, is not the end of the matter. There is another argument to be made, but it must be an argument that is altogether different from the familiar ones that, by virtue of enduring and regular repetition, have achieved the status of ritual incantations of a difference—of course, a spurious difference, hence no difference at all, as we have suggested—between Theology and Religious Studies.[12] The proposition to be argued, rather, is this: the data that is classified as religious *can* be, indeed *must* be, open to analysis from epistemological vantage points and theoretical commitments, and to disciplinary regimes *other* than those that constitute Religion as Religion and Religion's postulated data as religious and the religio-theological epistemological and disciplinary practices that are defined by a religious constitution of Religion as an object of study. This *other than* is required by the general humanistic, social-scientific, critical *raison d'etre* of the secular and public academy whose mandate is to generate and disseminate knowledge about and explanations of the material and social world. In other words, conceding Religion to the religio-theologian does not diminish, much less obviate, the general humanistic intellectual mandate to study the religio-theologian's religious objects in terms *other than* how they are classified and often represented, studied, and taught in Religious Studies departments. To theologians may belong the category, the demarcating circle of Religion, but such a concession does *not* imply their exclusive ownership of the stuff—the heterogeneous, quotidian human *arts de faire*[13]—that they may place *in* that circle.

Making intelligible, giving plausible and credible accounts of, the variety of human expressions and representations that, by applying one or another religious criterion, some people name "religious" or "religion" is, must be, part of the data that comprises humankind, data that is no less subject to the scrutiny of the secular academy than any other, putatively *non*-religious, expressions and representations.

Herein, however, lies a second problem that consists of a double neglect. One side of the neglect is that secular universities generally have not been resolutely committed to appropriating (confiscating?) the stuff inside the Religion circle as touchable data in their humanistic and social-scientific disciplines. That is, not only the Religion circle but the stuff inside the circle is systemically ceded to the Religion experts in the secular academy, even, we suspect, when a given university or college has no Religion experts or department. When, on the other hand, "religious" elements of human practice *are* taken up in disciplines such as sociology, anthropology, history, literature, archaeology, and so forth, it is usually done with a disciplinary "failure of nerve."[14] That is, the analysis of "religious" data is not usually done with unflinching adherence to the theoretical principles and methodologies that define these humanistic and social-scientific disciplines, but in *ad hoc* fashion and, more seriously neglectful, with tacit deference to, even reverence for, these elements as theologically pre-positioned elements that stand alone or apart precisely *as* religious. Hence the familiar "*of* Religion" courses—Anthropology *of* Religion, History *of* Religion, Philosophy *of* Religion, Sociology *of* Religion—or "*and* Religion" courses—Literature *and* Religion, Law *and* Religion, Art *and* Religion, Women *and* Religion. Here irony perches on irony, for apparently Theology (= Religion) is allowed comfortable, even if marginal, living space *on Religion's terms* in the secular academy's explicitly secular workshops. Religion is treated as Religion where in theory and disciplinary practice it is quite possible to give intelligible, plausible and relevant *non*-religious account of items of data contained in the Religion circle.

There remains, therefore, a contingent necessity for the continued existence of religion courses, even Religious Studies departments or programs, in secular academies as a necessarily interdisciplinary (and non-disciplinary) *corrective* to the unselfconsciously theological underpinnings of the concept of Religion in the non-theological disciplines and area studies of the public, secular academy. Indeed, this corrective orientation has been the hallmark of the most useful and theoretically sophisticated work being done by scholars of Religion today.[15] Our characterization of the genealogical and epistemic foundations of religious studies and its systematic constitution should not be taken as an indictment of the many scholars in the field using the rubric of Religious Studies as opportunities to work against the grain. Let it be clearly understood, however, that the necessity for work of this sort and for the programs and courses that sustain it is political and provisional, not principled and epistemological. As such, courses in Religion should then become a *contrepoint*, an enunciation that is deliberately set against the grain of the epistemological foundation and disciplinary logic that defines the object of interest and study as *extra* to anything else, as Religion or religious, whether in Religion departments or any other disciplinary precinct in the academy. This, we suggest, truly would be the "irony of Religious Studies"—with a wink at Don Wiebe (1991). In this ironical key, the aim of Religious Studies at the theoretical level is a fundamental deconstruction of its object, Religion. Religious Studies, as we posit its need, plays something like the role of the idiot, the unorthodox fool, to the serious "straight man" in the asymmetrical, uneven double act of Religious Studies in the academy. The introductory course, for example, thus is not a venue for introducing students to Religion or vice versa, but a forum for addressing issues of conceptualization and misconceptualization that have constituted Religion as a stand-alone object, for introducing classificatory thought and systems, for giving accounts of the historical and contemporary conditions that gave rise to and sustain Religious Studies in the secular academy, of the reasons why the academy in general is so resistant to lay hands on its mandate to study the stuff of Religion in non-religious terms.

This conception of the analytic vacuity of Religion as well as especially its consequences for scholarship have already been adumbrated in a celebrated passage from the work of Jonathan Z. Smith:

> [W]hile there is a staggering amount of data, of phenomena, of human experiences and expressions that might be characterized in one culture or another, by one criterion or another, as religious—*there is no data for religion*. Religion is solely the creation of the scholar's study. It is created for the scholar's analytic purposes by his imaginative acts of comparison and generalization. Religion has no independent existence apart from the academy. For this reason, *the student of religion, and most particularly the historian of religion, must be relentlessly self-conscious. Indeed, this self-consciousness constitutes his primary expertise, his foremost object of study*. (Smith 1982: xi; emphasis added)

The point may be pushed even further. As an idea, religion itself is the very embodiment of a failure or refusal to think seriously and rigorously about certain classes of human practice. The study of religion as religion, then, without the self-consciousness of which Smith speaks, is defined by the failure of nerve that Wiebe rightly laments.

Notes

1   This chapter was co-written with William E. Arnal.
2   See, e.g., Masuzawa: "[T]he disciplinary establishment of so-called religious studies, for whatever reason and with whatever justification, seems to hold fast to this bottom line: Religion is found everywhere; it is an essential and irreducible aspect of human life; it should be studied" (2005: 317).

3   The emphasis on irony here is a (friendly) reorientation of the use of the term by Donald Wiebe (1991). Wiebe argues that Theology is an ironic discipline, applying the techniques of reason to the fundamentally irrational or "primitive" mental processes of Religion. Theology thus is a rational Trojan Horse in the walls of religion. With Wiebe, however, the irony is standing on its head. It must be turned right side up again.

4   Leaving aside the historical *origins* of the concept, on which see especially Jonathan Z. Smith (2004: 179–196). For the argument that Religion is a modern and Christian-derived category, see Asad (1993: 27–54). For the claim that Religion as a taxon in its modern form is a fundamentally political category, see Arnal (2000: 21–34; 2001: 1–19). Recently, Daniel Boyarin has argued that "Religion," while a Christian construct, is not a product of the early modern period, but of late antiquity (2004: 11–17, 203–204).

5   This is in fact Durkheim's definition of religion in *Les formes élémentaires de la vie religieuse* (1968 [1912]: 50–57): the practice of religion is the set of practices involved with this more or less arbitrary segregation of some objects as aspects of the realm of the sacred that is set apart from the realm of the profane.

6   This is precisely why we find in Religious Studies so much effort spent on the naively postulated and politically motivated "reductionism versus non-reductionism" debate, and why, more often than not, "reductionism" is regarded as a "dirty word" that is equated with an anti-religious "'holier-than-thou' self-righteousness" (Dawkins 1982: 113), even though "reductionism" is a scientific virtue (see Sperber 1996: 5–6; cf. Alton 1986).

7   Masuzawa adds: "What is at stake here is far more fundamental than the problem of border violations between historical science and theology; rather it is a question of whether the world religions discourse can be in any way enlisted, and trusted, on the side of historical scholarship" (2005: 326).

8   In the North American context this relationship is controversial and subject to some of the most heated "turf wars"—really a sibling rivalry for privilege on the same turf—in the academy, for which the famous older debate between Canadian scholars Charles Davis and Donald Wiebe continues to set the terms (Davis 1975: 205–221; 1981: 11–20; 1984: 393–400; 1986: 191–196; Wiebe 1984: 401–422; 1988: 403–413; 1999). See also Bruce Alton's (1986), Lorne Dawson's (1986), and Hans Penner's (1986) meditations on this exchange and now the thoughtful reflection on the terms of the debate by the Belgian scholar, Lieve Orye (2005). In this debate, for which the Davis-Wiebe exchange is a synecdoche, the core controversy consists of arguments over demarcating or diminishing the line of difference between the study of Religion as a secular, humanistic, social-scientific, even scientific undertaking, and Theology as a confessional, hermeneutic, even ecstatic endeavor. At root it is a purity issue for people such as Donald Wiebe who regard Theology in Religious Studies departments as dirt, as "matter out of place," in Lord Chesterton's terms made famous by Mary Douglas (1984 [1966]: 35; 1975: 50). And it is an issue of tolerance, pluralism for those who argue that theological inquiry is a sub-discipline of the study of Religion lest the study of Religion becomes an arid, even meaningless effort "wherein there is no ecstasy," as Davis argued.

9   See, for example, Wilken (1989: 700) on how the choice of "prepositions 'of' and 'about' portend a profound redefinition of the subject matter [religion] that requires in turn a new relation between the scholar and the thing studied." Wilken suggests that the preposition "of" entails a relation where the scholar speaks "for" religion in the sense of "on behalf of" or "care for," while the preposition "about" implies an adversarial stance "care against religion," a phrase that Wilken approvingly takes from Wendy

Doniger O'Flaherty (1986) as semantic shorthand for Enlightenment-inspired critical distance, detachment that excludes love of the thing studied (Wilken 1989: 702). For a defense of "criticism" and criticism of the scholar as "caretaker" see Mack (2001); McCutcheon (2001); Lincoln (1996).

10 We take as axiomatic here that "religion" *eo ipso* is neither a substantive nor a taxonomic "unique beginner." Rather, the *summum genus* that comprises the *arts de faire* of human kind is "culture," i.e., all the data, bar none, that comprises humankind (see Smith 2000: 39). Insofar, and it is usually far indeed, as Religion has been classified as a genus or a species of culture, i.e., has been made an object *of* classification, it is a taxonomic deke, a move that has given disciplinary import to the fact that "Religions ... are themselves powerful engines for the production and maintenance of classificatory systems" (Smith 2000: 38). In such cases, that is, the "religious" data itself has imposed its own taxa onto a disciplinary system to which those taxa are not native.

11 So Asad (1993: 54): "The anthropological student of particular religions should therefore begin from this point, in a sense unpacking the comprehensive concept which he or she translates as 'religion' into heterogeneous elements according to its historical character."

12 On "difference" as a politically charged rather than a theoretically justified term in the debates on theological versus non-theological or religious versus non-religious study of Religion, see Smith (1988: 231–44; 1997: 60–61).

13 *Arts de faire* is taken from de Certeau (1974); see also Braun (2000: 11–15).

14 This opportunistically, and egregiously, redirects the "failure of nerve" argument made by Donald Wiebe in "The Failure of Nerve in the Academic Study of Religion" (1984).

15 Offering a criticism of the category "religion" in many ways very similar to that suggested here, Timothy Fitzgerald (2000: esp. 12–15) likewise qualifies his criticism by noting that actual departments of Religious Studies and the scholars in these departments have been responsible for the application of non-phenomenological theoretical and disciplinary approaches to "religious" data.

References

Alton, Bruce (1986). "Method and Reduction in the Study of Religions," *Studies in Religion/Sciences religieuses* 15: 153–164. https://doi.org/10.1177/000842988601500203

Arnal, William E. (2000). "Definition." In Willi Braun and Russell T. McCutcheon (eds.), *Guide to the Study of Religion*, 21–34. New York: Cassell.

—— (2001). "The Segregation of Social Desire: 'Religion' and Disney World," *Journal of the American Academy of Religion* 69: 1–19. https://doi.org/10.1093/jaarel/69.1.1

Asad, Talal (1993). "The Construction of Religion as an Anthropological Category." In *Genealogies of Religion: Disciplines and Reasons of Power in Christianity and Islam*, 27–54. Baltimore, MD: Johns Hopkins University Press.

Boyarin, Daniel (2004). *Border Lines: The Partition of Judaeo-Christianity*. Philadelphia, PA: University of Pennsylvania Press. https://doi.org/10.9783/9780812203844

Braun, Willi (2000). "Religion." In Willi Braun and Russell T. McCutcheon (eds.), *Guide to the Study of Religion*, 3–18. New York: Cassell.

Davis, Charles (1975). "The Reconvergence of Theology and Religious Studies," *Studies in Religion/Sciences religieuses* 4: 205–221. https://doi.org/10.1177/000842987500400302

—— (1981). "Theology and Religious Studies," *Scottish Journal of Theology* 2: 11–20.

—— (1984). "Wherein There is No Ecstasy," *Studies in Religion/Sciences religieuses* 13: 393–400. https://doi.org/10.1177/000842988401300402

—— (1986). "The Immanence of Knowledge and the Ecstasy of Faith," *Studies in Religion/Sciences religieuses* 15: 191–196. https://doi.org/10.1177/000842988601500206

Dawkins, Richard (1982). *The Extended Phenotype: The Gene as the Unit of Selection*. San Francisco, CA: Freeman.

Dawson, Lorne (1986). "Neither Nerve nor Ecstasy: Comment on the Wiebe-Davis Exchange," *Studies in Religion/Sciences religieuses* 15: 145–151. https://doi.org/10.1177/000842988601500202

de Certeau, Michel (1974). *L'Invention du quotidien*, vol. 1: *Arts de faire*. Paris: Union générale d'éditions.

Doniger O'Flaherty, Wendy (1986). "The Uses and Misuses of Other Peoples' Myths," *Journal of the American Academy of Religion* 54: 219–239. https://doi.org/10.1093/jaarel/LIV.2.219

Douglas, Mary (1984) [1966]. *Purity and Danger: An Analysis of the Concepts of Pollution and Taboo*. London: Ark/Routledge and Kegan Paul.

—— (1975). "Pollution." In *Implicit Meanings*. New York: Routledge & Kegan Paul.

Durkheim, Émile (1968) [1912]. *Les formes élémentaires de la vie religieuse*. 5th ed. Paris: Presses Universitaires de France.

Fitzgerald, Timothy (2000). *The Ideology of Religious Studies*. Oxford: Oxford University Press.

Gellner, Ernest (1992). *Postmodernism, Reason and Religion*. London: Routledge.

Lincoln, Bruce (1996). "Theses on Method," *Method & Theory in the Study of Religion* 8: 225–227. https://doi.org/10.1163/157006896X00323

McCutcheon, Russell T. (1997). *Manufacturing Religion: The Discourse on Sui Generis Religion and the Politics of Nostalgia*. New York: Oxford University Press.

—— (2001). *Critics Not Caretakers: Redescribing the Public Study of Religion*. Albany, NY: State University of New York Press.

—— (2003). "Autonomy, Unity, and Crisis: Rhetoric and the Invention of a Discipline." In *The Discipline of Religion: Structure, Meaning, Rhetoric*, 54–82. New York: Routledge.

Mack, Burton (2001). "Caretakers and Critics: On the Social Role of Scholars Who Study Religion," *Council of Societies for the Study of Religion Bulletin* 30: 32–38.

Masuzawa, Tomoko (2005). *The Invention of World Religions; Or, How European Universalism Was Preserved in the Language of Pluralism*. Chicago, IL: University of Chicago Press. https://doi.org/10.7208/chicago/9780226922621.001.0001

Orye, Lieve (2005). "To Be or Not to Be Scientific is Not the Question: A Science Scholar's Challenge for the Study of Religion," *Council of Societies for the Study of Religion Bulletin* 34: 14–18.

Penner, Hans H. (1986). "Criticism and the Development of a Science of Religion," *Studies in Religion/Sciences religieuses* 15: 165–175. https://doi.org/10.1177/000842988601500204

Pope, Alexander (1733). *An Essay on Man*, 4 vols. London: printed for J. Wilford.

Smith, Jonathan Z. (1982). *Imagining Religion: From Babylon to Jonestown*. Chicago, IL: University of Chicago Press. https://doi.org/10.1177/000842988401300403

—— (1988). "'Religion' and 'Religious Studies': No Difference at All," *Soundings* 71: 231–244. https://doi.org/10.1017/S003441250001951X

—— (1997). "Are Theological and Religious Studies Compatible?" *Bulletin of the Council of Societies for the Study of Religion* 26: 60–61.

—— (2000). "Classification." In Willi Braun and Russell T. McCutcheon (eds.), *Guide to the Study of Religion*, 35–44. London: Cassell.

―― (2004). "Religion, Religions, Religious." In *Relating Religion: Essays in the Study of Religion*, 179–96. Chicago, IL: University of Chicago Press.
Sperber, Dan (1996). *Explaining Culture: A Naturalistic Approach.* London: Blackwell.
Wiebe, Donald (1984). "The Failure of Nerve in the Academic Study of Religion," *Studies in Religion/Sciences religieuses* 13: 401–422.
―― (1988). "Why the Academic Study of Religion? Motive and Method in the Study of Religion," *Studies in Religion/Sciences religieuses* 17: 403–413.
―― (1991). *The Irony of Theology and the Nature of Religious Thought.* Montreal and Kingston: McGill-Queen's University Press.
―― (1999). *The Politics of Religious Studies.* New York: St. Martin's Press.
Wilken, Robert L. (1989). "Who Will Speak For the Religious Traditions?" [American Academy of Religion 1989 Presidential Address], *Journal of the American Academy of Religion* 57: 699–717. https://doi.org/10.1093/jaarel/LVII.4.699

3

Introducing Religion

> Das Bekannte überhaupt ist darum, weil es *bekannt* ist, nicht erkannt. [For the very reason that the familiar is familiar it is not known.]
> —G. W. F. Hegel (1928 [1805]: 28)

Many disciplines, including Religious Studies, are undergoing a period of lamentation over a perceived slippage in, or fragmentation of, disciplinary identities. The reasons are multiple. Older notions of disciplinary knowledge systems have been destabilized by forces that are familiar to us all. Indeed, the notion of disciplinarity itself is under question (Hertz 1994; Messer-Davidow et al. 1993; Thompson Klein 1996). In Canada at least, economically imposed anorexic regimens in the universities during the last three decades have left the human sciences, Religious Studies among them, scrambling for institutional space, resources and, therefore, license (see Gadaz 2006). And, this scramble entails in part disciplinary self-scrutiny as a matter of (often self-defensive) rationalizing of Religious Studies' intellectual contributions to the academy's study of humankind across time and space.

As is often the case, situational changes do present opportunities for reviewing disciplinary practices, even for inventing new ones. So, this occasion does represent an opening for wading into what I take to be a combination of cliché-ridden ennui and ideational unrest, if not anxiety, concerning questions on what distinguishes the study of religion as an academic field. That is, on what account is the study of religion to live another day in the academy of learning? How does the scholar of religion define the *raison d'être* of her or his labors? My meditation to follow does not lay out a full answer, not even the elemental forms of an answer, but addresses the question of stance, or intellectual disposition, that might direct the disciplinary practices of Religious Studies, especially the attitude, the intellectual angle that is appropriate to introducing religion, a matter on which Jonathan Smith has thought and advised throughout his career.

* * *

A common frustration for scholars of religion concerns the restrictions, often self-restrictions explicitly invoked or tacitly obeyed by students at all career stages, that are placed on curiosity: the "better not ask" or "better not go there" affective stances that are put down as obstacles to the pursuit of a disciplined drive toward a cogent intelligibility of human practices we have come to call, in virtue of some stipulated markers, "religion" or "religious." The Pandora of myth is still censured in the academy, it seems, as the arch- or original sinner, the anti-model of intellection, that evil woman (it *would* be a woman, of course) whose curiosity released a can of toxic worms that kills cats, rather than as the mythic hero of curiosity as the giver of everything—which is what *Pandora* means. This restriction of curiosity, especially prevalent in the study of religion, poses an important threat to academic freedom, perhaps the greatest threat, since it does not come from institutional strictures, but from a cultural censure of unbounded curiosity, that might in fact be diagnosed as a gendered anxiety about the corrosive effect of the Pandora complex. Within the study of religion the Pandora complex is seen as a veritable toxin that might kill the power of the gods. Hence Pandora is a metaphor that chidingly stands as a warning against an anthropocentric scholarly stance and analytic preference in the study of religion. It is this stance, anxieties over it, and resistance to it, about which I want to worry briefly, for it is crucial in introducing religion in the collegiate domain.

* * *

By "anthropocentric stance and analytic preference" I mean something like the following: There is no religion in-it-self apart from people who do things that either those who do them or scholars of religion (or both) call "religious," though with different meanings of the term "religious." In that sense, religion does not exist (let's not conflate nomenclature and ontology; Steinthal 1863, 5); all that exists for our study are people who do things that we classify as "religious" by means of various definitional criteria (see Arnal 2000). For the scholar of religion this entails, first, that the gods are not given a say in our sense-making of religious affairs; it entails that the gods are truly regarded by religion scholars as among the deaf and mute, to speak biblically (1 Cor. 12:2). I am alluding here to what Hans Penner articulates in this volume with reference to the study of myths:

> After many years of false starts we should do our best to put aside the long tradition that translates myth as a revelation of a mystery, a code that must be decoded, or a complex multivalent symbolic system of some deep psychological or metaphysical domain. In brief it is best to put aside all the intellectual effort, which at times has been brilliant, that tried to demonstrate that the basis, the foundation, of the meaning of myth is referential, or, representational. (Penner 2008: 418)

Second, it entails that the proper object of the scholar's study consists of the "religious" behavior of people, a study that consists of description and explanation in general anthropocentric terms. In the words of Alexander Pope (1733): "presume not God to scan / The proper study of mankind is Man." Thus, even when we study objects that in the religious doings of religious people represent themselves as the "presence" of the gods, it is *people* who make this re-presentation of "presence." For example, as I tell my students who come into my course on the New Testament and other early Christian writings, even when we study the Bible—the "word of god"—we shall be studying the *human interests in representing texts (or anything else) as divine rather than human* and the historical, social, and political effects of these representations.

As a scholar of religion I find that this is a crucial conceptual threshold that many students find difficult to cross and one, therefore, that must take up a significant amount of time in the religion scholar's work, whether in the study or in the classroom. This is not the place to worry at length over the reasons for this difficulty, but only to surmise that they are rooted in at least three complementary default affects:

1. A general inclination toward idealism which regards ideas—and beliefs, experiences, sentiments associated with these ideas—as an autonomous realm of things apart from social contexts and, therefore, that ideas ought to be examined in their own terms. Or, stated conversely, there is a diminution of materiality insomuch as the tangible world of human doings is seen merely as the transitory site where the otherwise autonomous ideational entity is housed, expressed, symbolized, and practiced.

2. A general inclination, induced by the forces of our culture, to regard religious ideas in hyper-idealist terms, such that we are seduced into a desire for an analytic that is commensurate with religious ideas' topical orientation toward gods and ghosts and inscrutable human hearts—that is, the topical "it" of religious discourses rather than people and societies that constitute, rationalize, defend, contest, and identify themselves in complex ways by means of these discourses in socially, materially, and historically, located contexts.

3. A general inclination to set off these hyper-idealist religious ideas as the privileged articulation of timeless, self-validating truth, rather than thinking of ideas *too* as practices, that is, ideas as *effects of* and *subject to* or complexly *in the service of* human practices (see Stowers 2008).

Despite the prevalence of these default assumptions, it ought to be said that ideas are not autogenetic; they don't think *themselves*; they do not self-evidently communicate their own meaning. And, even once they are thought and articulated by thinkers, they do not have practical force unless they are given force by people (see further Arnal and Braun 2004). History is, after all, littered with graveyards of rusty and never-mobilized ideas, much like many rural Alberta highways are decorated with rusted, dead automobiles.

Taking seriously that it is people who think and do things and that ideas do not think themselves means that we should adopt a thorough-going "anthropocentrism," in which our object of study are the people (which includes their behaviors and their institutions) who discursively think the gods into existence. In turn, this means that one's dealing with religious phenomena in the very least begs for an examination of these idealist affective stances—not to speak of offering some of the conceptual tools for proceeding with such an examination, and, at its strongest, resisting inclinations for severing ideas, even right godly ones, from social provenances and processes.

With reference to introducing religion in an anthropocentric key—indeed, as an anthropological category—this means that we paraphrase a point made by the anthropologist John Comaroff on the relationship between "history" and "anthropology": A theory of religion which is not at the same time a theory of society is hardly a theory of religion at all (Comaroff 1982: 143–172; see also Comaroff and Comaroff 1992: 13–18). The reverse also holds true, I suggest: a theory of society that is not at the same time a theory of religion is hardly a theory of society at all, given that all so-called "religious" practices are an integral part of the societies in which they are found.

That this must entail that the scholar of religion becomes a certified social scientist, an ethnographer or anthropologist, as I am sometimes told—most recently by an anthropologist, who, equating anthropology with ethnography, suggested to me that I should not use the word "anthropological" unless that means doing ethnography in the field—is not evident to me. Which ethnography, in any case? Riding which theory of ethnography? As if ethnography is a self-evident stand-in for theorizing religion, or as if ethnography is itself not something that is riding on or in service of a theory. I would most certainly demur against a concomitancy between anthropocentric-social study of religion and a certain *kind* of ethnography, the symbolist-hermeneutic-ethnographic anthropology that Marvin Harris labeled "emic" (1980: 32–41). I get very nervous when the term "ethnography" is short-hand for the view that the scholar must go "native" in a quest for empathetic replication of the epistemologies of adherents to whatever religion the scholar is studying, such that the scholar is then in a position to speak *for*, perhaps speak *the* (no preposition needed) adherent. This kind of ethnographic motive is the re-appearance or afterlife of the legacy of the so-called phenomenological approach that continues to dominate much of the academic study of religion, currently often under transmuted terms in which the phenomenologist's desire for protecting an ontological Religion live on. I am thinking of terms such as "post-colonialism," "indigeneity," "alterity" and/or "authenticity" (Adorno 1964; Griffiths 1989; Sayeed 1995; McCutcheon 2003)—recognizing, of course, that these terms are themselves divergently thought and contested. This kind of ethnographic motive strikes me as suspect for two reasons. First, no amount of ethnography, however empathetic, will fulfill the desires which motivate it, that is, the desires of the ethnographer to know not only *what* but exactly *how* the informant knows what he or she knows. Second, to persist nonetheless in the quest for an intersubjective convergence between ethnographer-anthropologist and native-informer, such that the former might then be able to ventriloquate the subjectivity of the latter, strikes me as conceit bordering on hubris. I have therefore decided that I cannot go there.

Rather, I use the term "ethnography" as a general shorthand for gathering information or data, and specifically to gather the kind of information that is not available to the scholar except by ethnographic techniques such as observation and interviewing. Ethnography is simply a means, a method, of gathering, describing, and classifying what people say and do; once I have that information it is up me to subject it to explanation with respect to conceptual scheme or a theory-in-progress that is of my own devising. That is, I would like to make it clear that when we try to subject to our thought the information thus gathered, it is *we* who try to understand the data for *our* explanatory purposes. The "natives" (people who practice religion) do not need me and it is an act of academic hubris, bordering on imperialism or at the least unflattering paternalism, to presume that they do; they already know what they do and why they do it; at least, whatever their knowledge about what they do and why they do it is sufficient and true for them. Even the late Clifford Geertz, who wanted to understand the Balinese cockfight from the "native's point of view," said this in response to an interviewer's question whether the ethnographer should "go back to the natives and show them one's results":

> In general, no! ... They are not interested in social science or alternative understandings ... of what they are doing. They are not interested in the hermeneutics of cockfights. They already know what it [the cockfight] means to them. What I want to do is tell somebody, who does not already know what the cockfight means, what it means. (Geertz in Micheelsen 2002: 10)

Just so! Let this notion of an "anthropocentric study of religion" stand for a kind of declaration, a thesis statement. Admittedly it is a statement with an attitude that generates either nervous or resisting responses from colleagues in the field and students in my classroom. Let me illustrate this nervousness with reference to two lengthy review articles on the *Guide to the Study of Religion* (Braun and McCutcheon 2000), which tries, with "attitude," to set forth the case for a thoroughly anthropocentric study of religion that owed much to Smith's conceptual instruction on what the religion scholar's work is about. One commentator characterizes this attitude with the term "gnosticism," which I take to be in part a metaphor for immodesty regarding the certainty of knowledge presumed to be entailed in this attitude (see Desjardins 2001: 139–150). Another commentator worried about the *Guide*'s "totalizing" desire that betrays an excess of confidence in the "certainty of modernity," that is, a certainty that has not been sufficiently chastened by the postmodern critique of the bullet-proof epistemologies of post-Enlightenment or "modern" scholarship (Whitcombe 2001: 151–160). This same critic finds fault with what is perceived to be an imperious sense of "superior wisdom" hidden in this "attitude," a superiority marked by "a striking disrespect" for and "snub" of the knowledge of religious people about their own religiosity.

* * *

What I take to be the crucial issue here is a worry over scholarly "attitude" as a desire for intellectual monarchy or theoretical imperialism. I accept the equivalence, but do not share the worry, neither in my scholarly work nor as a teacher in the classroom. Concepts (that enable us to establish relations between apparently unlike things), theories (that enable us to account for the relations), and the methods of assembling and analyzing the objects of our scrutiny (which are none other than the disciplined acts by means of which theories are put into practice), once we commit ourselves to them, act like jealous lovers who insist that we permit them "the kind of monomaniacal power or imperialism that a good method has when we are honest about it" (Smith 2007: 93). Theoretical mix-and-match, methodological profligacy, a come-one-come-all ecumenical generosity with respect to "approaches" or elemental presuppositions are, in the final analysis, not in my lexicon of scholarly or pedagogical virtues. Why not? My answer begins once more with a quote from Smith:

> Without the experience of riding hell-bent for leather on one's presuppositions, one is allowed to feel that methods have really no consequences and no entailments. Since none of them is ever allowed to have any power, none of them is ever subjected to any interesting cost accounting. (Smith 2007: 93)

In other words, a theoretical and methodological "fusion cuisine" (fashionably and ubiquitously called "pluralism"), sometimes prescriptively adjured as a requirement of plain human decency or, perhaps more typically, thought to be mandated by a pseudo-postmodern abnegation of strong critical judgment, is corrosive of the very possibility of determined, disciplined, non-promiscuous explanatory intellection with respect to human, including religious, "practices of everyday life" (*arts de faire*), as de Certeau (1984) calls them.

In the realm of *Religionswissenschaft* (though also in other disciplines) this view takes the side of the methodological reductionists in their long (and mostly tedious) debate with the anti-reductionists. Why "reductionism" is so often regarded as a "dirty word" that is equated with a "'holier-than-thou' self-righteousness" (Dawkins 1982: 113; cf. Sperber 1996: 5–6), and often associated with critiques arising from the work of interpretivists of what are considered the non-reducible, incommensurable religious whispers "in" or "behind" our data, is something that I find more amusing than puzzling, although in the classroom "reductionism" is always a good entrée into the problematics of explaining human phenomena in translated terms, that is, in terms other than those in which the phenomena present themselves. Given that all scholarship involves disciplined acts of description, translation, and redescription (terms used in the Smithian sense), the terms "reductionism" and "anti-reductionism" should actually be retired without any loss for the academic study of religion. The binary, therefore, has devolved into something that is about as interesting as observing early Christians calling their marvels "miracles" and other people's miracles "magic"— such terms are social devices that tell us nothing interesting about the object so named, but tell us much about the interests of the namer. Thus other terms are preferable, such as "translation" of phenomena that seemingly and passively present and promulgate themselves in asocial, ahistorical, natural, idealist, non-anthropocentric terms, coming to understand them instead in terms of social, historical, material, anthropocentric categories.

So, "attitude," which I equate with "monomaniacal" theorizing of religion (or anything else, for that matter) is good; it is a requirement of intellection itself. But lest readers are not convinced or, worse, lest they are tempted to take umbrage over this "attitude," allow me several amplifications and clarifications.

1   Riding one's theory "hell-bent for leather," whether in what one writes or in the classroom, is to be differentiated from social or political imperialism or even generalized intellectual imperialism. Riding like a bat out of hell, especially on the track (academy) to test the limits of machine (theory) and rider (scholar), is not an example of "road rage" that aims to run other riders off the track. Although one should expect some abrasion—with Smith: "You have to allow me some measure of monomania if I am to get anywhere. I can't do my work when I have to stop and entertain every other opinion under the sun. This is why such work must always be done in a corporate setting, so that the monomania's mutually abrade against, so that they relativize each other" (2007: 98).

2   Strong theorizing is not equivalent with presenting one's theory from behind bullet-proof armor of dogmatism. Presuppositions and the theories and methods that they generate are corrigible generalizations and they should be held and presented as corrigible. Indeed, corrigibility and rectification are strong concomitants of monomaniacal theorizing, just as they are rather weak concomitants of all-inclusive, pluralist investigations of religious (or any other human) "practices of everyday life." Only what is truly tested can be corrected. How to put this aphorism into pedagogical practice is a challenge with implications for syllabus design, for student project design, and for managing the intellectual and affective mix of losses suffered and gains achieved.

3   Monomaniacal theorizing is not the same as an analytical monism that can account for all jots and tittles of "religious" social practice by means of a single analytical category, such as "exchange theory" or "rational choice theory" or "ritual theory" or any other theory. For example, the social-historical processes by which some tales become authoritative myths and some authoritative myths devolve into mere tales may require a different explanatory scheme than why some people religiously justify going to war as a holy activity and other religious people think it is unholy. Nor does monomaniacal theorizing require that a general, all tidied-up theory of society and culture (if such is even possible) be in place prior to accounting for religion, religions, and religious doings in broadly social terms. *Corrigible theoretical monism is compatible with plural analytics or methodologies*, I propose. Think, thus, of the analytic categories and methods of the human and social sciences as a tool shed for anthropocentric-social explanations of religious practices. The tools in the shed may need fixing, adapting, constant scrutiny as to their utility, but there is no other shed with a different equipment set.

4   I am not persuaded of the critique that monomaniacal theorizing is a mode of modernist self-assertion of certainty that cannot

withstand the critique of postmodernism. This is not the place
to parse the modernism vs. postmodernism debate, except to say
that my view of the knowledge produced by the academic study of
religion, and the means of producing this knowledge, resists the
either/or of modernism and postmodernism. My view of making
knowledge in *Religionswissenschaft* is not modern if by modern one
means a foundational, ahistorical, "universal human reason," i.e.,
knowledge and knowing that is historically unsituated and unaware
of the conditions in which knowledge is produced, a view that
seems, unfortunately, to be regaining currency in the worst of the
cognitive science of religion. It is not postmodern either, however,
if by postmodern one means the valorization of "whatever," of
untranslatable "difference" or "wholly other" as self-legitimated
transcendentals of sorts. Rather, in my rejection of essentialism or
foundationalism—hence my importuning "corrigibility" above—I am
postmodern; in my recoursing to so-called Enlightenment regard
for the possibility of conceptuality by means of intellectual labor—
both testable and corrigible, of course—as a matter of "becoming
answerable for what we say" (Wolfart 2001)—I am a modernist
who stands to be corrected. And as such, I am suspicious of any
invocation of postmodernism where I sense that it is used either as
a rhetorical device to place some taste, preference, practice, belief,
or self-representation beyond criticism, or as an incantation of the
dubious premise of what Ernest Gellner calls the "egalitarianism of
all thought-systems" as the basis for an uninterrogatable admission
of "whatever" into venues of critical thought (see Gellner 1992:
55). This is simply a kind of vulgar liberalism turned into compost
for growing things that I find very frightening, not only because of
what they bode for thought itself, but also what they imply socially
and politically. By "things that frighten" I have in mind the very
conditions that enchanting priests of postmodernism present as
epicurean delight: the "dedifferentiation" of all things, which, as
Fredric Jameson (1991) diagnostically points out, might be seductive
(the allure of the exotic) and addictive (the allure of the authentically
personal), but which constitutes the conditions for and the effects of
the global voracity of late capitalism. For example, permitting myself
a hunch (see Antonio 2000): it is the increasingly dedifferentiated
world that is perhaps the foundation for the current "rebirth of
the tribe," of the rise of nativisms, presenting themselves in forms
of nostalgic, utopian nationalisms and by means of rhetorics of
recuperation of something lost (laden with yearning language of
origin, indigenism, authenticity, uniqueness, incomparability, and so
forth, as markers of difference and identity), all in defense against
the agonies of global capitalism's "empire of blur" (Jameson 2003:
74–76; phrase owed to Rem Koolhaas).

The above four points are a way of saying that the study of religion is fundamentally an activity of thought that is not beholden to an *a priori* foundational premise. It is thus an activity that, to my mind, has not yet given up on the idea of the university as a place for persistent examination and criticism of our and others' (including the university's) cultural sacralities, and for offering its students some resources for explaining the mechanisms and modes whereby these sacralities assume, maintain, or lose their sacredness and the multi-layered cognitive, social, and political effects of super-valuing something *as* sacred. All this, too, is a long exposition of my unease concerning the oft-repeated lamentation that an anthropocentric study of religion disrespectfully sneers at religious thought-systems and, therefore, at the people for whom those systems function as organizers of personal and social identities and practice.

This kind of lamentation is to blame Pandora all over again; it is ultimately to consider curiosity, and its disciplined and intrusive activation, as uncivil, perhaps even inhumane. Allow me clarify what I mean.

As a matter of record and as a plea for a stipulation: the motive force behind representing the study of religion as a non-religious endeavor is neither to pan religion(s) nor to praise religion(s), neither to snipe at religion(s) nor to snuffle for religion. That is to say, the perception of "disrespect" and "snub" is entirely a side issue, a kind of peripheral turbulence that appears to be hyper-felt in the study of religion, though it is an endogenous effect of critical thought itself. This kind of the discomfort of the turbulence is not a reason to still the wind of critical theorizing, neither in the study of religion nor in the study of anything else.

This turbulence accounts, I think, for why one is often asked, in more or less explicit ways, to have the "other" side presented as a "balance" to what they perceive to be a "one-sided" or "unbalanced" representation of the study of religion. Students intuitively prefer to be gatherers and samplers of "meanings." Motives may vary, ranging from unreflected desire to evade the risk of "reductionist" demystification of their cherished meanings to an articulate preference for what we might call the school of hermeneutic/symbolist anthropology which, now commonly validated by some understanding of "postmodernism," likes to collect and sniff meanings—though, so my impression, often remaining majestically cagey ("impartial") with respect to pronouncing whether meanings' bouquets are pleasant or stinky.

My response, condensed here but doled out *ad hoc* in bits and bites throughout my work in the study and in the classroom is something like this:

1. "Meanings" indeed are as numerous as a thousand flowers in the garden, so let's stipulate a pluralism of meanings. But the many meanings do not stand in symmetrically "balanced" relationship to each other for those who have and hold a meaning. At the level of status and function, that is, meanings generally are not held with a sentiment of pluralism or relativism. To be sure, they may be regarded, in one sense, as "provincial" insofar as "other" "provincial" meanings are recognized, even tolerated, but this concessive tolerance of "other" meanings generally does not de-mean or

relativize "my/our" provincial meaning-complex. The thousand flowers in the garden thus reveal themselves as a thousand provincial absolutes, not as a thousand "sympathetic relativisms," as Gellner puts it (1992: 50). Religious meanings are always *somebody's* meanings and they have the status of meanings precisely because they cannot be rendered less weighty by the counter-weight (balance) of an *other's* meaning. What, then, is the scholar to do if he or she frets to do something more interesting and intellectually challenging than merely count and catalogue the flowers of meaning in the garden?

2 Meanings are notoriously inaccessible. I will let Gellner's truculent words carry on: "one of the temptations to which the hermeneutic school is prone, and to which practitioners of postmodernism succumb with ecstasy ... [is that] they become so enthusiastic and inebriated with the difficulty of explicating the Other that in the end they don't even try to reach it, but content themselves with elaborating the theme of its inaccessibility, offering a kind of initiation into a Cloud of Unknowing, a Privileged Non-Access ... a mystery all its own" (Gellner 1992: 56). I agree.

3 Hence, I suggest, we might learn a lot more about religious meanings by paying attention not so much to the flowers in the garden but to the gardener and the gardener's (human) processes of planting, cultivating, fencing off and reaping meanings.

All this to make the point that the problem of a buffeting turbulence effected by anthropocentric-social-historical theorizing of religion is best solved pedagogically by scrutinizing the problem itself and thoughtfully minding the intrusive nature of introducing thought into the domain of the familiarly-known and the exotically strange and other (Smith 2003), of introducing as "poking and prying with a purpose" (Hurston 1942), rather than by permitting the problem to frighten us into abandoning our hell-bent-for-leather theorizing ride.

* * *

And so we ride on, knowing full-well that this "attitude" is not representational of the field of Religious Studies as a whole, either of its past or its current constellation of practices. If this manner of introducing religion is thought to be too imperialistic, I would agree only if I am permitted to qualify my imperialism with a coda expressed in Toni Morrison's words:

> I want to draw a map, so to speak, of a critical geography and use that map to open as much space for discovery, intellectual adventure, and close exploration as did the original charting of the New World—*without the mandate of conquest.* (Morrison 1993: 3; emphasis added)

Empires are built on and continuously shored up by what Wilfred Sellars calls "the myth of the given" (Sellars 1997; see also Penner 2000). The truly imperial modes of imperializing are assertions of power and rhetoric of assimilation—that, of course, might well represent themselves in various platitudinous nods toward "pluralism" (see Brown 2006) but such that "pluralism" is sharply contained either with reference to the "private" or to the "personal"—or a way of talking to ourselves among ourselves within (concessively acknowledged but ignored) earshot of the noise of other folks talking to themselves. Hence an imperialism that represents itself as corrigible is actually quite an oxymoron, thus not an imperialism at all. Because the academic field of *Religionswissenschaft* is at this time actually ruled by different disciplinary attitudes, the stance recommended here is merely an assertion of a kind of work on religion that refuses to be assimilated, the kind of work that insists on "a trained and scrutinized consciousness" as the *sine qua non* in the academy's human and social sciences, including Religious Studies. And what is this? Nothing grander than "sheer survival" of the most humane road to understanding human societies, what J. Z. Smith calls "the hard road of understanding" (1985: 546), because it must labor for its insights and contend for them in the arena of public argument in the academy, rather than wait passively for visions and revelations.

What this means for the disciplinary practices of scholars of religion, particularly the mandate of introducing religion in the context of a general education, can here be indicated only briefly in terms of clues. It means, I think, finally (finally!) restraining ourselves from employing taxonomies of religion that are binary in structure, either qualitative binaries such as true vs. false, revealed vs. natural, universal vs. particular, ours vs. theirs, or historico-evolutionary binaries such as prehistorical vs. historical, primitive vs. advanced, animist vs. rational, cosmotrophic vs. soteric (Alles 1994: 104–106), and so forth. These binaries—and others we might think of—are ethnocentrically prejudiced (Rüsen 2004). As Tim Murphy has reminded us, in these bi-modal taxonomies the "paired oppositions ... are not equally weighted ... [B]inary pairs actually form hierarchical oppositions" (2006: 202). Moreover, not only do they fail to have empirical and sound logical warrant, but they are also inhumane. It means too, I suggest, creating and using definitions of our object(s) without creating essences, something that is quite possible to do (see Stowers 2007). Essences are born out of a mythic imagination, but when deployed ideologically and politically, they are not just "acts of metaphysical aggression," as Dubuisson would say (2003: 167; see profitably also Fitzgerald 2000), but pernicious tools of apologetics, vilification, and conquest. And that too is inhumane.

This entails, as a third clue, that the vast data field of what we by some stipulated set of markers nominally call "religion" or "religious" (or by some other name for a beyond-history and beyond-language—i.e., nonhuman = inhuman?—*ontos*) is not subject to a single capital-T Theory of religion because such a theory would need to presuppose a generic and thus non-historical human being. In that case the theory would not be able to escape being a "disincarnate idealization" (Dubuisson 2003: 110) and thus offer no aid at all in the description and understanding of the parochiality, particularity, and historicality of social formations and their practices in various times and places. But it is only thus that these parochial, private experiences are given their human and humane due—a scholarly due that the scholar of religion donates to the project and prospect of humanity (see Saxton 2006).

References

Adorno, Theodor W. 1964. *Jargon der Eigentlichkeit: Zur deutschen Ideologie*. Frankfurt am Main: Suhrkamp.
Alles, Gregory D. 1994. *The Iliad, the Ramayana, and the Work of Religion: Failed Persuasion and Religious Mystification*. University Park, PA: Pennsylvania State University Press.
Antonio, Robert J. 2000. "After Postmodernism: Reactionary Tribalism," *American Journal of Sociology* 106: 40–87. https://doi.org/10.1086/303111
Arnal, William E. (2000). "Definition." In Willi Braun and Russell T. McCutcheon (eds.), *Guide to the Study of Religion*, 21–34. London: Cassell.
Arnal, William E. and Willi Braun (2004). "Social Formation and Mythmaking: Theses on Key Terms." In R. Cameron and M. Miller (eds.), *Redescribing Early Christianity*, 459–469. Society of Biblical Literature Symposium Series, 28. Atlanta, GA: Society of Biblical Literature; Leiden: Brill.
Willi Braun and Russell T. McCutcheon (eds.) (2000). *Guide to the Study of Religion*. London: Cassell.
Brown, Wendy (2006). *Regulating Aversion: Tolerance in the Age of Identity and Empire*. Princeton, NJ: Princeton University Press. https://doi.org/10.1515/9781400827473
Comaroff, John (1982). "Dialectical Systems, History, and Anthropology: Units of Study and Questions of Theory," *Journal of Southern African Studies* 8: 143–172. https://doi.org/10.1080/03057078208708040
Comaroff, John and Jean Comaroff (1992). *Ethnography and the Historical Imagination*. Studies in the Ethnographic Imagination. Boulder, CO: Westview.
Dawkins, Richard (1982). *The Extended Phenotype: The Gene as the Unit of Selection*. San Francisco, CA: Freeman.
de Certeau, Michel (1984). *The Practice of Everyday Life*. Steven Rendall (trans.). Berkeley, CA: University of California Press.
Desjardins, Michel (2001). "Teaching with the *Guide to the Study of Religion*," *ARC* 29: 139–150.
Dubuisson, Daniel (2003). *The Western Construction of Religion: Myths, Knowledge, and Ideology*. W. Sayers (trans.). Baltimore, MD: Johns Hopkins University Press.
Fitzgerald, Timothy. (2000). *The Ideology of Religious Studies*. Oxford: Oxford University Press.
Gardaz, Michel (ed.) (2006). *Religious Studies in Canada: Past, Present, and Future*. Special issue of *Studies in Religion/Sciences Religieuses* 35(3–4). https://doi.org/10.1177/000842980603500301
Gellner, Ernest (1992). *Postmodernism, Reason and Religion*. London: Routledge.
Griffiths, Gareth (1989). "The Myth of Authenticity: Representation, Discourse and Social Practice." In C. Tiffin and A. Lawson (eds.), *De-scribing Empire: Postcolonialism and Empire*, 70–85. London: Routledge.
Harris, Marvin (1980). *Cultural Materialism: The Struggle for a Science of Culture*. New York: Vintage.
Hegel, G. W. F. (1928) [1805]. *Phänomenologie des Geistes*. Dritte Auflage. Leipzig: Felix Meiner.
Hertz, Judith (ed.) (1994). *Fields and Boundaries: The Shifting Space of Disciplinarity*. Ottawa: Canadian Federation for the Humanities/Fédération canadienne des études humaines.
Hurston, Zora Neale (1942). *Dust Tracks on a Road*. Urbana, IL: University of Illinois Press.
Jameson, Fredric (1991). *Postmodernism, or, The Cultural Logic of Late Capitalism*. Durham, NC: Duke University Press. https://doi.org/10.1215/9780822378419
—— (2003). "Future City," *New Left Review* 21 (May–June): 65–79. https://doi.org/10.7208/chicago/9780226922621.001.0001

McCutcheon, Russell T. (2003). "The Jargon of Authenticity and the Study of Religion." In *The Discipline of Religion: Structure, Meaning, Rhetoric*, 167–188. New York: Routledge. https://doi.org/10.4324/9780203451793_chapter_8

Messer-Davidow, Ellen, David R. Shumway, and David J. Sylvan (eds.) (1993). *Knowledges: Historical and Critical Studies in Disciplinarity.* Charlottesville, VA: University Press of Virginia.

Micheelsen, Arun (2002). "'I Don't Do Systems'": An Interview with Clifford Geertz," *Method & Theory in the Study of Religion* 14: 2–20. https://doi.org/10.1163/157006802760198749

Morrison, Toni (1993). *Playing in the Dark: Whiteness and the Literary Imagination.* New York: Knopf.

Murphy, Tim (2006). "Cultural Understandings of 'Religion': The Hermeneutical Context of Teaching Religious Studies in North America," *Method & Theory in the Study of Religion* 18: 197–218. https://doi.org/10.1163/157006806778553525

Penner, Hans D. (2000). "Interpretation." In Willi Braun and Russell T. McCutcheon, *Guide to the Study of Religion*, 57–71. London: Cassell.

——— (2008). "What a Difference Theory Makes." In Willi Braun and Russell T. McCutcheon (eds.), *Introducing Religion: Essays in Honor of Jonathan Z. Smith*, 418–433. London: Equinox.

Pope, Alexander (1733). *An Essay on Man*, 4 vols. London: printed for J. Wilford.

Rüsen, Jörn (2004). "How to Overcome Ethnocentrism: Approaches to a Culture of Recognition by History in the Twenty-First Century," *History and Theory* 43: 118–129. https://doi.org/10.1111/j.1468-2303.2004.00301.x

Saxton, Alexander (2006). *Religion and the Human Prospect.* New York: Monthly Review Press.

Sayeed, S. M. A. (1995). *The Myth of Authenticity: A Study in Islamic Fundamentalism.* Karachi: Royal Book Co.

Sellars, Wilfrid. (1997). *Empiricism and the Philosophy of Mind.* Cambridge, MA: Harvard University Press.

Smith, Jonathan Z. (1985). "Jonathan Z. Smith on William J. Bennett's 'To Reclaim a Legacy: A Report on the Humanities in Higher Education,'" *American Journal of Education* 93: 541–546. https://doi.org/10.1086/443822

——— (2003). "Why Compare Religions?" Unpublished paper presented at the Conference in Honor of John F. Wilson, Princeton University.

——— (2007). "The Necessary Lie: Duplicity in the Disciplines." Afterword in Russell T. McCutcheon, *Studying Religion: An Introduction*, 73–80. New York: Routledge.

Sperber, Dan (1996). *Explaining Culture: A Naturalistic Approach.* London: Blackwell.

Steinthal, H. (1863). *Geschichte der Sprachwissenschaft bei den Griechen und Römern, mit besonderer Rücksicht auf die Logik.* Berlin: F. Dümmler's Verlagsbuchhandlung.

Stowers, Stanley (2007). "The Concept of 'Religion,' 'Political Religion' and the Study of Nazism," *Journal of Contemporary History* 42: 9–24. https://doi.org/10.1177/0022009407071628

——— (2008). "The Ontology of Religion." In Willi Braun and Russell T. McCutcheon (eds.), *Introducing Religion: Essays in Honor of Jonathan Z. Smith*, 434–449. London: Equinox.

Thompson Klein, Julie (1996). *Crossing Boundaries: Knowledge, Disciplinarities, and Interdisciplinarities.* Charlottesville: University Press of Virginia.

Whitcombe, Anne (2001). "Seeking Guidance: One Student's Critical Reflection on Using the *Guide to the Study of Religion*," *ARC* 29: 151–160.

Wolfart, Johannes C. (2001). "Becoming Answerable for What We Say: Colonialism and the Pax AAR," *Studies in Religion / Sciences Religieuses* 30: 381–388. https://doi.org/10.1177/000842980103000309

Part II

Particularities

4

Jesus and Addiction to Origins

> There is no primordium—it is all history.
> —J. Z. Smith, *Imagining Religion* (1982: xiii)

> I don't need to be a global citizen
> because I'm blessed by nationality
> I'm member of a growing populace
> we enforce our popularity
> there are things that seem to pull us under
> and there are things that drag us down
> but there's a power and a vital presence
> that's lurking all around
> we've got the American Jesus
> —Bad Religion, "American Jesus" (1993)

The history of the Christianity's relationship to and evaluation of Jesus presents us with a fascinating case study for the place of "history" in Christian discourses about their past. "History," in Christian thought, is an ambiguity that wants to slip into a contradiction or, at least, into an antagonistic tension. The ambiguity concerns the status of "history" and where to draw the line on its usefulness, how to arbitrate the excess of historical Jesuses (see Price 2000), and how to bail out if the encounter with documentary history should threaten to topsy-turvy the imaginary artifice of "history," when the encounter with the documentary traces of the past rattle away at understandings of "the truth of history" which believers seem to know quite apart from historical studies, sometimes despite what they learn through historical studies.

On the one hand, "history" is a deeply valued, even normative concept in Christian self-understanding. Historical inquiry would thus seem to be grounded in the very fabric of Christianity itself. It presents itself as an historic and historical religion; it plots its origin from the life of a real person; it has from the beginning insisted on "history" as an essential ingredient for theological imagination and other discourses by which Christians re-present to themselves their own religious constitution. Viewed from this end of the paradox, the end that says history matters, one would expect that the effort to identify by all possible means the man who stands at the point of historical beginnings would be of central importance, even essential for intra-Christian inquiries and discourses in order to examine not only theoretically the notion of "origins" of religious/social movements (see Masuzawa 2000) but also what possible material, social, and cultural conditions and interests in the first-century Mediterranean world help to account for the Jesus-phenomenon in its multiple and diverse forms.

On the other hand, the category of "history," the grime and grit of "human doings in the past," to define history in Herodotus' terms (Herodotus 1:1; see Martin 2000: 74), and the recovery or reconstruction of the stuff of those "human doings" has been regarded with hedging wariness, at best, and outright suspicion, at worst. Let me illustrate each with a very generalized and exaggerated sketch of how the "historical Jesus" has been dealt with in the history of Christian thought.

In the first view, most sharply expressed in the "orthodox" creedal christologies, history appears to be important at first blush; the historicality of Jesus is stressed, but his history is severely limited and interest in him as an historical figure is rather more instrumental and strategic than it is substantial. The interest in history is limited because it is only necessary to vouchsafe the "that" of Jesus' humanity and the "that" of his death, rather than to supply the full "what" of his life and the varied and multiple effects the "what" of his life and death had on his contemporaries and those who lived on in his memory. Here history merely supplies a name (Jesus), a vague sense of time and place, and a crucial anecdote (crucifixion). The pre-Pauline creed (1 Cor. 15:3-5), the Philippian Christ hymn (Phil. 2:5-11), indeed, the entire Pauline Christ-imagination had little use for the life of Jesus at all beyond needing him dead so that he could be raised to the mythic status of cosmic savior (see Mack 1988: 100–113; 1995: 79–87). The creedal christologies carry the Pauline christology forward in such a way that Nazareth has little do with Nicea and Chalcedon beyond an instrumental value of asserting the necessity of belief in the Christ's humanity (or God's incarnation) and beyond functioning as a strategic counterpoint to the claims of the Marcionites, the Gnostics and other "heretics" in Christian antiquity and countless other Christian "deviants" throughout Christian history.

At this point one might want to object and point to the "lives" of Jesus, the narrative gospels, as a way of insisting that here we have the other side of the story, the "what" of Jesus's life missing in Paul and the creeds. This is partly true. Certainly in the development of the christological imagination, the mythic Christ of Paul needed to be narrativized (i.e., set in time and space, which should not be equated with historicization), to be brought down to earth, so to speak. The person who achieved this with a "last word" kind of effect was, of course, the writer of the gospel of Mark, because for 2000 years Mark's story of Jesus has served ordinary Christians and learned theologians, even non-confessional historians, as the true story of the real Jesus and as the real story of how it truly all began (Mack 1988).

But after William Wrede (1971 [1901]), Albert Schweitzer (1910 [1906]), and more recently, Burton Mack (1988), to name just a few watershed figures, we know that this view of Mark no longer holds. Rather, what Mark did was to superimpose the Pauline Christ myth onto his Palestinian Jesus stories. Whether one wants to call Mark's story an historicized myth or a mythic history—or "mythistory," to use McNeill's (1986) neologism—matters little: in either case, history is subservient to myth, and Jesus to the Christ, and what you get is a story with a kerygmatic core claim, the story of a god-man who gave his life as a ransom for many (Mark 10:45).

It is the narrative version of the Nicean or Chalcedonian creed and its astonishing genius is that it appears to satisfy the "history" requirement of Christian faith without, however, adjusting, even in the least, the weight and core of the creedal christological imagination. Here the ambivalence toward the category of "history" or "biography" manifests itself in a creative theological, myth-making historiography not only compatible with but deeply congenial to mainline Christian belief in matters christological—which is itself, of course, "a sophisticated form of mythic thinking" (Mack 1996: 251). The divide between myth and history was bridged; the Jesus of history and the Christ figure of the Pauline savior myth were more or less conflated and made to appear identical. It is essentially the Markan god-man Jesus-Christ who has provided some of the most central and familiar and normative categories by which christological thought is organized and articulated. The divine Jesus-as-God-incarnate is the pillar of the doctrine of revelation; a theologized cross stands at the heart at what Jesus was all about; a *theologia crucis* is the common denominator of various models of salvation; the humiliated-yet-vindicated Christ becomes the model and rationale for Christian character and moral formation; and so forth.

That the Galilean Jesus would hardly have recognized himself in the Markan hero, the crucified god-man savior Jesus-Christ, is the claim of a second kind of historical investigation that has turned the category of "history" into a problem subject to suspicion, strategies of dismissal or often even hostility for those who are heavily invested (believers) in the first "history." History matters but it better be the right kind with the right outcomes! I am speaking here of the post-Reformation and post-Enlightenment history of questing for the historical Jesus that began with Reimarus (1694–1768) and that has in recent decades resumed with flood-like volume to the point where it is increasingly necessary to produce books that make sense of the books about Jesus (e.g., Borg 1994; for a journalists' attempt to report on contemporary Jesus scholarship see Allen 1998). There is not time here to review this history, except to say that the effort to exhume the historical Jesus beneath layers of Christian imagination about him has rarely been welcomed by ordinary believers, nor has it made a tremendous impact on the theologians' effort to articulate the role of Jesus in Christian theology, nor, I should add, has it made a remarkable impact on non-confessional descriptions of Christian beginnings, though there are notable exceptions (see, for example, Cameron 1994; Mack 1996, cf. Mack 2000; Riley 1997).

The reasons for this likely are neither single nor simple, but we should not be far off by suggesting that at the heart of them stands an almost unshakable commitment to the Pauline/Markan christological paradigm that is undergirded by firm preferences for creedal orthodoxy and by the "sacred persistence" (Smith 1982: 36–52) of the fact of the biblical canon and the canonical epistemology derived from this fact. (The term "canonical" does not refer only to the physical fact of the biblical canon nor to the school of canonical criticism, but it also contains the ideas of normativity, orthodoxy, and a hermeneutic driven by the self-evident nature of privileged theological truths that drive historical inquiry rather than derive from it.)

Through the perspective of this lens it is almost impossible to imagine, much less to embrace or take serious account of, some remarkable findings of those who study early Christianity. Again, this is not the time to review them in detail; let me just list a few to make the point. (For a core starting bibliography, consider Cameron 1990; Jacobson 1992; Kloppenborg 1987, 1994; Kloppenborg and Vaage 1991; Mack 1988, 1993, 1995).

Recent source and literary stratigraphical analyses have brought to light several more or less reconstructible charter documents of early Palestinian Jesus groups which make it quite clear that it was possible to remember Jesus and live on in his memory and effect without speaking of him in incarnational terms, i.e., without attributing to him titles implying divinity and without connecting him to a theologized soteriological cross. The Sayings Gospel Q and the oldest strata of the Gospel of Thomas are the best known of these memory traditions. Q, especially strikes me as a very interesting document, not only for the historian of the emergent phase of Christianity, but also for intra-Christian reflection, because of its insistent call for a hermeneutic of practice (see Robinson 1993). The Jesus of Q is neither imagined as *christos* nor remembered in Pauline/Markan kerygmatic terms. Q has no interest in the death of Jesus beyond implying that a violent death often is the outcome of someone who lives the life of a prophet. There is no saving-significance attached to his death. Indeed, there is no saving-language at all; what we find instead is the language of coming to Jesus, to see and hear him, and to follow him.

The Q memory tradition was not the only one that kept the idea of Jesus alive without the Pauline kerygmatic trappings. Jesus the "living" mystagogue (Valantasis 1997) of the Gospel of Thomas is a teacher of saving wisdom for which death, resurrection, and future parousia are not necessary as credentials (Cameron 1999). Similarly, the *Didache* (or "The Teaching of the Lord through the Twelve Apostles"), more or less contemporary with the canonical gospels, entirely glosses over Jesus' death and resurrection. To this other, more fragmentary memory traditions may be added.

To this literary evidence one can also add the iconographic witness. In his greatly under-appreciated book on *Archaeological Evidence of Church Life before Constantine* (1985), Graydon Snyder documents that the cross and symbols of sacrifice, suffering, and death do not appear in Christian art until the fourth century. Rather, the typical early images used to represent Jesus are those of shepherd, philosopher or wonder-worker—a variety of images that appear to contain an understanding of Jesus as a kind of mobile consultant in the art negotiating the vicissitudes and treacheries of life in a rather confusing and unstable world. Snyder concludes: "With the evidence at hand there appears a clear Christology for the *ante pacem* era. Jesus was not understood in a promise-fulfilment nexus, nor in a guilt-redemption pattern, but in an alienation-deliverance structure. Understood in this manner, we can see why motifs of ... [the cross and sacrifice] cannot be found in the data except by those who insist on cryptosymbol systems" (Snyder 1985: 165–166).

It would seem, therefore, that the kerygmatic Christ, the creedal Christ came into his own, rose to victory, as it were, in the post-Constantinian church. The fact that this Christ looms so large in the New Testament canon is not surprising given that this canon is itself a Constantinian fact.

What does one do with this? The question might be asked at several different levels, depending on the discursive context (who is doing the talking? where and to whom? who might be listening? what is being pleaded for or negotiated?—and depending also on the kind of questions we want to work out in the historical realm and, finally, on the historiography (theory of history) that we will use to determine what stockpile of goodies get stuffed into the bag labelled "history." In other words, whether one stands inside the Christian tradition (or any other tradition) or whether one stands outside will make a difference not only in how "history" is constituted in our minds, but also in where our questions will focus. Let's take one level, for example: the rhetorical and ideological situation of the theological college or seminary. Given the normativity of the originary period of Christianity for Christian self-constitution, how "historical" might our inquiry be in the attempt to reconstruct and creatively assess some long-forgotten Christian memories of Jesus by which a good number of early Christian groups defined themselves, and quite well, it seems? One might muse here, in addition, that inasmuch as the creedal-canonical christology was, at least in the first several centuries, the preferred christology of the learned and lording elite of the church, it is more of a litmus test for right belief than a mimetic ideal for Christian praxis; Christian adherence to it seems to be driven primarily by a canonical epistemology that may not always be most advantageous to a practical Christianity. The stakes in this re-imagining of Christian origins are high—highest perhaps for those deeply invested in a theological appropriation of Christian beginnings. What is involved is not only adjustment or minor modifications of the "orthodox" christologies, but a willingness to consider the possibility of a different christological hermeneutic altogether. What is at stake is the very myth of Christian origins that is so self-evidently true that its mythic character, its coming to be by means of "fictioning" (from the Latin *fingere*, to make or invent, which, as Theodore Sarbin points out, is etymologically a "distant cousin" to *facere*, to do or to make, from which the word "fact" is derived; Sarbin 1998b: 299–300) in the history of Christian thinking and liturgical and other ritual doings, is neither questionable nor evidently mythic but indubitably historical.

However, rather than pursuing how emic (insider) and etic (outsider) stances might generate different histories of the same archival stuff, let me rather muse a bit at one level of abstraction up, in order to make sense of the possibility that the same archival stuff constitutes a pantry for different "historical" concoctions. Let's therefore move up to the level of historiography that can take thicker account of the production of history that in one of its "moments" includes the fictioning (fashioning) of historical narratives.

For, historical narratives don't just happen. They are made—fictioned. How might we think of this making? I would like to suggest that we locate our thinking about this making within a view of a theory of prolongated historical production, on which a bit more shortly. To get us there, I begin by citing Eric Hobsbawm's book *On History*: "history," he claims, "is the raw material for nationalist or ethnic or fundamentalist [or any "religious"] ideologies, as poppies are the raw material for heroin addiction. The past is an essential element, perhaps *the* essential element" (Hobsbawm 1997: 5) in ideology formation, just as ideology formation, in turn, is essential for constituting social and "convictional worlds" (a phrase owed to Donaldson 1997) in the present. "If there is no suitable past, it can always be invented" (Hobsbawm 1997: 5). Or if there is a past, as there usually is, it can be tinkered with to properly permit and vindicate a state of affairs in the present (see Lincoln 1989: 21–23). Hobsbawm goes on to say that, insofar as this is the case, historiography is not disentangled from politics, just as the historical narrative is not an unprejudiced re-presentation of the past, and just as the historian cannot shed the role of the political actor, whether within the commonwealth of a religious community or within any other group. In addition to being a reference to data in the chronological past, the term "history" thus always is also a catchment of the social, political, or religious interests of those who "do history"—whether professional historians or ordinary people who make less specialized forays into the past, for whatever reason. This means, however, that history, in the full sense that includes our assembly of it and our re-presentation of it by means of narratives, is not *just* "back there," ready-made and waiting to be toted into our present location in time. Rather, history is made largely in retrospect and thus subject to the inventive, occluding, refractive ramifications of retrospection, and, as studies on remembering retrospection have shown, "memory is as much or more creative reconstruction as accurate recollection, and, unfortunately it is impossible to tell where one ends and the other begins" (Crossan 1998: 59). It is from our present location in time that we, in retrospect, turn poppy seeds into heroin. Or, if you find Hobsbawm's metaphor too seedy, that is when we fashion potatoes into poutine (a popular Québécois dish, consisting of a mixture of French fries and cheese curds doused with gravy)—i.e., that is when we cook raw history by larding it with an immaculate origin (a mythologoumenon; Masuzawa 2000) and meaning, by straining out the murk of contingency of human history (on which see Heller 1993: 1–35), by seasoning it with order and ontology, by stirring in teleology and all such things that make history tasteful (useful) to us as an alibi for *our* interests, interests that include forging and maintaining group identities, emplacing ourselves on a line of continuity between primordial past and a plenary future (Urzeit-Endzeit), and so on. In this sense, Paul Veyne is surely correct. People, he suggests, "do not find the truth; they create it, as they create their history" (1988: xii). "History" thus, whatever else it is, is primarily a discursive means of social formation and contestation. This is why it is not surprising, for example, that the emergence of strong nationalist interests goes hand in hand with scrutinizing and tinkering with the history curricula in the schools (such as we have seen in Quebec in recent years) and why recent provincial election campaigns in Quebec have been fought with frequent, explicit, and passionate references to "the past," a past that may be substantively vague in popular memory, but that is rhetorically evocative nonetheless—the "je me souviens" motto on every Quebec vehicle license plate is the reminder that the past provides license and authority for the (perceived) need of national emancipation from the colonial past and the ongoing instrument of colonization: the Canadian federation.

Notions of invention, fictioning, or cooking suggest, of course, that historical production is a human artifact, though I hasten to add that I attach no connotation of arbitrariness, meaninglessness or falsehood to the artificiality of historical narratives. Let me suggest the contrary anecdotally. When my daughter was in high school she was assigned by her literature teacher to write a snippet from her past: a limited exercise in autobiography. She asked me to read it, and, though I recognized the event described in her narrative, it struck me as highly invented. Moods, motives, detailed thought processes of the past were neatly dramatized and, by means of literary fictioning, tethered to a single theme. "Is this how it really was?" I asked. "No," she conceded, "I couldn't remember how it actually was, and the teacher told me that the story must have a theme, and so I made some things up so I could write a story." "But," she continued, "the story is true, it really is about me." (Just as, incidentally, the anecdote I have just told is a product of fictioning the long ago facts of a conversation with my daughter!) *Factere* and *fingere* may be "distant cousins" but in my daughter's activity on the past they seemed to have romanced each other to become a single process of narrative re-presentation, such that the result was a fictioned factual story, a "believed-in imagining" (Sarbin 1998a) about the past. Anyone who has tried to write her or his autobiography will probably recognize at least some truth in what I am talking about. Artificiality thus is not something to be avoided in historical production; on the contrary, history in the fullest sense of the term is artifice; the result of human artificing. One should recall that, although the notion of the invention of history sounds heretical from the vantage point of a modernist, positivist-empirical historiography, it is quite in keeping with a strong tradition of ancient historiography in which the presentation of the past was considered a rhetorical art (e.g., Cicero, *De legibus* 1.5; see Bowersock 1994: 12–13; Worthington 1994), a view, indeed, that remained dominant until the French Revolution (White 1976: 23–24), and one that has regained currency in recent theoretical work on the relationship between history-writing and the production of fictive narratives and rhetoric (see Berkhofer 1995; Easthope 1993; LaCapra 1985; Stone 1979; White 1976, 1978, 1987).

Artificiality enters historical production at several different junctures and it takes different forms. Let's consider only one form: amnesia, either intentional or unintentional forgetting or deliberate or social-structural suppression and ideological silencing of human doings (for what follows I am indebted to Trouillot 1995). Any historical production is at once a bundle of what it says and what it does not say; any historical narrative, whether religious or not, thus is a "bundle of silences" (Trouillot 1995: 27). Loss happens in at least four stages—or, what Trouillot calls "moments" where "moment" should be thought of as an abstraction for the purposes of analysis rather than as an indicator of time—of historical production, and the losses are cumulative and overlapping. And, since the four "stages" are analytical components of an elongated notion of the making of history, the four moments of loss should also be imagined as always simultaneous.

(a) *Making the facts* (sources). This is the moment of actual human doing, of lived history, in space and time. It is the moment of evoking sentiments and interests, of turning those sentiments into motivations for actions and practices, of marshalling those motivations and converting them into intentional personal and social actions by which people construct their everyday material and social worlds as well as the ideational superstructures in terms of which they think of and contest those worlds. At this level, all people are history-makers; all people are fact/source-makers. But not everyone's doings (facts, sources) and not all doings of anyone get validated and recorded, for the validation and recording takes place in social contexts in which who and what count as valuable and recordable is determined by mechanisms of marginalization and silencing that are linked to status, power, and influence, something we know well enough even without having read Marx, Nietzsche, or Foucault. At this stage, history, including early Christian history, is full of unrecorded doings (facts).

(b) *Assembling the facts.* Think of this as creating the "archive" by retrospective selection that heralds some facts, side-lines others, and forgets some entirely. Not all recorded doings are archived. History thus suffers a second moment of attrition at the archiving stage.

(c) *Retrieving the facts.* "Archives" are the sources for making the "narrative" that organizes the archival grab-bag of knowledge into a connected just-so story. Again, there is loss, for narratives valorize some knowledge, trivialize other, resignify and fiction all archival stuff.

(d) *Signifying the facts.* This is the moment of making history in the fullest sense. It is the moment of canonizing both archives and narratives, which of course entails at the same time marginalizing or forgetting many sources and many narratives. A most important achievement at this stage is that the canonical narrative turns into a kind of "simulacrum," a hyper-reality that signifies nothing but itself (Baudrillard 1994)—myth and history become an indistinguishable, confused entity, such that the narrative and real history are about identical. This is precisely why it is hard for believers and many learned historians to imagine early Christian history in any other way than the writer of the gospel of Mark tells it. (Mack 1996 and Lightstone 1997 describe this as the "catch-22" that hampers historical redescription of early Christianities and Judaisms.) This is precisely why "history" is a shibboleth in Christian dealings with their past, a kind of pet term that must be carefully kept on a leash.

What to do with all this? One could pursue all kinds of questions: what to do with the discarded, marginalized archival traditions? It seems self-evident that the amnesia in historical production is linked to power and thus evokes questions about who makes, assembles, retrieves and signifies the facts. To serve whom and what interests? If this view of historical production is allowed to stand, we have much work to do, not least of which is to pursue our historical interests, whether this is focussed on Jesus or any other set from the past, with a committed bent on historiographical theorizing and to link such theorizing to social analysis. For, if the view of historical production that I have outlined is allowed to stand, our own dealing in the past is itself a moment in historical production that is rife with special interests that do not belong in the past at all (see Arnal 1997, 2005; cf. Braun 1997).

Much more could and ought to be said. For there is much entailed here for how we study early Christianities, how we understand "canon," and how we engage the canon. I forfeit here indulging in these questions, except to say that it strikes me as an extraordinarily interesting and worthwhile thing to do to read the early Christian literature as exemplars, cases in point, of a theory of historical production that begins with real, intentional "human doings" in the past and ends with the creation of the simulacrum of the canonical historical narrative in the present. Observing the processes at work in this sort of elongated chronology of production puts us in a good position to think deeply about the question why we invest so much in the past and why it is so important that the past looks just so, rather than just any old way, and why it is apparently necessary to forget as much as we remember, and why what and how we remember is not so much a matter of "the past" as it is a matter of *our* present.

The "our" is most important. If history, including its repertoire of symbols—yes, including the "sacred" shibboleths in Christianity's theologies and narratives about its supernatural origin and providential history—is a human production from beginning to end, then there is no place to hide from the imperative to take responsibility for history, both in terms of our lived doings in the present and in terms of how we describe and use "the past" to rationalize our doings, worldviews, social arrangements, and the multitudinous instrumentalities, material and symbolic, by which we contrive powerful tangible worlds in accordance with our imagined worlds. There are no proxies—slippery abstractions such as "nature," "teleology," "God," "Destiny," that are reified, i.e., endowed by human imagination with a rock-solid concreteness, and placed in tamper-proof, beyond-argument creeds and canons—which might allow us to avoid exercising our franchise, to cast our vote, as frankly and transparently as we can. This should not be misunderstood. I am not implicitly pleading for a Promethean view of human performance, which by heroic dint and huff, can unfix and refix the theatre of our lives at will. That would be to fall under the spell of fantasy that overlooks the complexities of the cultural and material forms and forces that place constraints both on the potential (power) and forms of human doing. No, the point of this little discourse on the Christian production of "Jesus" as an opening for reflecting on the idea of the human production of history is precisely to begin to expose the complexities of history-making, then to plead for the historiographical axiom that the Christian Bible and post-biblical narratives of Christian history are not historical histories of anyone's real past (see Thompson 2000) as much as a mythography of origins that represents identifiable interests. Most obliquely, this entails a future for the study of Christian beginnings and history that is situated firmly within, rather than beyond, the messy mix of historical human performance, a locating that requires as a start, and at least within the situation of the secular and public academy, to scrutinize, reconsider, and rectify assumptions that the history of Christianity is in fact and in imaginative-narrative representation nothing more than an instance of ordinary human history-making.

The American Jesus

That Jesus is manufactured in the millennia-old discourse of the "historical" Jesus sheds some light on the long-standing American fascination with Jesus. Indeed America is a "Jesus nation" whose roots go back to Thomas Jefferson and the founding of the nation itself (Prothero 2003; Mack 2003, for example). Influenced by the work of the British Unitarian Joseph Priestly, especially his *An History of the Corruptions of Christianity* (1782), *An History of Early Christian Opinions Concerning Jesus Christ* (1786), *A General History of the Christian Church from the Fall of the Western Empire to the Present Time* (1802 and dedicated to Thomas Jefferson) and *Socrates and Jesus Compared* (1803), Jefferson (1743–1826) drew a sharp distinction between "the philosophy of Jesus of Nazareth"—whom Jefferson called "the first of human Sages" long before Robert Funk and other members of the famous Jesus Seminar would again argue the "Jesus the Sage" thesis (see below)—and the "distortions" and "mutilations" of Jesus' real teachings by the gospel writers and Paul and their Platonizing metaphysics and mysticisms (see Adams 1983; Smith 1990; Prothero 2003). Taking razor blade to a King James version of the New Testament, Jefferson excised what he took to be the authentic tidbits (about one of every ten verses of the gospels) of teachings of the Galilean sage from the gospels, a task that he found as "obvious and easy" as picking "diamonds in a dunghill" (Adams 1983: 352; Prothero 2003: 24). The result was a little booklet, the not well-known and belatedly discovered predecessor to the famous Jefferson Bible, that Jefferson considered a "precious morsel of ethics." Shorn of any hints of miracles, virgin birth, crucifixion and resurrection or other supernatural accoutrements, Jefferson's Jesus could serve as a natural (rather than supernatural) moral foundation for an emerging nation without threatening Jefferson's other achievement, namely the constitutional removal, by means of the First Amendment, of religious and ecclesiastical participation in the affairs of state.

While it would be a mistake to credit Jefferson alone for the subsequent iconization of Jesus in the United States, he created a set of cultural possibilities, aided by constitution and law, that permitted Jesus to become the ubiquitous eponym for whatever is considered righteous and moral in America, to become a trans-religious figure that is neither identifiable with historic Christianity or any of its particular denominational formations in the US and at the same time making him adoptable, and hence as "multiform as Proteus," by non-Christian immigrants to America for whom embracing Jesus is a way of reckoning with America's central symbol, thus a quintessentially way of embracing America itself, while continuing to remain Jews, Muslims, Buddhists, and so forth (Adams 1983: 291).

Unlike any other nation on the globe, Jesus is alive and well in every sector of American culture, whether lowbrow or highbrow. As M. Hagevi (2002: 763) reports, "In the United States ... more than two out of three of every citizens say they have made a 'personal commitment to Jesus Christ' and approximately three out of four report they have sensed his presence." He is present in the debates on almost any national issue; one can find him as easily the priest of American nationalism, the champion of a secular humanist morality, the symbolic potentate who authorizes global American might, the prince of peace who stands in judgment over America's warring inclinations, the personal savior of countless millions of born-agains, the liberator of historically and current American poor, down-trodden and marginalized. Choose an issue, a moral preference, a social vision on the political left or the right or on some sectarian extreme, then take any side of the issue, preference or vision and Jesus will be your ally and friend. He is "a vital presence / that's lurking all around / we've got the American Jesus," sings the punk rock band Bad Religion. "I was educated in a small town / taught to fear Jesus in a small town," belts out the rock singer John Mellencamp. "No, they ain't makin' Jews like Jesus anymore," sings Kinky Friedman, alternative musician and leader of the Texas Jewboys, with a satirical sneer. Mick Jagger and Bono alike have looked for the Buddha but found Jesus instead, for he is so much easier to locate. Jesus was a "freak" and "hippie" of the 1960s and 1970s drop-out generation; he was and still is "Jesus Christ, superstar" and the star of other wildly popular rock operas; he continues to be a Hollywood celebrity and the attraction in a Jesus theme park, the Holy Land Experience, near Disney World in Florida. Charles Sheldon's novel, *In His Steps: What Would Jesus Do?* (1897), about an American town that committed itself to live an entire year just as Jesus lived, was a best-seller for 60 years, with over eight million copies in print. Dan Brown's novel, *The Da Vinci Code*, has sold more than double that and the "code craze" shows no signs of spending itself. At the level of cultural fads that regularly sweep across the United States one might mention only the WWJD (What would Jesus do?) craze that by which American Evangelicals marked themselves in the 1980s and 1990s. And precisely because Jesus is such a powerful American celebrity he is of course often a subject for news reporters, appearing regularly in such influential mainstream magazines as *Time*, *Newsweek*, *The Economist* and *Atlantic Monthly*, in the most important dailies such as the *New York Times*, *Wall Street Journal*, *Washington Post* and the *Los Angeles Times*, but also in fashion magazines such as *GQ* and countless lesser periodicals, as well as in the electronic media, most influentially in the PBS series, *From Jesus to Christ* (1998).

Not surprisingly, New Testament scholars, historians of early Christianity and other academics in the Jesus Nation could not and would not resist entering the cultural discourse with their own claims. Despite numerous and cogent arguments at least since Albert Schweitzer's moratorium (1910 [1906]) on quests for the historical Jesus, influentially confirmed by Rudolf Bultmann in the first half of the twentieth century (1958 [1926]), that "the search for the real Jesus is a dead-end street" (Keck 1971; see also McDonald 1980; Ghiberti 1982), scholars were not deterred from trying again on a massive scale, launching a "renaissance in Jesus Studies" in the 1980s that continues unabated to the present day, including the launching in 2003 the scholarly *Journal for the Study of the Historical Jesus* (see Borg 1988, 1994; Charlesworth 1986; Kümmel 1988–1991; Evans 1989; Tatum 1982; Thompson 1998; Telford 1998; Porter 2001). The "quintessentially American" (Prothero 2003: 33). Jesus Seminar has been a major player in this renaissance, itself predominantly American.

The Jesus Seminar

The Jesus Seminar (JS) was convened in 1985 by the prominent New Testament scholar and former President of the Society of Biblical Literature, Robert Funk, and continues to function under the auspices of the Westar Institute, also directed by Funk until his death. At the inaugural meeting at the Pacific School of Religion in Berkeley, California, Funk announced the Seminar's task in his typically hyperbolic way:

> We are about to embark on a momentous enterprise. We are going to inquire simply, rigorously, after the *voice* of Jesus, after what he really said. ... Our basic plan is simple. We intend to examine every fragment of the traditions attached to the name Jesus in order to determine what he really said—not his literal words, perhaps, but the substance and style of his utterings. We are in quest of his *voice*, insofar as it can be distinguished from many other voices also preserved in the tradition. (Funk 1985: 7)

The group consisted of 35 scholars at the first meeting, but its membership and number of participants has varied over the years and, at one time or another involved over 100 scholars, including many of the most prominent New Testament scholars in North America, such as, for example, John Dominic Crossan who for some time co-chaired the JS, Marcus Borg, Harold Attridge, Karen King, John Kloppenborg, Marvin Meyer, Vernon Robbins, James M. Robinson (an early roster of the Seminar was published in Funk and Hoover 1993). The group met twice a year to examine particular sets of sayings attributed to Jesus with the aid of previously circulated position papers written by members of the Seminar. The aim was to come to the most rigorous, best-considered judgment on the authenticity or non-authenticity of each of the sayings. After discussion each scholar was asked to vote on the issue of authenticity, occasionally (but with great publicity effect) by throwing a colored bead into a box. Four choices, each worded in two ways were stipulated. As published in *The Five Gospels*:

1. (Red) I would include this item unequivocally in the database for determining who Jesus really was; or, Jesus undoubtedly said this or something very like it.

2   (Pink) I would include this item with reservations in the database; or, Jesus probably said something like this.

3   (Grey) I would not include this item in the database, but I might make use of some of the content in determining who Jesus was; or, Jesus did not say this, but the ideas contained in it are close to his own.

4   (Black) I would not include this item in the primary database; or, Jesus did not say this.

Each category or color would be assigned a rating (red = 3; pink = 2; grey = 1; black = 0), and the results would be tabulated to achieve a "weighted average" on a scale of 1.00 (0.7501 and up = red; 0.5001 to 0.7500 = pink; 0.2501 to 0.5000 = grey; 0.0000 to 0.2500 = black) to make sure that each vote counted in achieving the grade-point result to reflect not unanimity among seminar members but to give as accurately as possible a measure of expert scholarly opinion (for procedures and analyses of the voting results see Anon 1990; Borg 1994: 161–164). After six years of labor the JS finally published its results in a new kind of "red-letter" edition of the gospels (including the Gospel of Thomas), *The Five Gospels: What Did Jesus Really Say?* (Funk and Hoover 1993). A second phase of the project examined the actions of Jesus, using a similar procedure; these labors were published as a second "red-letter" edition, *The Acts of Jesus: What Did Jesus Really Do?* (1998).

Although the results achieved immense publicity, deliberately sought by Funk and his colleagues by means of provocative press releases and pot-stirring, irreverent references to Jesus as the "bastard messiah" (i.e., not born of a virgin) and "the first Jewish stand-up comic" (i.e., a master of witty retort and humorous parable), for example, the manner of achieving those results were neither eccentric nor novel; the results were the remains of paring the Jesus tradition using the standard tools of critical source, form and redaction criticism, along with delicate use of the old criteria of dissimilarity and multiple attestation. Nor should critically trained gospel scholars, especially those with familiar with the long history of criticism, be dismayed by the rather low rate of survival on the JS cutting table. Only 18 percent of sayings were given the red or pink rating; only 16 percent of the actions of Jesus attributed to him in the Jesus traditions are rated red or pink.

What did survive and make it into red or pink print sketches a Jesus that, for historically informed Americans, at least, could pass as *déjà vu*: in general the Jesus exhumed by Funk and the JS is remarkably similar to Jefferson's Galilean sage. Jesus emerged from the JS as a Galilean peasant with a remarkable gift for Cynic-like cunning repartee and witty story (no member of the JS ever claimed that Jesus was a Cynic, as is often charged) that, by use of humor, paradox, double entendre and exaggeration, was aimed to startle and shock people into taking a subversive social posture that imagined an inverted world by means of the cipher of "the kingdom of God." A laconic sage and poet, not an apocalyptic visionary, a man who did not attribute titles of divinity to himself, nor expect the world to end in his lifetime, a religious and social gadfly, an iconoclast, a subversive peasant preacher, no more son of God than you and I, no virgin-born, no miracle worker (although a few healing stories receive at least pink or grey codes), and of course no resurrection and no ascension, and, though a crucifixion, no historical "passion." Like Jefferson's moral philosopher, Funk's Jesus has been severely demoted from the status he has in the gospels, in the early Christian creeds, and in the hearts of millions of American Bible-believing evangelical Christians (Funk 1996: 21ff., 306).

From the Jesus of History to the Jesus of Symbolic Discourse

How is the work of the Jesus Seminar to be judged? The Seminar's historical achievement, that is, its success in using historical methods to reconstruct a real person of the past is unremarkable, which is itself not unexpected, given the nature of the evidence that is such that it seems to require a priori stipulations, grounded in religious or ideological preferences, as to what will constitute evidence in the first place. At best, the Seminar has retrieved, reiterated, and re-argued evidence and conclusions that are already in the thick dossier of *Leben-Jesu-Forschung*, though often more sharply and cogently. At this level there is no breathtaking gain in knowledge.

This is not to say that the Seminar has been unsuccessful, though its successes are unexpected, inadvertent effects. For the success does not lie in a startlingly novel reconstruction of the historical Jesus, but in focusing attention on matters that have contributed significantly to our knowledge about the world of early Christianities. One should, for example, regard the spate of work on the Sayings Gospel Q and the Gospel of Thomas as driven in part by the Seminar's Jesus-quest, given the importance Q and Thomas have as evidentiary sources for the JS. We now know much more about the social, political and economic realities of first-century Galilee and surrounding areas than we did before the Seminar did its work. John D. Crossan's magisterial life of Jesus has established a cogent model for historical work that historians of early Christianity should read attentively quite apart from his conclusions about Jesus, for it represents a brilliant, even if not unproblematic, fusion of theoretical and ethnographic studies in cultural and social anthropology, pre-industrial peasant societies, patron-client relations, and more: all intellectual and methodological building blocks for the historian's *plausibly imaginative* historical reconstruction (Crossan 1991). The field of New Testament scholarship has been deeply enriched by the Jesus Seminar and its many and varied spin-off publications.

Besides that? The Jesus Seminar is an immensely interesting example of American cultural contest in which Jesus seems to be an unavoidable "before" that can authorize and fix some, almost any, religious, ideological and moral "after." The fact that Funk, like Jefferson (to whom Funk dedicates *The Five Gospels!*) before him, righteously swings his historical Jesus as a battle axe against the fetters of traditional Christian creeds and institutions, which for him reach their inglorious apogee in the American Christian fundamentalism in which he was raised, does not render any less probable or plausible the JS's portrait of Jesus as a subversive Galilean sage and moralist, but it does expose this historical Jesus as an attempt at re-founding a myth of origins in which the value-added function of "history" is to oppose the Jesus portraits and Jesus traditions that Funk would like to see retired from the American cultural scene.

In theory, though, it is not necessary to invoke Jesus as friend of this and enemy of that cultural practice or value. Our world, after all, is ours to make and to keep, ours to criticize, ours to cultivate or destroy, as I suggested above.

After all, the historical Jesus is dead, his body gone to dust. His *ipsissima verba* have vanished, as all oral utterances do the moment they are spoken. His *ipsissima vox* is so superimposed with the cacophonous static of his multitudinous ventriloquists, beginning with the gospel writers and ending, say, with Robert Funk and his Jesus Seminar, that one should be profoundly skeptical about any claims to have reliable voice recognition technology that will recover the voice of Jesus. The irony, of course, is that the historical Jesus is required neither for theological reasons, as the early apostle of Christ, Paul, should have taught Christians, nor for secular historical accounting of the formation of early Christian associations, for any historiography that is fundamentally staked to the assumption that one individual can kick-start a socio-religious movement that is as varied and polythetic as early Christianity is theoretically naive. "And so," stressing the recent advice of the Canadian scholar William Arnal:

> [P]erhaps the quest for the historical Jesus should be abandoned once again. Not because scholars cannot agree on the reconstructions. ... Not because the investigation has been biased; bias is unavoidable, here as elsewhere. Not even because reasonable conclusions are impossible in the light of our defective sources, though this may indeed be the case. But because, ultimately, the *historical* Jesus does not matter, either for our understanding of the past, or our understanding of the present. The historically relevant and interesting causes of the development and growth of the Christian movement will be found, not in the person of Jesus, but in the collective machinations, agenda, and vicissitudes of the movement itself. And the Jesus who is important to our own day is not the Jesus of history, but the symbolic Jesus of contemporary discourse. (Arnal 2005: 76–77)

Indeed! Jesus—R.I.P.

References

Adams, Dickenson W. (1983). *Jefferson's Extracts from the Gospels: The Philosophy of Jesus and the Life and Morals of Jesus*. Princeton, NJ: Princeton University Press.

Allen, Charlotte (1998). *The Human Christ: The Search for the Historical Jesus*. New York: Fress Press.

Anon. (1990). "The Jesus Seminar: Voting Records, Sorted by Gospel, Chapter, and Verse," *Foundations and Facets Forum* 6: 3–55.

Arnal, William E. (1997). "Making and Re-Making the Jesus Sign: Markings on the Body of Christ." In William E. Arnal and Michel Desjardins (eds.), *Whose Historical Jesus?*, 308–319. Studies in Christianity and Judaism—Études sur le christianisme et le judaïsme, 7. Waterloo: Wilfrid Laurier University Press.

—— (2005). *The Symbolic Jesus: Historical Scholarship, Judaism, and the Construction of Contemporary Identity*. New York: Routledge.

Bad Religion (1993). "American Jesus," from the album *Recipe for Hate*. Hollywood, CA: Epitaph Records.

Baudrillard, Jean (1994). *Simulacra and Simulation*. Sheila Faria Glaser (trans.). Ann Arbor, MI: University of Michigan. https://doi.org/10.3998/mpub.9904

Berkhofer, Robert F., Jr. (1995). *Beyond the Great Story: History as Text and Discourse*. Cambridge, MA: Harvard University Press.

Borg, Marcus J. (1988). "A Renaissance in Jesus Studies," *Theology Today* 45: 280–292. https://doi.org/10.1177/004057368804500303

—— (1994). *Jesus in Contemporary Scholarship*. Valley Forge: Trinity Press International.

Bowersock, G. W. (1994). *Fiction as History: Nero to Julian*. Berkeley, CA: University of California Press.

Braun, Willi (1997). "Socio-Rhetorical Interests: Context." In William E. Arnal and Michel Desjardins (eds.), *Whose Historical Jesus?*, 92–97. Studies in Christianity and Judaism—Études sur le christianisme et le judaïsme, 7. Waterloo: Wilfrid Laurier University Press.

Bultmann, Rudolf (1958) [1926]. *Jesus and the Word*. New York: Scribner.

Cameron, Ron (ed.) (1990). *The Apocryphal Jesus and Christian Origins*. Semeia 49. Atlanta, GA: Scholars Press.

—— (1994). "Alternate Beginnings—Different Ends: Eusebius, Thomas, and the Construction of Christian Origins." In Lukas Bormann, Kelly Del Tredici and Angela Standhartinger (eds.), *Religious Propaganda and Missionary Competition in the New Testament World: Essays Honoring Dieter Georgi*, 501–525. Supplements to Novum Testamentum, 74. Leiden: Brill.

—— (1999). "Mythmaking and Social Formation in the Gospel of Thomas," *Method & Theory in the Study of Religion* 11: 236–257. https://doi.org/10.1163/157006899X00041

Charlesworth, James H. (1986). "From Barren Mazes to Gentle Rappings: The Emergence of Jesus Research," *Princeton Seminary Bulletin* 7: 221–230.

Crossan, John Dominic (1991). *The Historical Jesus: The Life of a Mediterranean Jewish Peasant*. New York: HarperCollins.

—— (1998). *The Birth of Christianity: Discovering What Happened in the Years Immediately After the Execution of Jesus*. San Francisco,. CA: HarperSanFrancisco.

Donaldson, Terence L. (1997). *Paul and the Gentiles: Remapping the Apostle's Convictional World*. Minneapolis, MN: Fortress Press.

Easthope, Antony (1993). "Romancing the Stone: History-Writing and Rhetoric," *Social History* 18: 235–249. https://doi.org/10.1080/03071029308567875

Evans, Craig A. (1989). *Life of Jesus Research: An Annotated Bibliography*. Leiden: Brill. https://doi.org/10.1163/9789004379831

Funk, Robert W. (1985). "The Issue of Jesus," *Foundations and Facets Forum* 1: 7–12.

—— (1996). *Honest to Jesus: Jesus for a New Millennium*. San Francisco, CA: HarperSanFrancisco.

—— (1998). *The Acts of Jesus: What Did Jesus Really Do?* San Francisco, CA: HarperSanFrancisco.

Funk, Robert W. and Roy W. Hoover (eds.) (1993). *The Five Gospels: What Did Jesus Really Say? The Search for the Authentic Words of Jesus*, 533–537. New York: Harper.

Ghiberti, G. (1982). "Überlegungen zum neueren Stand der Leben-Jesu-Forschung," *Münchener theologische Zeitschrift* 33: 99–115.

Hagevi, Magnus (2002). "Religiosity and Swedish Opinion on the European Union," *Journal for the Scientific Study of Religion* 41: 759–769. https://doi.org/10.1111/1468-5906.00160

Heller, Agnes (1993). *A Philosophy of History in Fragments*. Oxford: Blackwell.

Hobsbawm, Eric (1997). *On History*. London: Weidenfeld & Nicolson.

Jacobson, Arland D. (1992). *The First Gospel: An Introduction to Q*. Foundations & Facets: Reference Series. Sonoma, CA: Polebridge.

Keck, Leander E. (1971). *A Future for the Historical Jesus*. Nashville, TN: Abingdon.
Kloppenborg, John S. (1987). *The Formation of Q: Trajectories in Ancient Wisdom Collections*. Studies in Antiquity & Christianity. Philadelphia, PA: Fortress Press.
—— (ed.) (1994). *The Shape of Q: Signal Essays on the Sayings Gospel*. Minneapolis, MN: Fortress Press.
Kloppenborg, John S and Leif E. Vaage (eds.) (1991). *Early Christianity, Q and Jesus*. Semeia 55. Atlanta, GA: Scholars Press.
Kümmel. Werner G. (1988-1991). "Jesus Forschung seit 1981," *Theologische Rundschau* 53 (1988): 229-249; 54 (1989): 1-53; 55 (1990): 21-45; 56 (1991): 27-53, 391-420.
LaCapra, Dominick (1985). "Rhetoric and History." In *History and Criticism*, 15-44. Ithaca, NY: Cornell University Press.
Lightstone, Jack N. (1997). "Whence the Rabbis? From Coherent Description to Fragmented Reconstruction," *Studies in Religion/Sciences Religieuses* 26: 275-295. https://doi.org/10.1177/000842989702600301
Lincoln, Bruce (1989). *Discourse and the Construction of Society: Comparative Studies of Myth, Ritual, and Classification*. New York: Oxford University Press.
Mack, Burton L. (1988). *A Myth of Innocence: Mark and Christian Origins*. Philadelphia, PA: Fortress Press.
—— (1993). *The Lost Gospel: The Book of Q & Christian Origins*. San Francisco, CA: HarperSanFrancisco.
—— (1995). *Who Wrote the New Testament? The Making of the Christian Myth*. San Francisco, CA: HarperSanFrancisco.
—— (1996). "On Redescribing Christian Origins," *Method & Theory in the Study of Religion* 8: 247-269. https://doi.org/10.1163/157006896X00350
—— (2000). "Social Formation." In Willi Braun and Russell T. McCutcheon (eds.), *Guide to the Study of Religion*, 283-296. London: Cassell.
—— (2003). "The Historical Jesus Hoopla." In *The Christian Myth: Origins, Logic, and Legacy*, 25-40. New York: Continuum.
Martin, Luther H. (2000). "History, Historiography and Christian Origins," *Studies in Religion/Sciences Religieuses* 29: 69-89. https://doi.org/10.1177/000842980002900105
McDonald, J. I. H. (1980). "New Quest–Dead End? So What about the Historical Jesus?" In E. A. Livingstone (ed.), *Studia Biblica*, II. *Papers on the Gospels*, 151-170. Sheffield: Sheffield University Press.
Masuzawa, Tomoko (2000). "Origin." In Willi Braun and Russell T. McCutcheon (eds.), *Guide to the Study of Religion*, 209-224. London: Cassell.
McNeill, William H. (1986). "Mythistory, or Truth, Myth, History, and Historians." In *Mythistory and Other Essays*, 3-22. Chicago, IL: University of Chicago Press. https://doi.org/10.2307/1867232
Porter, Stanley E. (2001). *The Criteria for Authenticity in Historical-Jesus Research: Previous Discussions and New Proposals*. Sheffield: Sheffield University Press.
Price, Robert M. (2000). *Deconstructing Jesus*. Amherst, NY: Prometheus.
Prothero, Stephen (2003). *American Jesus: How the Son of God Became a National Icon*. New York: Farrar, Straus & Giroux.
Riley, Gregory J. (1997). *One Jesus, Many Christs: How Jesus Inspired Not One True Christianity, But Many*. San Francisco, CA: HarperSanFrancisco.
Robinson, James M. (1993). "The Jesus of the Sayings Gospel Q." *Occasional Papers of The Institute for Antiquity and Christianity*, 28. Claremont, CA: Society for Antiquity and Christianity.
Sarbin, Theodore R. (1998a). "Believed-In Imaginings: A Narrative Approach." In Joseph de Rivera and Theodore H. Sarbin (eds.), *Believed-In Imaginings: The Narrative*

Construction of Reality, 15–30. Washington, DC: American Psychological Association. https://doi.org/10.1037/10303-001

——— (1998b). "The Poetic Construction of Reality and Other Explanatory Categories." In Joseph de Rivera and Theodore H. Sarbin (eds.), *Believed-In Imaginings: The Narrative Construction of Reality*, 297–307. Washington, DC: American Psychological Association.

Schweitzer, Albert (1910) [1906]. *The Quest of the Historical Jesus: A Critical Study of its Progress from Reimarus to Wrede*. Trans. W. Montgomery. London: A. & C. Black.

Smith, Jonathan Z. (1982). "Sacred Persistence: Toward a Redescription of Canon." In *Imagining Religion: From Babylon to Jonestown*, 36–52. Chicago, IL: University of Chicago Press.

——— (1990). "On the Origin of Origins." In *Drudgery Divine: On the Comparison of Early Christianities and the Religions of Late Antiquity*, 1–35. Chicago, IL: University of Chicago Press.

Snyder, Graydon F. (1985). *Ante Pacem: Archaeological Evidence of Church Life before Constantine*. Macon, GA: Mercer University Press.

Stone, Lawrence (1979). "The Revival of Narrative: Reflections on a New Old History," *Past & Present* 85: 3–24. https://doi.org/10.1093/past/85.1.3

Tatum, W. Barnes (1982). *In Quest of Jesus: A Guidebook*. Atlanta, GA: John Knox Westminster Press.

Telford, William R. (1998). "Major Trends and Interpretive Issues in the Study of Jesus." In Bruce Chilton and Craig A. Evans (eds.), *Studying the Historical Jesus: Evaluations of the State of Current Research*, 33–74. Leiden: Brill.

Thompson, Thomas L. (2000). *The Bible in History: How Writers Create a Past*. London: Pimlico.

Thompson, William M. (1998). *The Jesus Debate: A Survey and Synthesis*. New York: Paulist Press.

Trouillot, Michel-Rolph (1995). *Silencing the Past: Power and the Production of History*. Boston, MA: Beacon.

Valantasis, Richard (1997). *The Gospel of Thomas*. London: Routledge. https://doi.org/10.4324/9780203295090

Veyne, Paul (1988). *Did the Greeks Believe in Their Myths? An Essay in the Constitutive Imagination*. Paula Wissig (trans.). Chicago, IL: University of Chicago Press.

White, Hayden (1976). "The Fictions of Factual Representation." In Angus Fletcher (ed.), *The Literature of Fact: Selected Papers from the English Institute*, 21–44. New York: Columbia University Press.

——— (1978). *Tropics of Discourse: Essays in Cultural Criticism*. Baltimore, MD: Johns Hopkins University Press.

——— (1987). *The Content of the Form: Narrative Discourse and Historical Representation*. Baltimore, MD: Johns Hopkins University Press.

Worthington, Ian (1994). "History and Oratorical Exploitation." In Ian Worthington (ed.), *Persuasion: Greek Rhetoric in Action*, 109–129. New York: Routledge.

Wrede, William (1971) [1901]. *The Messianic Secret*. J. C. G. Creig (trans.). Cambridge: J. Clarke.

5

Christian Origins and the Gospel of Mark: Fragments of a Story

Within the field of New Testament and early Christian writings there is a consensus that "Christian origins" temporally means the first century CE. Every college introductory textbook on the New Testament or early Christianity assumes this. I note as an example the most widely used introductory textbook, Bart Ehrman's *The New Testament: A Historical Introduction to the Early Christian Writings* (2008). Despite the explicit announcement that the introduction will be historical, he assumes a first-century origin of Christianity, even though it can be argued that no first-century text that was eventually included in the Christian canon was written by authors who identified themselves as "Christian." Even more noteworthy, and ironic, is the splendid work of Burton Mack, who has devoted much of his later career to the effort of "redescribing" Christian origins, to show that the Gospel of Mark, indeed, the entire New Testament represents a myth of origin, rather than a history of beginnings of Christianity (Mack 1988, 1996a, 1996b, 2001). The Christian myth was constructed in the first century by Paul and the writers of the gospel of Mark and the writer of Luke and Acts, Mack thinks. What follows after the first century is the "legacy" of the original, first-century myth. In this sense, and only in the sense of temporally placing Christian origins in the first century, Mack's redescription turns out to be a historiographical reinscription. Let the exceptional historical work of Ehrman and Mack's origin-legacy model stand as signal examples of how difficult it is to re-imagine the first century outside the framework of Christianity's own myth of origins, that of course is mythically and, it turns out, historically focussed *en arche* or *ab origine* (Mark 1:1; John 1:1). The dominant default in the field of the formation and history of emergent Christianity is the assumption of this mystique of first-century origins. Christianity's own myth of origins *de facto* has become the universal scholarly history of Christian beginnings. Fiction indeed has become history, in much modern scholarship, just as it was in antiquity, as Glen Bowersock has shown so well (1994; see also Demoen and De Temmeran 2016).

In what follows, I look at just one literary example, the Gospel of Mark, to see if it can bear the burden of the Christian myth of origin.[1]

* * *

First, on accounting for the literary move from heterogeneous "archival" Jesus stuff to a *bios*, a biography-like narrative: Burton Mack, in *A Myth of Innocence*, has satisfied me on *how* Mark did it—that is, Mack has outlined convincingly both a narrative and a social-cultural logic that accounts for Mark's biography-like narrative. Arnaldo Momigliano has given the best possible *general* surmise that permits near-satisfaction on why Jesus adherents *too* produced *bios* exemplars in the first century and beyond. Thus Momigliano:

> Biography gained prestige in the Imperial age for contradictory reasons. Biography was the natural form of telling the story of a Caesar. On the other hand, biography was a vehicle for unorthodox political and philosophic ideas. (Momigliano 1993: 99; see also Demoen and De Temmeran 2016)

"The writers of biography created a meaningful relationship between the living and the dead," argues Momigliano, as a way of drawing genetic linkages between a mythic ἀρχή (mythic origins in Mark's sense) and whatever social formation is imagined as normatively desirable (1993: 104).[2] Mark's option for the *bios* genre for achieving this kind of coupling is novel on the landscape of production of Jesus literature, but categorically there is nothing especially novel or counter-intuitive in choosing this genre.[3]

The motivational force behind Mark partially can be uncovered in the narrative itself: I am attracted to the crisis scenario, elaborated in Mack's *A Myth of Innocence* (see especially chapter 12), as the most compelling motive-set for the ultimately apocalyptic logic of Mark, so sharply focused, as it is, on the devastation of Jerusalem and the Temple and other fall-outs caused by the Jewish War. Surely, for the writer of Mark we must reckon that there was a set of issues that had enormous stakes for him, issues that can hardly (to my mind) be construed as benign, mundane quibbles over this or that preference in an ethnically and religiously and socially heterogeneous locale (such as the Galilee or the Levant). The heat of the adversarial rhetoric and the shrill tone of Mark's justification of the truth of his story suggests otherwise.

Indeed, I prefer to suggest as my stipulation the view argued by William Arnal, namely that Mark is a narrative "reflection on exile and identity" (2008). Arnal notes that despite enormous labors over more than a century,[4] the Gospel of Mark "strenuously resists our usual procedure of positing a (usually "Christian") *community* and making inferences about the author's agenda in terms of interaction with that community" (2008: 59). So he abandons the explanatory assist of a "Markan community" whose social interests and social-formational agenda are somehow encoded in the gospel-cum-myth-cum-social charter.[5] Rather, he takes from Burton Mack the point that Mark is the work of a scholar (Mack 1988: 231) and suggests that the "what's he up to?" question posed by Mark's narrative might be answered more satisfactorily if we "focus on the intellectual problems solved by Mark, rather than the role of Mark in a distinct Christian group whose essential characteristics can be recovered by us" (Arnal 2008: 59). The occasion for Mark's reflection, Arnal argues on the basis of a persistent and multi-faceted preoccupation in Mark's narrative, is "the Jewish War and the fallout subsequent to the War" (Arnal 2008: 60). The gospel is Mark's answer, in narrative form,

> to the questions raised by the War, with its attendant dislocations, exiles, and opportunities for re-imagining identity, nation, and location. Mark's massive

> emphasis on the War, the destruction of the temple, and the peculiar movements made by Jesus between Gentile, semi-Jewish, and Jewish regions, and between Galilee and Judea, all point to the possibility that Mark is engaging in post-traumatic re-imagining of identity in his ... Jesus-narrative. (Arnal 2008: 60)

Arnal then offers the "tentative" suggestion, based on oft-overlooked but telling details in Mark, that in answer to the question of to what kind of real-world historical author we might attribute the Markan "reflection," we might think of someone who is doubly exiled[6]: once, by virtue of a somehow tainted Jewish identity, thus a stranger in the Judean homeland; twice, from a destroyed, temple-less homeland from which he or she is now finally displaced and forced to make a home and identity in a strange land where homeland and temple do not, cannot, function even as nostalgic treasures (2008: 61–66).

What I like about this argument is that it correlates the form and content of Mark's narrative, an authorial agenda, a highly plausible historical "situational incongruity" (to use J. Z. Smith's phrase) that appears to be of "crisis" proportions to the author, and an equally plausible real person whom one can envision as thinking about the situation in about the way that Arnal proposes. And all this without having to postulate, contrary to what Mark allows us to do, a discrete community that is urgently engaged in its own formation with reference to a social charter encoded in a Jesus-*bios*.[7] Mark appears to be a local story with a local agenda for its author; it does not strike me as a myth of origins for a community, but rather a reflection by an author on the fly on matters of incongruity and urgent concerns associated with the Jewish War and its aftermath.

* * *

I move on to a second remark that is also part of the set-up for the central point of this essay. I would like for you to permit me to suggest that NT-Mark (as I will call canonical Mark) is, in a complex way that is only opaquely discernible, a product of the second century, when it was pressed into now rather explicitly "Christian" duties that it did not carry at the point of initial composition. These duties were largely of a political sort, that are either ignorant of, or more likely, egregiously dismissive of the authorial agenda of whoever first created the initial Markan narrative as an exercise in thought on matters about as elaborated by Mack or Arnal.

That Mark had a literary history both prior to NT-Mark (= the Nestlé-Aland or UBS Greek text) and after NT-Mark is well known, even if the precise stages of this history and NT-Mark's placement in this history is unclear and hence contested.[8] What matters to me is that this history can *not* be understood as a text that is changing, growing, shrinking or expanding in the hands of a single school or community over time, adapting or altering its own "myth of origins" to suit changing sociological realities within the group and changing self-perceptions of the custodial group in a larger social environment—analogous to the composition history of, say, Q, a product of staged composition and (likely) exegetical tinkering by a discrete "community" or Jesus School over time, nor perhaps somewhat like the composition of the Gospel of Thomas, where compositional stages are admittedly not as literarily apparent, nor analogous finally in the manner of the Johannine corpus, which is generally still seen as a production, encompassing several literary genres, over time by a discrete, even evolving and changing "Johannine community." No, rather than seeing the literary history (and reception history) of Mark as an organic unfolding of a "trajectory" (to use a precious term in our field), possibly in coordination with the social history of a particular Christian group, I see it as a history of confiscation and assimilation.[9] I offer several familiar examples in support of this generalization:

1. The writers of the gospels of Matthew and Luke purloined Mark's general literary structure as well as most of the discrete parts of his narrative, thus paying respect to Mark's literary genius, but erasing or refracting Mark's argument about the import of Jesus for Mark's agenda. In short, Matthew and Luke confiscated Mark's literary form and structure and erased, by overwriting, his thought. Think, for example, of the erasure of Mark's aggressive assertion that "I (alone) am he [Jesus Christ]" (13:6) over against which all other such claims are condemned as πλανή, as an error, an assertion taken up by Matthew and Luke, to be sure, but now presumably turning Mark's accusation against him and treating his gospel as an error that needs to be corrected.

2. The critically reconstructed *editio princeps* of the ending of Mark's gospel as presented in the Greek text of the Nestlé-Aland or UBS editions is not how canonical Mark ended, as every first-year NT student knows. Mark 16:9-20 is a second-century addition by an unknown author who "made use of the [other] 'NT' Gospels in order to make his addition to Mark resemble documents that had attained at least some level of popularity in certain Christian communities" (Kelhoffer 2004: 10; 2000). A case can be made that the beginning of NT-Mark (Mark 1:1-3) also has been subject to editorial tampering (Elliott 2000). It certainly was prefaced later by the anti-Marcionite Prologue (ca. 160–200) (where Mark gets his slurry nickname κολοβοδάκτυλος, lit. "stump-fingered," which is repeated by Hippolytus of Rome as a known derogatory moniker, suggesting that it had its origins prior to Hippolytus [*Refutation of All Heresies*, 7.18]).[10] If so, both ending (16: 9-20) and beginning (1:1-3), that is, the two most crucial reading-bias storage sites in any literary work, show the work of secondary scribal/authorial activity.

3. I raise another example that some might well see as a red flag or stinky fish: I'm talking about Clement of Alexandria's fragment of a Letter to Theodore and its reference to and citation from the infamous "Secret Mark" circulating in Alexandria. The authenticity of this letter is heatedly disputed for a variety of reasons, many

of which need not concern us here.[11] Someone named Mark as the eponymous founder of a Christian association in Egypt,[12] and the use of some version(s) of the Gospel of Mark there, are often enough remarked in the patristic sources (for complete inventory see Humphrey 2006). Since I can't think of any tendentious motive for making up especially the latter item, its historical veracity is likely in the range of the probable.[13] If Clement's Letter to Theodore is genuine,[14] I see two things of interest in Clement's rebuke of the Carpocrations' "unspeakable teachings"—which apparently included "things they keep saying about the divinely inspired Gospel according to Mark" (Smith 1973a: 446)—and his remarks on the making of Mark's gospel. The first is that Mark had a three-stage composition history, the other that in some Alexandrians' reading of the gospel, Mark was considered a mystagogue and his gospel a source of "the hierophantic teaching of the Lord" suitable for progressive (three-stage) initiation into "knowledge." Thus, the first edition, in Rome, consisted of "an account of the Lord's doings ... for increasing the faith of those who were being instructed"; the second, in Alexandria, aimed at enabling "progress toward knowledge," and was a "more spiritual Gospel for the use of those who were being perfected"; the third, also in Alexandria, consisted in additions of "certain sayings of which he [Mark] knew the interpretation would, as a mystagogue, lead hearers into the innermost sanctuary of that truth hidden by seven veils" (Smith 1973a: 446).

Given the uncertain historical value of Clement's letter, firm conclusions are inappropriate, but a conjecture of reasonable probability is not. This is that NT-Mark is a second-century confiscation-by-redaction of some Alexandrians' Gospel of Mark, a confiscation accomplished by partially excising (if one holds to the authenticity of "Secret Mark") or editorially muting (if one does not believe in "Secret Mark"), however sloppily, Alexandrian Mark's μυστήριον ("mystery") accent and giving it a new introduction (1:1-3) and a proper "canonical" ending. I say "partially" and "sloppily" because the μυστήριον accent remains a strongly evident feature in NT-Mark—in the so-called "secrecy" motif first isolated by W. Wrede in 1901, and most remarkably in Mark's peculiar parable theory that imagines Jesus as an esoteric mystagogue: the insiders have been given τὸ μυστήριον τῆς βασιλείας ("the mystery of the kingdom"); the outsiders hear everything ἐν παραβολαῖς ("in parables") thus seeing but not perceiving, hearing but not understanding (Mk 4:10-12). As it is, in NT-Mark Jesus hums vestiges of a bi-phonic tune: he is both purveyor of secret knowledge and an apocalyptic prophet of judgment—a combination that is not unique to Mark, of course.

We know from Paul and the Sayings Gospel Q that *mysterion* and *apocalypsis* are convergently variable accents of Wisdom genres that may congenially hold hands in the same authorial work, just as we know that *mysterion* and *apocalypsis* may be divergently similar modes of reflection on and responses to similar social situations in two separate authorial minds—as William Arnal convincingly demonstrated for both Q and the Gospel of Thomas (1995). It is possible that both of these accents in Mark could have been a feature of the originary Markan narrative. If so, one option is to suppose further that the relation of these aspects in Mark is similar to the way Burton Mack imagines the relation of these same aspects in Q: Mark contains trace signals of the social history of a Markan group that somewhat like the Q1 school, and somewhat like the Thomas school, had its genesis as a group that experimented with a social program with reference to its secret knowledge; this program failed and Mark shifted its stance, taking on the tenor and tropes of an "apocalyptic solution to the failure of the program [which] meant that all of the original desires were abrogated, sacrificed to the new desire for self-justification" (Mack 1988: 331). The problem with this scenario, as possible as it is in theory, is that *it's not arguable* with reference to evidence of (a) a Markan community and (b) with reference to indicators of literary stratification (e.g., analogous to Q) that are amenable to coordinating Mark's literary history with the social history of a Markan group. We do not know, nor can we know, the specifics of the "program" imagined by Mark as the aim of some "original desires"—that is, if by "program" we have in mind a social formation as an implemented, enacted social exemplum (a "community," if you will) of a desired "world" that is at odds with the real world.

And so I continue to ask for consideration that NT-Mark is a second-century confiscation-by-redaction of some Alexandrians' Mark. The Markan story, I suggest, appears to have been a variable "cultural operator,"[15] ending up as a kind of hapless child in second-century intra-Christian custody battles. In its wandering from the first century to the latter part of the second century Mark evidently picked up and dropped differentiable diacriticals, all-important accents. It is not too difficult to imagine, for instance, that the bi-phonics (*mysterion* and *apocalypsis*) in Mark could be exploited in some Alexandrian Christian "mystery" context, perhaps even enhanced by redactional activity so as to render the Markan narrative as a clearer source and elaboration of "the *mysterion* of the kingdom of God"—whether the *mysterion* is the motive and subject for intellectual "research" or the focus of initiation rituals, or possibly both.[16]

* * *

Let me now move toward the core issue of the Markan example by reconsidering the two best-attested data items about Mark in the second century. Both are well known and often remarked in scholarship; together, however, they pose a most interesting incongruity that begs for some thought.[17] The first is the near-absence of evidence for use of Mark as a text of intrinsic interest for exegetical, apologetic, or liturgical purposes by the Christian *literati* in the second and early third centuries (and beyond), in marked contrast to their extensive use of Matthew, Luke and John.[18] There is not a single trace of evidence that there ever was anything like a Markan school or "textual community," that is, a micro-society organized around a script (Stock 1990: 23),[19] in which Mark enjoyed place, much less pride of place—with the exception, perhaps, of the second-century Alexandrian group that Clement anathematizes in his *Letter to Theodore*. In lieu of a long recitation of a survey of the sources here, I piggy-back on the splendid work of Brenda Deen Schildgen on the reception history of the Gospel of Mark. I string together her bottom-line statements on what she calls Mark's "absent-presence"[20] in the early Christian documentary record:

> [T]he gospel was present in the canon, but essentially absent from attention ... [without] "intrinsic" merit ... The references or allusions to the gospel [of Mark] in citations and lectionary cycles in the patristic period point conclusively to the absence of Mark as a major text in the early Church ... The actual count of the citations ... shows that if there is a stepchild in the canon, Mark is the one about whom the Fathers spoke most infrequently. (Schildgen 1996: 36–41)

All in all, Augustine's off-hand dismissal of Mark as *breviator*, in the context of proposing his two-source theory of gospel relationships, reflects the judgment about Mark in the centuries preceding Augustine: "separately, he has little to record" (*De consensu evangeliorum*, 1.2). Whatever ideational, ideological, social, or political work the gospels were made to perform in post-first-century Christian formations, Mark's narrative, and much more so his myth, were a silent sideline presence—with the possible Alexandrian exception already mentioned.

Why then is Mark in the canon at all? The second datum concerning Mark in the second century, and the Patristic period in general, provides the answer.[21] The answer has to do with how Mark became a "prestige good" without intrinsic value.[22] This is what I want to make of the patristic tradition of insisting that what the author of Mark wrote derived from Peter. I am referring to the Mark as the ἑρμηνευτὴς Πέτρου ("Peter's interpreter") postulate, first claimed by Papias in the middle third of the second century (in Eusebius, *Historia Ecclesiastica* 3.39.15, citing Papias's *Exegesis of the Lord's Oracles* [ca. 140 CE]), then repeated with some variation in detail by Justin Martyr, Irenaeus, Tertullian, Origen, and on and on into the third and fourth and fifth centuries, becoming a fact by means of repeated recitation until the onset of modern (post-Enlightenment) biblical criticism (Humphrey 2006; Schildgen 1999).[23] In terms of historical authenticity the claim that Mark was the ghost writer of what is really Peter's gospel is probably bogus, but that is quite beside the point of my interest. What *is* of interest is that this claim is made, then repeated so often that it seems to reach the status of taken-for-granted and undisputed fact.[24]

Why? Based on the scholarly commentary record, one recurring answer is that the argumentative value of the Mark–Peter connection is "to uphold the integrity and worth of Mark," in Hugh Anderson's words (Anderson 1976). "Integrity and worth," however, are put under serious doubt by the striking lack of interest by anyone in actually *reading* Mark (above-noted possible exception notwithstanding), a lack, moreover, that is not alleviated by what appears to be such certain knowledge that Mark's text really is Peter's gospel. Hence, I would think that the Petrine connection as a credo had little to do with "the integrity and worth" of Mark, at least not with reference to its intrinsic value.

Let's amplify the incongruity. It is also difficult to explain Petrine authorship of Mark by supposing that the status ascendancy of Peter in the second century and beyond should be appropriately recognized by a gospel, which, though he did not actually write one, nonetheless would be his ἀναγραφή ("record"; playing on Clement of Alexandria's term; *Hypotyposes*, in Eusebius, *Historia Ecclesiastica* 6.14.5-6). This would require us to believe that Peter was responsible for a "record" that, on the evidence from Mark's narrative, is most anti-Petrine, matched only by the anti-Petrinism in Paul and, perhaps, in John 1-20 (Weeden 1901).[25] It is in this connection that I find most amusing a tiny bit of slippage in the credulity of one of Clement's rehearsals of the Mark-is-Peter's-amanuensis credo; there he intimates that Mark's ἀναγραφή may have been a case of an "unauthorized memoir." I paraphrase what Clement said to accent the amusement factor: "When Peter learned of this [Mark's project of writing out the εὐαγγέλιον that Peter had been preaching in Rome], he said 'I won't stop him, but I sure as hell wouldn't give him any encouragement either'" (*Hypotyposes*, in Eusebius, *HE* 6.14.6).[26]

So, here we have the incongruity: Mark—a prestigious narrative by virtue of its emplacement in the emerging canon; Mark—apparently without intrinsic value in the very canon that bestows prestige on it, hence as really absent, even though present; Mark—presented as Peter's ἀναγραφή, but without any consequence for Mark's influence; Mark—presented as Peter's ἀναγραφή despite the fact that Mark's story features Peter as a rather dense, misunderstanding figure.

* * *

A different tack is called for. It is of interest to me to see, as others are seeing as well, an appreciative, even rehabilitating, reconsideration of the once "heretical" argument made by F. C. Baur long ago that Paul, and his theology of "Christ crucified" and his view that Torah was passé in the new *Christos*-era, represented not a wide-spread, much less central view among the earliest Christian groups, but a sectoral, and embattled view, and a rather lonely voice crying in the proverbial wilderness.[27] With respect to Mark, it is just as interesting to observe, as Joel Marcus and others have pointed out, a remarkable return to "the question of the relation between Mark and Paul" (Marcus 2000: 473), a question that had been considered as answered in Martin Werner's 1923 refutation of Gustav Volkmar's 1857 thesis that Mark's gospel is an allegory in which Jesus is really Paul (Werner 1923; Volkmar 1857; Marcus 2000: 472 n. 1). My supposition is that a re-examination of the question would allow us to stake out an answer somewhere between Volkmar's view that Mark is an allegory of Paul and Werner's view that Mark is uninfluenced by Paul. That is, I am suggesting that *Mark* can be re-construed not as a Petrine but as a Pauline ἀναγραφή.[28] In fact, Joel Marcus has already gone a long way in that direction, though he does not use the same term:

> [T]here are on the face of it a number of striking similarities between Paul and Mark. Both, for example, make the term εὐαγγέλιον a central aspect of their theology (e.g. Mark 1.1; Gal 1.6-9; Rom 1.16-17). Both stress the significance of Jesus' crucifixion as the apocalyptic turning point of the ages … , although neither ignores the resurrection either. Both highlight Jesus' victory over demonic

powers (the Markan exorcisms; Rom 8.38-9; 1 Cor 15.24; etc.) and see his advent as the dawn of the age of divine blessing prophesied in the Scriptures (e.g. Mark 1.1-15; Rom 3.21-2). ... Both emphasize the importance of faith in Jesus and in God, sometimes picturing this faith in a dualistic way as a new mode of seeing that God grants to his elect people while condemning outsiders to blindness (Mark 4.10-12; Rom 11.7-10; 1 Cor 2.6-16). In both cases, however, such dualism sometimes yields to a universalistic perspective (e.g. Mark 10.45; Rom 11.25-32). Both Mark and Paul have negative things to say about Peter and about members of Jesus' family (e.g. Mark 3.20-1, 31-5; 8.31-3; Gal 2). Both assert that Jesus came not for the righteous but for ungodly sinners (e.g. Mark 2.17; Rom 4.15; 5.18-19), on whose behalf he died an atoning death (Mark 10.45; Rom 3.25; 5.8), and that he came for the Jews first (πρωτον) but also for the Gentiles (Mark 7.27-9; Rom 1.16; cf. Rom 11). And both think that the widening of God's purposes to incorporate the Gentiles was accomplished by an apocalyptic change in the Law that had previously separated Jews from Gentiles, a change that included an abrogation of the OT food laws; in the new situation that pertains since Jesus' advent, all foods are pure (Mark 7.19; Rom 14.20).[29] (Marcus 2000: 475–476)

I think Marcus is right in general.[30] And if so, why not try another move and seriously consider the possibility that Mark should be placed on the same side of what Joseph Tyson, in his consequential book on *Marcion and Luke-Acts*, calls "the defining struggle" over marking a Christian "center" in the second century (2006). This is the side of Marcion and his Paul, something that apparently was at least a presumed, if not a known fact in the late second century—witness the anti-Marcionite prologue to Mark. Mark's originary local problems in all their poignancy, and his urgent response to them, were transposed into, confiscated for, a struggle over defining later Christian centers. Originary Mark was a local story and it seems to have survived not because of its merits as a story (cf. Dewey 2004), nor because it was a Christian myth of origin and a social charter for first-century Jesus community. NT-Mark merely serves a structural function that is not tied to the merits of the narrative itself. One might think of it as analogous to the structural completion of the College of the Twelve by the enrolment of Matthias in this College to replace Judas (Acts 2:15-26).

* * *

I end with some comments of a methodological and conceptual kind on critical historiography and origins. Of course, these comments have in view Christian "origins," but analogies abound for the study of origins in other religions, nation states, or the political, interactional and situational processes of what Rogers Brubaker calls "group-making" (2004: 13–14). For, all of these entities do things, often with considerable force, to establish categories, or usurp available myths, narratives, or texts in order to pose a past that is able to authorize interests in the present.

The notion of a Markan community engaged in mythmaking as rationalization of its diagnosis of an incongruous social situation and of its remedial social experiments/formations is inadequate to account for the prestige or status value of the gospel of Mark as a second-century artifact. The eventual production of canonical

Mark, and its emplacement in the canon, was a precipitate of intra-Christian internecine squabbles over centers and margins at a time after the first century, when, echoing Marshall Sahlins and Bruce Lincoln, actors with distinct myths of origin relate their actions to each other, with sentiments of affinity or sentiments of hostility (Sahlins 2005; Lincoln 2014b: 6–9). Looking at NT-Mark as a bone in the mid- to late-second-century Christian dogfight over alpha-dog status does not require us to abandon NT-Mark as an interesting, though problematic, datum for early (originary, emergent) Jesus adherents. But looking at it as a *second-century artifact* does well up a different set of descriptive requirements and conceptual challenges for a scholarly redescription of the conventional myth of Christian origins.

New Testament scholars have overstressed their expectation of Mark as a key witness for "Christian" mythmaking in the *first* century. The reasons are partly due to Mark's eventual achievement of "first gospel" status in post-Enlightenment gospel criticism, and partly due to the displacement of its historical evidentiary value, by means of the invention of the Petrine connection and the canonizing process. Mark is in motion across time, place, and social setting; and the shifting, contingent, and local historical realities through which the gospel passed are not best thought of in terms of *continuities* and *trajectories*, which obscure precisely those *contingencies* of greatest interest to us about Mark's historical work (or work in history) (Brakke 2012). NT-Mark is but a stop in this story's whither, hither, and yon—a stop that effectively "centers" Mark, where, standing shoulder to shoulder with Paul and John, for example, the gospel is largely muzzled concerning whatever original problem its author tried to think about, and where NT-Mark repudiates the interests of its most avid readers in exchange for acting as a ceremonial guard of the Christian palace that was under construction in the face of threatening Christian outposts (in the minds of the palace constructors), among whom Mark appears to have been one.

Perhaps counter-intuitively, consider a historiographical stance that may help us to conceive of the second century preceding the first. This is not to say, I hasten to add, that nothing happened in the first century, but it is to say that whatever happened in the first century is massively mediated to us by what happened in the second century (and later, for that matter). In that sense, the first "Christian" century is a creation of the second century and beyond. In the process of creating myths of the past, linkages, trajectories, successions, traditions go not forward in time, but backward; they are categories made for, indeed made in, a retrospective mode that is in the mood for "first times." This holds true not only for Christian origins, but for all quests for origins of religion, a religion, or any other valued institution (such as nation or ethnicity) that needs to be perennially established "in the beginning" that is retroactively projected into the past only once the institution exists. I would suggest that these terms, to which one might add others, especially canon, canon-making, and legacy-making, might become subject to what J. Z. Smith calls "the rectification of categories."[31] Thinking of the text of the author of Mark—as a pawn in tactics and strategies not of his own making, and far removed from his originary interests and laments—as an example by means of which to think about these matters makes a great deal of sense.

As Bruce Lincoln finely states it: "All institutions, like all groups, tell stories about their beginnings. Such tales are oft repeated, finely wrought, and usually much beloved" (Lincoln 2014b: 1; see also Lincoln 2014a). Origin, especially as thought of in much past and contemporary thought and practice in the critical study of religion, is an extraordinarily overloaded term (Masuzawa 2000; McCutcheon 2015). Although origin can carry diverse meanings, in the study of religion it is a privileged, mythic, theological category—perhaps in distinction to "beginning" or "emergence."[32] As Tomoko Masuzawa has shown in her *In Search of Dreamtime*, the so-called fathers of the modern academic study of religion— say, for example, David Hume, Friedrich Max Müller, J. G. Frazer, Friedrich Hegel, Sigmund Freud, Émile Durkheim and, with melancholic anxiety over the scholar's inability to reach the origin of religion, Mircea Eliade—were in one way or another engaged in a quest for the origin of religion, where origin is the *plenum*, the site of the true explanation of the beginning and development of religiosity in human societies (Masuzawa 1994). It follows that when scholars write the history of a particular religion that "origin" in the sense of absolute beginning is a prominent (and troublesome) point of preoccupation, even devotion. And, since origin tends to mean in "the beginning," the possibility that origins are retrospective constructions has immense historiographical implications for the history of religions, Christianity included, of course.

Notes

1 What follows is an expansion and revision of parts of Braun (2010).
2 How this coupling plays itself out on the surface of Mark's narrative is demonstrated by Schildgen (1996).
3 Cf. Arnal (2008: 58), "It is the author of the Gospel of Mark … who first decided to present the import of Jesus the teacher in the certainly novel and perhaps counter-intuitive format of a biography—and specifically, a biography culminating in the teacher's death."
4 In lieu of a long bibliographic note, see Barton (1992), Donahue (1992), Bird (2006). I would underscore as still valid John Donahue's conclusion that "there is no consensus on the setting of Mark, nor is there a method agreed upon for describing the social makeup of a given community on the basis of the text" (1992: 1).
5 "The problem is not that Mark provides us with no clues about his context: it is that he provides us with so little data about the existence of a discrete 'Christian' group— the omnipresent 'community'—which is affected by this context and to which he is, more or less particularly and uniquely, directing his writing. … Indeed, Mark provides *so* little information about his audience that we cannot even be sure that he has *any* discrete Christian group in mind. Mark is simply not amenable to explanation in terms of precise intra-Christian developments" (Arnal 2008: 59).
6 Arnal here makes productive use of Benedict Anderson's story of and reflection on a certain Mary Rowlandson, an English colonist abducted in 1675 in Massachusetts, thus becoming a double exile, a displaced colonial and a kidnapping victim (Anderson 1994: 314–327).
7 For a criticism of the pervasive assumption that the New Testament texts and other early Christian writings "mirrored communities," see Stowers (2011: 238–256).

8   "Even without appealing to the evidence of *Secret Mark*, the New Testament *Canonical Mark* has long appeared to many to be a secondarily redacted document" Sellew (1991: 247–257, see 257 n.17 for bibliography). See also Humphrey (2006) and Burkett (2004).
9   E.g., Sellew (1991: 254–255) in a hedged statement: "The *Secret Gospel of Mark* no doubt differs *somewhat* from *Canonical Mark* ... though the two stages probably *differ to a greater extent* than is admitted by Koester and Crossan, *Secret Mark* should *not be seen as unrepresentative* of the originary impulses and interests that operated within the Markan tradition from the start. We must think in terms of *lines of development* ('trajectories') *rather than disruptive external redaction or tampering*" (emphasis added). Cf.: "organic development" (Sellew 1991: 257).
10 On the origin of Mark's derogatory surname and its relation to the dating of the anti-Marcionite prologue, see the detailed discussion of "the disfigurement of the evangelist" by Kok (2015: 220–226).
11 The discovery of this letter and the claims for its authenticity are famously credited to Smith (1973a, 1973b). The three recent and central disputants concerning the authenticity of Smith's "Secret Mark" hypothesis are Brown (2005), Carlson (2005) and Jeffrey (2007). I will take Sellew's statement for my purpose: "Even without appealing to the evidence of *Secret Mark*, the New Testament *Canonical Mark* has long appeared to many to be a secondarily redacted document" (1991: 247).
12 For recent histories of Christianity in Egypt and Alexandria see Griggs (2000) and Jakab (2001).
13 See Smith (1973a, 1973b), Cameron (1982: 67–71), Koester (1983: 35–57; 1990: 293–303), Schenke (1984), Crossan (1986: 91–121), Sellew (1991) and Brown (2005). Just in case it needs to be said: the probability of a version or versions of Mark being used in Alexandria does not imply a preference on my part for Alexandria as the place where Mark's narrative had its compositional genesis.
14 Griggs claims that "the overwhelming majority of those who had written on the subject believe that the letter of Clement is genuine" (2000: 21). This is an exaggeration.
15 The phrase is from Boon (1972).
16 Note Stevan Davies's argument for the Gospel of Thomas's literary influence on Mark, notably visible in NT-Mark's interest in the "mystery" of its knowledge (1996). Although it is impossible to be sure exactly when and where literary crossings between Mark and Thomas took place, second-century Egypt is, as far as I know, the only place in which both gospels evidently were used in the second century.
17 See now the splendid book by Kok (2015).
18 For the raw data see *Biblica Patristica* (1975–1995). Signal works on the reception history of Mark in the second century include Koester (1983), Oden and Hall (1998), Schildgen (1999), Kelhoffer (2000), Dewey (2004), Braun (2010), Joynes (2011), Head (2012) and, most exhaustively, Kok (2015).
19 Stanley Fish speaks of "interpretive communities" (1980).
20 "Absent-presence" is Schildgen's re-use of Crossan's term (Crossan 1980).
21 I pass by altogether the discussion, beginning in the latter part of the second century, of the relation between the Gospel (truth) and the gospels (literary entities) and the emerging preference to think of this relation in the terms of Irenaeus's famous τετράμορφον τὸ εὐαγγέλιον formulation ('the gospel in four forms'; *Adv.haer.* 3.11.8); see Reed (2002) for a splendid study of "gospel" in Irenaeus. In this "one Gospel-four gospels" argument Mark merely serves a structural function that is not tied to the merits of the narrative itself.

22 See Paden for a Durkheim-influenced analysis of the process of turning mere goods into prestige goods: either turning into high-status goods things that have little or no inherent value (such as baseball bats, or cloth into flags or "sacred" head covers) or turning objects with intrinsic value into prestige objects without intrinsic value (Paden 2008: 412).

23 I note in passing that this tradition leaves traces in the manuscript evidence for Mark, explicitly in the so-called shorter secondary ending. I would be delighted to find MS. evidence for claiming that the curious καὶ τω Πετρῳ in Mark 16:7 is a secondary addition. Alas, there is none.

24 To my knowledge, the Petrine source for Mark's narrative is never questioned by early Christian writers, though not all who remark on Mark make a *positive and explicit claim* for its derivation from Peter (e.g., Augustine).

25 Allow me to say this for now without providing textual foundation or further elaboration.

26 The Greek text from Eusebius, quoting Clement: ὅσπερ επιγνόντα τὸν Πετρον προτρεπτικως μήτε κωλυσαι μήτε προτέψασθαι ('when Peter discovered this, he neither urgently put a stop to it nor urged it on'). See also Mitchell (2005: 50): "Peter appears rather oddly disposed to the gospel which Mark wrote on request of the Roman audience ... This text cannot be used as proof for an enthusiastic authorial or patronal dissemination of the gospel."

27 Marcus, commenting on Baur's thesis: "If Paul was a lonely and contentious figure rather than a universally approved one, it is more remarkable than it would otherwise be that Mark frequently agrees with him. Mark, too, has been portrayed in post-war scholarship as a polemical writer, and it is natural that sooner or later the attempt would be made to compare and even to draw lines of influence between these two contentious theologians" (Marcus 2000: 474–475). See also Vinzent (2011) and Snyder (2003).

28 I am here playing off Clement's term and Marcus's wonderful redirection of Papias's claim that Mark was Peter's interpreter; see Marcus (2000).

29 Note also Marcus's claims: "Let me conclude simply with a claim that I will not now try to substantiate in detail: a similar demonstration to the one I have just made could be constructed about other aspects of Pauline and Markan theology. Not everyone agreed with Paul that the Law was passé for Christians—but Mark did. And he even expressed this point in terms that are remarkably similar to those of Paul in Rom. 14 καθαρίζων πάντα τὰ βρώματα, Mark 7:19; compare πάντα μὲν καθαρά, Rom. 14:20). Not everyone was as negative as Paul about Peter and Jesus' family—but Mark was. And only Mark among the NT writers gives to one of his stories, that of the Syrophoenician woman, an interpretation that echoes Paul's formula "to the Jew first, but also to the Gentiles." If these are coincidences, they are amazing coincidences. If not—and I think not—they provide further evidence of Pauline influence on Mark" (Marcus 2000: 486–487).

30 We can say this much without making a commitment to specifying the nature of the linkage between Mark and Paul. Is the influence based on Mark's knowledge of the Pauline letters? An independent sharing of similar theological views?

31 In 1992, at a University of Toronto conference devoted to Wilfred Cantwell Smith's contribution to the academic study of religion, Jonathan Z. Smith presented a paper entitled "Scriptures and Histories" in which he rather laconically but evocatively provides both further foundation for the statement above, but also strategies for further thought, including about: distinguishing "chronology" as a temporal sequence of happenings and "chronology" as a timeline "of when we became interested in them

... [which] is a significantly different timeline than the one we are accustomed to—for example, [in the second timeline] the Sumerians would not appear until some 70 years ago" (Smith 1992: 100); excessive worry about recovery of "first times" as an operational credo in scholarly approaches in the history of religion. See also Brakke (2012).

32 "First is the notion of *beginning* as opposed to *origin*, the latter divine, mythical, privileged, the former secular, humanly produced, and ceaselessly re-examined" (Said 1975: xii–xiii).

References

Anderson, Benedict (1994). "Exodus," *Critical Inquiry* 20: 314–327. https://doi.org/10.1086/448713

Anderson, Hugh (1976). *The Gospel of Mark*. New Century Bible Commentary. Grand Rapids, MI: Eerdmans.

Arnal, William E. (1995). "The Rhetoric of Marginality: Apocalypticism, Gnosticism, and Sayings Gospels," *Harvard Theological Review* 88: 471–494. https://doi.org/10.1017/S0017816000031722

—— (2008). "The Gospel of Mark as Reflection on Exile and Identity." In Willi Braun and Russell T. McCutcheon (eds.), *Introducing Religion: Essays in Honor of Jonathan Z. Smith*, 57–67. London: Equinox.

Barton, Stephen C. (1992). "The Communal Dimensions of Earliest Christianity: A Critical Survey of the Field," *Journal of Theological Studies* 43: 399–427. https://doi.org/10.1093/jts/43.2.399

Biblica Patristica (1975–1995). *Biblica Patristica: Index des citations et allusions biblique dans la literature patristique*. 7 vols. Paris: CNRS.

Bird, Michael F. (2006). "The Markan Community, Myth or Maze? Bauckham's *The Gospel for All Christians* Revisited," *Journal of Theological Studies* 57: 474–486. https://doi.org/10.1093/jts/flj112

Boon, James A. (1972). "Further Operations in Cultural Anthropology: Synthesis of and for Debate," *Social Sciences Quarterly* 52: 221–252.

Bowersock, G. W. (1994). *Fiction as History: From Nero to Julian*. Berkeley, CA: University of California Press.

Brakke, David (2012). "Scriptural Practices in Early Christianity: Towards a New History of the New Testament Canon." In Jörg Ulrich et al. (eds.), *Invention, Rewriting, Usurpation: Discursive Fights over Religious Traditions in Antiquity*, 263–280. New York: Peter Lang.

Braun, Willi (2010). "The First Shall be Last: The Gospel of Mark After the First Century." In Panayotis Pachis and Donald Wiebe (eds.), *Chasing Down Religion in the Sights of History and the Cognitive Sciences: Essays in Honour of Luther H. Martin*, 41–57. Thessaloniki: Barbounakis.

Brown, Scott G. (2005). *Mark's Other Gospel: Rethinking Morton Smith's Controversial Discovery*. Waterloo: Wilfrid Laurier University Press.

Brubaker, Rogers (2004). *Ethnicity without Groups*. Cambridge, MA: Harvard University Press. https://doi.org/10.1017/CBO9780511489235.004

Burkett, Delbert (2004). *Rethinking Gospel Sources: From Proto-Mark to Mark*. New York: T & T Clark International.

Cameron, Ron (ed.) (1982). *The Other Gospels: Non-Canonical Texts*. Philadelphia, PA: Westminster.

Carlson, Stephen (2005). *The Gospel Hoax: Morton Smith's Invention of Secret Mark.* Waco, TX: Baylor University Press.

Crossan, John Dominic (1980). *Cliffs of Fall.* New York: Seabury.

—— (1986). *Four Other Gospels: Shadows on the Contours of Canon.* Minneapolis, MN: Winston/Seabury.

Davies, Stevan (1996). "Mark's Use of the Gospel of Thomas," *Neotestamentica* 30: 207-334.

Demoem, Kristoffel and Koen De Temmerman (eds.) (2016). *Writing Biography in Greece and Rome: Narrative Technique and Fictionalization.* Cambridge: Cambridge University Press.

Dewey, Joanna (2004). "The Survival of Mark's Gospel: A Really Good Story," *Journal of Biblical Literature* 123: 495-507. https://doi.org/10.2307/3268044

Donahue, John R. (1992). "The Quest for the Community of Mark's Gospel." In Frans van Segbroeck et al. (eds.), *The Four Gospels: 1992 Fetschrift Frans Neirynck*, 819-834. Leuven: Leuven University Press.

Ehrman, Bart (2008). *The New Testament: A Historical Introduction to the Early Christian Writings.* 4th ed. New York: Oxford University Press.

Elliott, J.K. (2000). "Mark 1.1-3: A Later Addition to the Gospels?" *New Testament Studies* 46: 584-588. https://doi.org/10.1017/S0028688500000345

Fish, Stanley (1980). *Is There a Text in this Class? The Authority of Interpretive Communities.* Cambridge, MA: Harvard University Press.

Griggs, Wilfred C. (2000). *Early Egyptian Christianity from Its Origins to 451 CE.* Leiden: Brill.

Head, Peter M. (2012). "The Early Text of Mark." In Charles E. Hill and Michael J. Kruger (eds.), *The Early Text of the New Testament*, 208-220. Oxford: Oxford University Press. https://doi.org/10.1093/acprof:oso/9780199566365.003.0007

Humphrey, Hugh M. (2006). *From Q to "Secret" Mark: A Composition History of the Earliest Narrative Theology.* London: T. & T. Clark.

Jakab, Attila (2001). *Ecclesia Alexandrina: Evolution sociale et institutionnelle du christianisme alexandrine (IIe et IIIe siècles).* Christianismes anciens, 1. New York: Peter Lang.

Jeffrey, Peter (2007). *The Secret Gospel of Mark Unveiled: Imagined Rituals of Sex, Death, and Madness in a Biblical Forgery.* New Haven, CT: Yale University Press. https://doi.org/10.12987/yale/9780300117608.001.0001

Joynes, Christine E. (2011). "The Sound of Silence: Interpreting Mark 16:1-8 through the Centuries," *Interpretation* 65: 18-29. https://doi.org/10.1177/002096431106500103

Kelhoffer, James A. (2000). *Miracle and Mission: The Authentication of Missionaries and Their Message in the Longer Ending of Mark.* Wissenschaftliche Untersuchungen zum Nuen Testament 2/112. Tübingen: Mohr-Siebeck.

—— (2004). "'How Soon a Book' Revisited: EUAGGELION as a Reference to 'Gospel' Materials in the First Half of the Second Century," *Zeitschrift für die neutestamentliche Wissenschaft* 95: 10. https://doi.org/10.1515/zntw.2004.005

Koester, Helmut (1983). "History and Development of Mark's Gospel (From Mark to *Secret Mark* and 'Canonical' Mark)." In Bruce C. Corley and John C. Hurd (eds.), *Colloquy on New Testament Studies: A Time for Reappraisal and Fresh Approaches*, 35-85. Macon, GA: Mercer University Press.

—— (1990). *Ancient Christian Gospels: Their History and Development.* London: SCM.

Kok, Michael (2015). *The Gospel on the Margins: The Reception of Mark in the Second Century.* Minneapolis, MN: Fortress Press. https://doi.org/10.2307/j.ctt9m0tkt

Lincoln, Bruce (2014a). *Between History and Myth: Stories of Harald Fairhair and the Founding of the State.* Chicago, IL: University of Chicago Press. https://doi.org/10.7208/chicago/9780226141084.001.0001

—— (2014b). *Discourse and the Construction of Society: Comparative Studies of Myth, Ritual, and Classification*. 2nd ed. Chicago, IL: University of Chicago Press.

Mack, Burton L. (1988). *A Myth of Innocence: Mark and Christian Origins*. Minneapolis, MN: Fortress Press.

—— (1996a). "Redescribing Christian Origins," *Method & Theory in the Study of Religion* 8: 247–269. https://doi.org/10.1163/157006896X00350

—— (1996b). *Who Wrote the New Testament? The Making of Christian Myth*. San Francisco, CA: Harper.

—— (2001). *The Christian Myth: Origins, Logic, Legacy*. New York: Continuum.

Marcus, Joel (2000). "Mark—Interpreter of Paul," *New Testament Studies* 46: 473–487. https://doi.org/10.1017/S0028688500000278

Masuzawa, Tomoko (1994). *In Search of Dreamtime: The Quest for the Origin of Religion*. Chicago, IL: University of Chicago Press.

—— (2000). "Origin." In Willi Braun and Russell T. McCutcheon (eds.), *Guide to the Study of Religion*, 209–224. London: Cassell.

McCutcheon, Russell T. (ed.) (2015). *Fabricating Origins*. Sheffield: Equinox.

Mitchell, Margaret M. (2005). "Patristic Counter-Evidence to the Claim that 'The Gospels Were Written for All Christians,'" *New Testament Studies* 51: 36–79. https://doi.org/10.1017/S0028688505000032

Momigliano, Arnaldo (1993). *The Development of Greek Biography*. Expanded ed. Cambridge, MA: Harvard University Press.

Oden, Thomas C. and Christopher A. Hall (1998). *Ancient Christian Commentary on Scripture: New Testament II (Mark)*. Downers Grove, IL: InterVarsity.

Paden, William E (2008). "Connecting with Evolutionary Models: New Patterns in Comparative Religion." In Willi Braun and Russell T. McCutcheon (eds.), *Introducing Religion: Essays in Honor of Jonathan Z. Smith*, 406–417. London: Equinox.

Reed, Annette Yoshiko (2002). "ΕΥΑΓΓΕΛΙΟΝ: Orality, Textuality, and the Christian Truth in Irenaeus' *Adversus Haereses*," *Vigiliae Christianae* 56: 11–46. https://doi.org/10.1163/15700720252984819

Sahlins, Marshall (2005). "Structural Work: How Microhistories Become Macrohistories and Vice Versa," *Anthropological Theory* 5: 5–30. https://doi.org/10.1177/1463499605050866

Said, Edward (1975). *Beginnings: Intention and Method*. New York: Columbia University Press.

Schenke, Martin-Hans (1984). "The Mystery of the Gospel of Mark," *Second Century* 4: 65–82.

Schildgen, Brenda Deen (1996). "The Gospel of Mark as Myth." In John C. Hawley (ed.), *Through a Glass Darkly: Essays in the Religious Imagination*, 3–23. New York: Fordham University Press.

—— (1999). *Power and Prejudice: The Reception of the Gospel of Mark*. Detroit, MI: Wayne State University Press.

Sellew, Phillip (1991). "*Secret Mark* and the History of Canonical Mark." In Birger A. Pearson et al. (eds.), *The Future of Early Christianity: Essays in Honor of Helmut Koester*, 247–257. Minneapolis, MN: Fortress Press.

Smith, Jonathan Z. (1992). "Scriptures and Histories," *Method & Theory in the Study of Religion* 4: 97–105. https://doi.org/10.1163/157006892X00084

Smith, Morton (1973a). *Clement of Alexandria and the Secret Gospel of Mark*. Cambridge, MA: Harvard University Press. https://doi.org/10.4159/harvard.9780674434493

—— (1973b). *The Secret Gospel: The Discovery and Interpretation of the Secret Gospel According to Mark*. New York: Harper & Row.

Snyder, Graydon (2003). *Ante Pacem: Archaeological Evidence of Church Life Before Constantine*, rev. ed. Macon, GA: Mercer University Press.
Stock, Brian (1990). *Listening for the Text: On the Uses of the Past*. Philadelphia, PA: Fortress Press.
Stowers, Stan (2011). "The Concept of 'Community' and the History of Early Christianity," *Method & Theory in the Study of Religion* 23: 238–256. https://doi.org/10.1163/157006811X608377
Tyson, Joseph (2006). *Marcion and Luke-Acts: A Defining Struggle*. Columbia, SC: University of South Carolina Press.
Vinzent, Mikael (2011). *Christ's Resurrection in Early Christianity and the Making of the New Testament*. Farnham: Ashgate.
Volkmar, Gustav (1857). *Die Religion Jesu*. Leipzing: Brockhaus.
Weeden, Theodore J. (1971). *Mark: Traditions in Conflict*. Philadelphia, PA: Fortress Press.
Werner, Martin (1923). *Der Einfluss paulinischer Theologie im Markusevangelium: Eine Studie zur neutestamentlichen Theologie*. Beihefte zur Zeitschrift für die neutestamentliche Wissenschaft 1. Giessen: Töpelmann. https://doi.org/10.1515/9783111327877
Wrede, William (1901). *Das Messiasgeheimnis in den Evangelien; Zugleich ein Beitrag zum Verständnis des Markusevangeliums*. Göttingen: Vandenhoeck & Ruprecht.

6

The Sayings Gospel Q and the Making of an Early Jesus Group

> Human history is created by intentional activities but is not an intended project; it persistently eludes efforts to bring it under conscious direction.
> —Anthony Giddens (1984)

Introduction

The recent record of scholarship on the early Christian Sayings Gospel Q has brought us to the point where the view of Q as both product of as well as reflective and productive of deliberate, thoughtful socio-mythic invention by a particular group no longer needs to be argued. That is, as articulated by William Arnal and me elsewhere, social formation is driven by "[s]ocial interest" that

> designates ... a desire to pursue ends and agenda shared with and relative to others within the same social body. The practice of forming subgroups is not an end in itself but is a particular type of intervention in the larger social body of which the subgroups form a part. (Arnal and Braun 2004: 462)

Mythmaking designates "a social intellectual activity whereby certain key terms, images, motifs, and idea complexes are elevated to a 'self-evidently' authoritative status" (Arnal and Braun 2004: 464).[1]

What E. P. Thompson said of the making of the English working class applies to Q—and any other early Christian group—as well: it "did not rise like the sun at an appointed time. It was present at its own making" (1963: 9). Burton Mack rightly speaks of Q (both as text and social entity) as a "precious" exemplar of "an entire history of an early 'Christian' community-in-the-making" (1995: 49). This view, amply warranted by recent literary and social studies of Q, stands as a reasonable presupposition that not only permits but also requires a move toward a new set of questions that would enable us to qualify and differentiate socio-mythic inventions and processes in antiquity at "local" (*Gospel of Thomas*, Q, etc.) sites by a necessarily complex toggling procedure: (a) fitting specific socio-mythic formations into a broader picture in order to save our "local" analysis from thin conclusions by acts of analogy and comparison, and (b) relying on local, particular socio-mythic formations to keep generalizations and typologies based on surveys of the larger cultural basin pliable and subject to adjustment. The second part of the toggle is linked to a concern for the categories "mythmaking" and "social formation" themselves as *our* theoretical constructs and as tools for social description and classification.[2] If they are going to sustain a prolonged and plausible redescription project we will have to be on guard against our categories exhausting themselves in their own vagueness, on one side, and against reification of either of its two prongs as abstract, formulaic tools that merely redecorate the "old, old gospel story" with a new vocabulary veneer, on the other.

With this notice of an alert of the methodological thicket that surrounds the project of redescribing early Christianities I begin the task of stalking—and this essay represents no more than a stalking exercise which, in the end, hardly gets beyond desultory reaches for toe-holds of a conceptual and methodological kind the Greco-Roman "schools" as arenas of socio-mythic formation to see if we find there some help with the question of how Q was actively present at its own making and, presumably, how the focus on "school" might help us to qualify the categories of mythmaking and social formation themselves.

At the beginning of this task, however, stands a desideratum: there are no self-evident, clear paths or unbroken lines between the contextual analogue of the Greco-Roman "school" and the socio-mythic project signified by Q. Analogizing clarification requires first a definition of "school" that will allow us to make discriminating selections of our analogues. We know well that as a bare term "school" is a tag on a bag of unsorted things. It is a label that encompasses a spectrum of possible referents, ranging from geographically and temporally diffused generalities, such as the philosophical schools of thought (αἵρεσεις) subsumed under φιλοσοφία as an omnibus of polymorphous theory-praxis systems and variegated set of cultural stances, to the concrete (spatial and social) locations, curricula and tutoring methods of the educational system during the Hellenistic era. In the in-between of "schools of thought" and the formal schools as instruments of training in letters and rhetoric were countless venues and modes of social discourse in which scholastic dimensions were integral in more or less disciplined ways: both φιλοσοφία as well as its technicalization and spectacle in sophistry, rhetoric and "handbook" production spilled from Academy, Garden, Stoa, or classroom into public spaces in town and city, into controlled-access spaces such as the many philosophical study circles (διδασκαλεία) that gathered around guru-like guides[3] and other voluntary associations of various kinds,[4] and into domestic locales of formal as well as everyday discourse.[5] Merely tallying the venues and practices that might be contained in the "school" bag is, however, hardly anything more than an exercise in list-production, a kind of sociography Clifford Geertz once lampooned as going "round the world to count the cats in Zanzibar" (1993: 16). Some initial calculation of our interest by which we could select particular "cats" for further inspection seems unavoidable.

These obstacles notwithstanding, the "school" label which Burton Mack (1995: 45) has attached to Q has commended itself not only as a descriptive term that reflects the Q-purveyors' scribal abilities, values, "wisdom" mode of research, and choice of the instructional genre as a means of textualizing that research,[6] but also as a term of strategic usefulness. What it does do is direct attention to the immanent as well as contextual dimensions of social emergence and formation that have to do with imaginative concept formation, diagnostic and prognostic self-reflection, the "heady" (to use a Mackianism) handling of the cultural repertoire to articulate both an emerging group's initial groans and then to develop a rhetoric to clarify and mobilize motive and initial shape of action. The "school" concept brings into analytic focus the role of the intellectual in social formation.[7]

The impulse to look to Greco-Roman "schools" in processes of social and ideological formation for purposes of clarifying comparison is of course not new. E. A. Judge's argument, now a half century old, for early Christian communities to be viewed as "scholastic communities" in which "distinctly intellectual" operations of a "scholarly kind" where the "methods" and "means" of forging social organization and group identities is an example worth noting. Thus Judge states in the concluding paragraph of his article:

> [A]t *each stage* of the [Christian] movement[s] *the initiative lay with persons whose work was in important respects of a scholarly kind*, and ... they [the scholars] accepted the status in the community that this required, and employed the *conventional methods of instructing and organizing their followers*. ... [T]he means to this end are *distinctly intellectual* ... Thus although the movement[s] may have drawn in persons of all social ranks, and though [their] principles may have been socially revolutionary or, as the case may be, conformist, it will not be these [social] aspects ... that determined necessarily [their] role in society at the time. (Judge 1960–1961: 136; emphasis added)

Judge's stress on the elevated status and functional importance of "persons of a scholarly kind" may strike us as an objectionable privileging of intellectual over social aspects in measuring the "initiative" and the "means" in early Christian groups' social formation. But that is not what he was up to. Rather, he wanted to set straight the "methods of social description" (1960–1961: 4) of the then still prevalent view of the proletarian beginnings of Christian associations and, by implication, that early Christian groups were *Lumpengesellschaften* (proletarian associations) who, though short in academic skills, contested the learned élites and the system, over which they presided to their disproportionate benefit, with the superiority of (self-evident) proletarian virtue that needed no great deal of thought or skilled articulation. One might bring in Karl Kautsky to testify to the conception which Judge criticizes as "misconceived":

> It is generally recognized that the Christian congregation originally embraced proletarian elements almost exclusively, and was a proletarian organization. ... There is not a single Christian thought that requires the assumption of a sublime prophet and superman to explain its origin. (Kautsky 1925: 323, 326)

It is a view, Judge argues, that obscures what the Christian writings should lead us to conclude, namely that this representation of a contest of humble virtue against mighty (cultured élite) depravity is itself a rather sophisticated Christian self-representation behind which stands perhaps not an intellectual "superman" but a scribal mythmaking intelligence and competence nonetheless (1960–1961: 4–5).

It is precisely in this strategic respect—criticizing theories of origin that obscure, diminish, or erase intellectual efforts and means in the highly complex process of producing grouped identities in the larger cultural arena—that Judge's argument for thinking of early Christian groups as "scholastic communities" who made themselves in part by disciplined (learned) instrumentalities of oral and textual discourse represents a significant regauging of the track for social description and for theorizing early Christian social formations.[8] The train of redescription along this track leads, by way of major outfitting pauses—redaction criticism, rhetorical analyses, cultural context studies and, more recently, general social theories—to the point where we are required to posit literate, literary, studied hermeneutical agency and rhetorical know-how at the earliest visible stages of the production of the Jesus traditions generally,[9] and the Q instantiation of this production in particular.

On the Formation of Q

With respect to Q, its production as a scholastic effort from its visible beginning to the point where we lose sight of it has been demonstrated well enough. Indeed, the history of recent Q scholarship is the history of the discovery of Q as a literary document and the Q community as an increasingly self-conscious and fairly sophisticated research collective. A schematic summary of the main and mutually supporting levels on which this demonstration rests should be sufficient here.[10]

Textuality

Q must be regarded as a written text, rather than a "source" consisting of oral traditions (Kloppenborg 1987: 42-51). By itself the written nature of Q does not require us to assume it as a school project, however we define school; a written text merely presupposes an author of a certain level of literateness. But it is nonetheless a significant starting point for appreciating the literary competency and instrumentality that was at work the production of Q, especially when its writtenness is conjoined with the recognition that it was written in Greek (Kloppenborg 1987: 51-64), and in a locale where competence in Greek can hardly be assumed for just anyone and where especially literary competence in Greek must be regarded as the property of a small "scholarly" sector.

Composition

Redactional and stratigraphical studies have shown that literary Q did not happen all at once but emerged in a series of at least three successive compositional "phases," as John Kloppenborg has shown,[11] where each phase (now conventionally designated Q1, Q2 and Q3) consists of material that was congealed with the material of the previous phase in a manner that cannot be regarded as some uncontrolled activity of quantitative expansion. That is, the literary techniques in Q's manner of phased composition is such that Q is neither mere list nor catalogue. This not only adds robustness to the requirement of learned authorship (contra the anemic authorial role in the form-critical model[12]), but it introduces the temporal dimension that bespeaks some perdurance of interest in returning to the same text again and again. While prolonged tinkering with a single text does not per force lead us to suppose "school production," it would seem to be prerequisite to a school hypothesis, for time is surely an important "environmental" element in forming a school entity.[13]

Genre

What James Robinson suggestively argued in his famous "LOGOI SOPHŌN" article (1971 [1964]), John Kloppenborg decisively demonstrated in his *The Formation of Q*, namely that Q belongs to the ancient instructional genre. Although Kloppenborg has not used Q's generic affiliation to argue a "school" hypothesis,[14] he does see it as an important clue concerning Q's purveyors and audience, an audience that has an identifiable research orientation dominated by scribal values documented in analogous wisdom texts.

> [T]he instructional genre itself is most frequently associated with palace and scribal schools, although occasionally more general audiences seem to be envisaged. The genre typically reflects the values of the scribal sector: a celebration of human learning, positive valuation of the process of tradition ... and concern for both the content of wisdom ... and the *origin, nature and means* by which wisdom is acquired. ... [T]he scribal penchant [is] to view both transmitted texts and contemporary reality, both physical and social, as fundamentally enigmatic and therefore the object of research. But whatever the means of acquisition, wisdom—both as a particular mode of conduct and as a vision of the divine—is for the scribe the redemptive medium itself. (Kloppenborg 1991: 82–83; emphasis original)

Kloppenborg then takes the generic clue a step further and examines the contents of Q itself. What he found is coherent with what the instructional form itself suggests: the contents of both major stratums of Q display scribal values, topics and techniques, despite the shifts in predominant forms, mood, and social posture from one stratum to the next.

School Technologies

When one turns from larger literary clues (textuality, compositional/redactional sophistication, genre) to examine the techniques of arrangement and manipulation of Q's constituent clusters and speech complexes, an older form-critical view of Q's inner creation by what Kloppenborg describes as a "block process, with complex blocks of sayings being created by quasi-organic forces, by 'growth' from individual sayings to small clusters to larger speeches" can no longer be held (1995: 7). Rather, the general Greco-Roman literary culture's value placed on "invention" (εὕρεσις; *inventio*) and the school-taught rhetorical techniques associated with that value seems to have been at work at both major stratums of Q, though there are differences in Q's argumentation from one stratum to the next.

"Invention" should be regarded in two senses that combine to give the term some leverage in arguing for a school scenario. At one level it refers simply to employment of Hellenistic school technologies for arranging sayings in suasive, argumentative patterns and for elaborating *chreiai* into arguments, and the like, many of which are present in Q with notable sophistication[15] and authorizing intent (Carruth 1995: 98–115). These are fairly advanced text-handling operations that would require of its practitioners "scribal literacy" rather than bare "craftsman's literacy."[16] In terms of training, one might think of the expertise of the *grammaticus*, someone with many of the skills and erudition of the rhetor, though not of the latter's status and access to élite social strata.[17]

On another level, invention concerns the question of whom to credit with the complex speech and argument construction one finds in Q: Q authors themselves or some pre-Q ghost composers? A conclusive answer is subject to further study, but Leif Vaage's argument, sharply stating earlier suggestions, that Q's inaugural sermon (Q 6:20-49) was likely not known prior to its appearance in Q1 (1995), and William Arnal's contention for similar *de novo* "fabrication" of John the Baptist's speech in Q2 (3:7-9, 16-17) (1995a), provide grounds for supposing a tradition/invention ratio in Q that is overbalanced in the direction of invention in all literary strata of the document.[18] Q's time frame itself favours the supposition of literary entrepreneurship, of the Q tradents composing their text largely from material they themselves generated in their history of research.[19]

Erudition, Power and Authorization

Whatever else they may be, societies are also "organized power networks" in which the ability to impose or to resist authority depends in part on abilities to manipulate the recognized cultural canon by means that are equally recognized as authoritative (Mann 1986: 1–33).[20] Relevant to our period generally: despite very uneven distributions and unbalanced levels of literacy and the higher scholastic competencies that presupposed literacy, even despite (and perhaps partly because of) wide-spread illiteracy over against which text-skills were valued as a scarce "golden gift," (Harris 1989: 337) the high social regard for intellectuals as displayed in the iconographic record (Zanker 1995) shows that Greco-Roman societies were scholastically-oriented societies, if only in the recognition that a kitbag of competencies derived from literacy was an important way to get one's hands on instruments of power in social discourse generally,[21] but also in dealing with the civic and imperial bureaucratic structures—and this whether deployed for conservation or for corrosion of the dominant cultural "facts." Q seems to recognize the power of letters in its apparently paradoxical insistence (remarkably accentuated in Q2) on reassuring its "knowledge," obtained outside of and in putschy opposition to the media associated with the sage and scholar (Q 10:21-22), by those very same repudiated media. An epistemology of revelation that stresses the immediacy of (superior) knowledge, self-evident modes of persuasion, and spontaneous articulation in situations that demand judiciousness of speech (Q 12:10-12) apparently needs to be sustained and legitimated by textualized, learned rationales and, pronouncedly in Q2 and Q3, with measured and competent recourse to Judaism's "canonical" repository, the so-called Great Tradition (Kloppenborg 1990: 45–60; 1991: 91–96; Arnal 1996). Q is not terribly unique in making a scribal return to an apparently repudiated scribal modality of discourse in order to empower its own self-evidences. Rough analogies abound: in other Christian circles;[22] in the massive production of more or less technical religious handbooks and compendia of specialized knowledge as a kind of replacement ritual activity where text replaces temple as the site of religious research (Smith 1993, 1995: 13–27; cf. Lightstone 1997); generally, in the late Hellenistic "rhetoric of dissent" exemplified by, say, Philostratus's literary (i.e., argued) doxography of Apollonius' self-authorized "display of truth" (ἐπίδειξις τῆς ἀληθείας) (Braun 1997)[23] or by the textualization of Cynic rhetoric of demonstrative action[24] as serialized aphoristic wit such as we find it in Diogenes Laertius or other gnomologia.

Along an adjunct vein, although early Q is evidently animated about standing at the brink of its own metaphoric and social "novelty" (the kingdom of God),[25] social novelties don't just happen on "the third day," as it were; they are "something con-structed, put together" (Lincoln 1989: 10–11) in a process of recursive reproduction of available cultural givens.[26] Recursive reproduction happens in Q in various ways, and is well enough charted in Q scholarship. Q's excitement about the new thus is tempered by the strategy of submitting the novel to some quick-aging activity so as to be able to construe the "new" as really something "old" and thus to claim for the "new" the power and sanctity of "tradition," a phenomenon Hobsbawm and Ranger try to evoke with the oxymoron, "the invention of tradition" (1983). The past is convertible to social power in the present—hence the variety of "instant-aging" maneuvers familiar to us from the early Christian groups we study (Wilken 1971b; cf. Braun 1999). "Strategic tinkering with the past" is a ubiquitous cross-cultural social rationalizing and formation device, as Lincoln demonstrates, and not restricted to times of social de- and rearranging out of which new groupings emerge (1989: 21). But moments of emergence demand it with accentuated urgency and provide exciting opportunity for tinkering, precisely because these are moments when the social world as it is experienced is exposed as fabricated (rather than self-evidently natural) and therefore also as fabricable.[27]

Persuasive tinkering with the past, however, is hardly imaginable as an easy activity that just anyone can do with equally forceful effect. It is a scholarly craft, for, once again, it demands not only familiarity with the contents of the cultural archives (myths, epics, wisdom collections, etc.), but equal familiarity with exegetical skills and hermeneutic specialties with which to correlate the old and the new. Q's ability, at its literary beginning (3:7b–9, 16b–17; from the Q2 stratum), to appropriate and evoke the Lot/Sodom narrative to map its own experience onto a reinterpreted story as a paradigmatic tale of divine protection in a scorched wasteland is, as Kloppenborg has demonstrated (1990), a masterful trick of metaphoric cartography, effective not only for displacing the regnant holy place but also for re-placing the sacred center in the Q circle itself. Appropriation of "Israel" in Q2, successionist linkages either in relation to the myth of Wisdom (*Sophia*) as a divine intermediary, the Hebrew patriarchs, or the line of abused prophets, then to place Jesus in these successions so as also to establish him as fountainhead of Q-to-come, does not quite add up the philosophical schools' self-understanding as venerable "successions," but the difference is not a difference of kind as much as of degree of explicitness and local particularity (Kienle 1961; cf. Mason 1996: 31–37). To speak Q as a διαδοχή (succession) may be a useful distortion for bringing into view Q's scribal-discursive bent in authorizing its novel discoveries in relation to a (revised) honored past and by means of treating its own text as an emerging literary διαδοχή that was both medium and product—and, as Q2 and Q3 show by their refractive study of Q1, also the source—of its meditations. That is, it seems possible to see in Q's collusive operations of social experience/formation and mythmaking all the interlinked "moments" of its own historical production, both social and literary: (1) fact-making (social experience and experiment), (2) fact assembly (an archive of remembered actions, rationales, etc.), (3) fact retrieval (crafting the narrative), and (4) signifying and valuing the narrative (the creation of history "in full," giving it its authoritative character of myth of origins, social charter, and myth of destination).[28] The competencies required to pull this off are hardly doltish!

Social Location and Status of the Q Scribes

The range of intellectual/scribal indicators in Q naturally has raised among Q scholars the question of the identity of Q's producers. Several issues are entangled in this question: the ethos of social radicalism articulated especially in Q1, the correspondence of this ethos to a real social stance and location (Galilean urban vs. rural), the social status (vagabonding beggarly types vs. settled, urban intellectual-professional types) of those who assumed the ethos of Q1 as a way of life, a postulation of motivations for the counter-cultural socio-mythic "world" imagined in Q, the range of competencies that the document Q requires us to assume of its producers. It is neither possible nor necessary here to recall and refereee the options on all these issues, especially as they are crystallizing themselves in the options of "itinerant radicalism" (Theissen 1973), given its fullest expression with help of the analogue of Cynic subversive virtue by Leif Vaage (1994), and what we might now call the "deracination" argument first suggested by John Kloppenborg (1991: 85–89), then worked out in great detail by William Arnal (2001). If the "itinerancy" option is not too insistently tied to a view of the Q1 purveyors/audience as peasants, itinerant laborers and tradespeople, nor overly committed to homologizing an "itinerant intelligence" (Vaage) and actual, physical roving of shoeless vagabonds, but understands "itinerancy" as a tropic imagination responding to perceived or real experiences of socio-economic, religious and intellectual *atopia* (Frischer 1982: 54),[29] it does not need to stand in opposition to the virtually unavoidable conclusion that Q1 and certainly Q as a whole represents the intellectual/scribal labors of people who had both competence and means for such labours. Parsed in other words, it is precisely by postulating Q as the product of intellectual, literary work that we are able to acknowledge and account for the putative "Cynic" aspects of Q without having to explain these aspects or Q as a whole as an effect of a mimetic idealization of a Cynic-like Jesus or as the literary mirror of an actual Cynic-like itinerancy.

The literary achievements evident in Q itself, along with close attention to indicators of social location in the document (Kloppenborg 1991; Piper 1995; Reed 1995), suggests a "clear homology" (Arnal 2001) between literary Q1 and a social group from the ranks of an urban retainer class of "middling" status (Kaster 1988: 106).[30] Indeed, Kaster's description of the social status of the grammarian (1988: 10–134) is perhaps of a general utility for trying to imagine the Galilean small-town scribal intelligentsia who had the combination of social affiliations, intellectual and literary competencies, and status ambiguities and disaffections for us to think of them as the conceptual, rhetorical and textual framers of Q.[31] The grammarian/ scribe was one of antiquity's ubiquitous, yet largely anonymous (as far as the documented historical record goes) and unsung "middling" figures, ranking well below other public intellectuals, such as the rhetorician, the sophist, the philosopher, on scales of public recognition, honor, income and opportunities of upward advancement, even though the grammarian/scribe shared some of the competencies for which the latter are known, competencies which, as I have noted, must be presupposed in relation to Q.

When Kaster characterizes the grammarian/scribe as occupying a level of "middling respectability" in the civic system he means several things:

1. *Social origins* were of a spectrum on the ladder of social rank and respectability, ranging from people of "low birth" to people of curial status,[32] though generally coming from the *mediocritas* level, people of at least enough resources and points of access to acquire the skills to qualify them for their professional demands (Kaster 1988: 107–111).

2. Kaster adduces evidence that suggests that grammarians enjoyed only a *modest social status*; their ascribed respectability derived chiefly from their professional competencies.

3. The grammarian's *class commitments* were ambiguous. On the one hand, he was dependent on the élite and circulated among their ranks in limited and controlled ways, but this controlled access indicated only that he was not one of them. On the other hand, in the course of his professional activity, contact with the lower-strata people required of this middling type to be the interface between the urban élite class and the lower-strata clients dependent on the civic/imperial system, but without the (literate) means to negotiate it. Kaster's notice that the grammarian thus was of torn loyalty, suffering from a double *atopia* owing to the double-surfaceness of his brokerage function, makes a great deal of sense.[33] In Q it is reflected in its "repertoire of topics that we know to have been directly the interest of scribes (divorce, debt, loans, petitions)" (Kloppenborg 2006: 7) that are at the same time the repertoire of worries of the agrarian or non-literate urban classes.

4   In terms of *wealth*, although the range of imperial evidence suggests "at least a modest surplus of wealth and comfortable standard of living" that allowed for "touches of civilized life" (Kaster 1988: 107–111) complaints about irregular income or unsatisfactory substitution of kind (alimentary goods) for cash (*salarium*; σύνταξις) were not unheard of (1988: 115–116).[34]

5   One is not surprised to see that grammarians were remarkably *mobile figures*, both geographically and in terms of the versatility of professional/scribal activities derived from their mastery of literate instrumentalities. A grammarian's move from the classroom to an assessor's post, advocacy, or other administrative portfolios is a matter of record (Kaster 1988: 124–125); a move from village administration to an urban tax collection job, such as one might suppose for some Q scribes, is likely. Kaster's prosopographic data indicates that a quarter of the grammarians moved from their homelands or changed their place of practice (1988: 126–128, 463–477). Presumably, mobility of both kinds is related to demographic and other socio-economic factors associated with urbanization and centralizations (or decline of centers) of administrative infrastructures that created a surplus of middling bureaucrats here while generating shortages elsewhere. For the scribe/grammarian whose mobility was encumbered by force of sentiment or by familial and social ties to native region or hometown, these same factors would contribute both to real and perceived sense of professional and personal devaluation and out-of-place-ness.

Looking For a Field of Analogies

It thus seems fitting to envisage both the social and the literary formation of Q in a school "space." That is, both the group and its document display an evident bent on investing in the power of text production (perhaps to be understood as ritual practice, though concerning Q this latter needs further thought[35]) as locus and means of social formation in response to the experience of displacement. Where to go from here? Does this provide any direction for contextualizing Q in a field of analogies? A few thoughts suggest themselves.

Assuming that the representation of the schooling of Q I have drawn above is plausible, the initial frustration about how to reflect on the formation of Q with reference to "school" analogies may be eased to some extent in that the representation may delimit and focus the analogical scope. Most generally, if one thinks of Q as a project that exemplifies what Jonathan Smith has called "trading places" (1995: 13–27), of responding to the experience of *atopia* by imagining re-emplacement in a reconfigured social space and enacted in scribal ways, one might look in the first place for comparisons with other instances where "the major sociological burden" of "alienation and deracination" (Frischer 1982: 53), however real or perceived and however severe either the reality or the perception, by a scribal/intellectual sector causes seguing toward alternate social visions, roles and arrangements in conjunction with literary activity and canon-making. Several examples may be enough to indicate directions in which to look for such comparative data.

First, Smith's own long and sustained effort both to document and reflect on such instances in Hellenistic-Roman antiquity may bring some previously unseen comparative possibilities into view. Who else would have thought, for example, that Q might have something to do with the creation of collections such as the Greek Magical Papyri (Smith 1995), or with Thessalos of Tralles's re-placement of defunct temple media and medical wisdom by an astro-herbal text that is both product and reproductive site of an alternate wisdom, wisdom which, much as in Q, is offered as unmediated goods, the result of meeting the god "one-on-one" (μόνῳ μοι πρὸς μόνον)?[36]

Second, Bernard Frischer's work on the Epicurean fraternities, although largely concerned with explaining their paradoxical recruitment practices, is cast within a sociological historiographical frame that permits him to eke out a redescription of the philosophical schools as socio-mythic formations in response to literal or perceived deracination of the philosopher as public intellectual (1982: 52–65, cf. 1–6; see also Bryant 1996). The emergence of Epicureans, Cynics, Pythagoreans, and possibly other philosophical/social associations should be good places where to think about the formation of Q and, more generally, about the phenomenon of scribal/intellectual re-emplacement strategies itself, and especially for noting and theorizing about the *different directions* these strategies can go concerning options on whether to secede from the "world" or to engage it a number of different ways, and on whether to embody the response to deracination in alternate community formation (Epicureans) or to shrink the sense of alienation and, hence, one's difference, to the level of pursuing individual cunning (μῆτις)[37] and virtue in a world perceived to be misguided and rotten (Cynics).

The point on difference as a theoretical challenge may be illustrated by noting an endemic problem in social-historical work that relies on comparison and typology-construction, namely the tendency toward assuming a predictable commensurableness between cultural conditions and social-formational reactions to it—if conditions "x" are in place, reaction "y" will follow; if reaction "y" is observed, conditions "x" must be supposed.[38] It is on this methodological issue alone that William Arnal, in his essay on "the rhetoric of marginality" in Q and the *Gospel of Thomas*, contributes a critical insight that should to be taken seriously, for there he demonstrates that a "shared critical stance toward [similar] distressing socioeconomic changes perceived to be taking place" generates diverging reactions, Q moving toward sectarian community formation rationalized with an apocalyptic rhetoric, the *Gospel of Thomas* taking a route toward "individualistic gnostic theology" (1995b: 492, 494). In view of their evident similarities at one stage of their respective histories, the difference in their final destinations—in J. Z. Smith's categories (1990), Q remaining locative to the end, and the *Gospel of Thomas* apparently preferring the utopia of its own deep head-space where it is able to "pass by" (*Gos. Thom.* 42) the world perceived to be a carcass (if this point can be drawn from saying 56; cf. 60, 80)—is all the more interesting and in need of explanation. If *Thomas* shows that it is possible to get from something like Q1 to a utopian hermeneutical school, Q2 stands as a puzzling difference, as the way not taken by *Thomas*, and therefore the evolution from Q1 to Q2–Q3 shows itself as not self-evidently in accordance with some inevitability, some "law" within the social formation and/or mythmaking process itself.

Although I do not wish here to belabor the Q1–Q2 problem too much, I do have some interest in pointing out that Q2 is not the *necessary* flowering of a seed germinating in Q1, even if Q2 appears, as it does, as a sensible and masterfully refracted appropriation of Q1. The point of the pointing is a social-theoretical one: it asks for an understanding of social formation that is perhaps best formulated in Anthony Giddens's proposition that

> [t]he flow of [social] action continually produces consequences which are unintended by actors, and these unintended consequences also may form unacknowledged conditions of action in a feedback fashion. Human history is created by intentional activities but is not an intended project; it persistently eludes efforts to bring it under conscious direction. (Giddens 1984: 27)

Speaking of Q, "it was present at its own making" (E. P. Thompson) with intentional action, but its final outcome is nonetheless on unintended project, a surprise, from the vantage point of earliest Q. Q's formational "teleology" is evident only in retrospect, from the vantage point of Q2 and Q3, and then it shows itself as imagined by Q's own "narrativization" of itself, where narrativization should be understood as a "moment" in the historical production of social and literary Q (cf. Trouillot 1995: 1–30).[39] Comparisons of Q's differences from analogous forms of emergent social/school formations likely will set before us in the first place the "fluidity of social formation" (Lincoln 1989: 18) driven at once by human intention to activate apparent interests and unintended consequences of those actions that then become junctures of renewed decision-making, as an unavoidable explanatory challenge that will hardly be met with formulaic invocations of group formation models.[40]

Third, we do know that the end of the Jerusalem temple in 70 CE meant that a large priestly-scribal sector lost not only jobs, but its fundamental social, intellectual and ritual *raison d'être*. This sector's "burden of alienation and deracination" can hardly be overestimated. We know the imaginative remaking of this group of itself as the formation of the rabbinic colleges which reconstituted a Judaism in which "temple" and the judiciary values based on temple were relocated in text and where textual talk about sacrifice and temple ritual becomes replacement ritual (Smith 1995: 22).[41] The description of this re-formation, however, is hampered by a similar historiographical "catch-22" that Burton Mack has exposed as a problem for reconstructions of early Christianities (1996). Thus Jack Lightstone: "Almost everything Mack says of the scholarly study of the New Testament and of related reconstructions of early Christianities holds true for the study of early rabbinic literature and the social reconstruction of early Rabbinisms"

(Lightstone 1997: 277). Commenting on modern scholarly accounts of the history of Rabbinism, Lightstone contends that

> in the main what one has is a scholarly refinement of rabbinic literature's own account of its own literary history. This [Rabbis' own] account, distilled and refined, becomes the [modern scholarly] description of the early rabbinic and proto-rabbinic social formation, in terms of which the literary history and character of the early rabbinic documents are explained, and in which framework their meaning is elucidated. "Catch-22!" (Lightstone 1997: 278)

The circular consensus of the Rabbis' self-account and scholarly accounts of Rabbinisms has produced a "historical narrative" in which literary history and corpus, embracing pre-70 "oral Torah," Mishna, and the later canons of the Babylonian and Palestinian academies, is "a largely self-consistent whole" (Lightstone 1997: 277, 279). Similarly, argues Lightstone, in this narrative the rabbis are a "synthesis" marked by a genealogical continuity between generations of pre-destruction Judean and Galilean sages, the Yavneh academy, and the school that produced the Mishna under the direction of Judah ben Simeon ben Gamaliel at the end of the second century CE. It is, as Lightstone points out, a picture of the social formation of Rabbinism that lacks "almost any resolution or acuity" (1997: 279). By means of a re-imagined historiography and socio-rhetorical procedures he had already developed earlier (1994), Lightstone attempts to work himself out of the confines "of what rabbinic literature says about itself, its own history and the history and social formations of those whom the literature claims as its progenitors" (1997: 281). Here we need to note only the results of Lightstone's kind of thinking. The literary and rhetorical analysis suggests that Mishna displays in (the selection of legal) substance and scribal-rhetorical technique "a priestly-scribal virtuosity of comprehensively mapping 'the world'" as a means of laying "claim to priestly-scribal authority for the College of Sages" (1997: 289). At the social level, Mishna "bespeaks finally managing to create or to find at the end of the second century a new institutional home for the exercise and perpetuation of that guild expertise" (1997: 291) once institutionalized in the Temple. When Lightstone turns to the question of the origin of the scribal/social formation documented in Mishna he notes that we must presuppose a portfolio of professional skills that "usually come from an institutionalized, social setting, where expertise is 'bought and paid for,'" and he suggests "that those persons who are at the largely veiled origin of Rabbinism are 'refugees' from the Temple-state's national bureaucracy and administration, who, having lost their institutional base, first tried to preserve and pass on their professional guild expertise" (1997: 290). In a note he makes clear what he means by "first":

> What I suggest is that preservation of the guild, through preservation of its characteristic virtuosity, "drove" the development of the earliest rabbinic movement—this more so than any motivation to define a Judaism without a functioning Temple and Temple-state, or to preserve the legal traditions of that Temple-state. (Lightstone 1997: 290 n. 36)

Lightstone's argument is remarkable—of course, for what it portends for a redescription of the emergence of rabbinic Judaism itself, but also because it opens up an analogy for Q's socio-mythic re-emplacement project by scribal-textual instrumentalities, an analogy, moreover, that is within the very Jewish scribal history in which Q contends its own claims, a history in which neither the post-70 temple scribal "refugees" nor the Q "research group" is the only example of scribal deracination that is mitigated by a deflected continuation of scribal activities.

Lightstone's point that group survival, including the preservation of relatively high-status expertise and social authority associated with it, may be a primary force behind a group's mythic inventions, can perhaps be dragged over to Q. Its trajectory from the aphoristic stage (if one is permitted to speak of that as a real stage in Q's literary *and* social history), certainly from Q1 to Q2 and unto Q3, appears to be moved in part by the centripetal force of the group's increasing attachment to *itself*. Put crudely, the constant in Q is not some bright star in the sky (myth; "kingdom of God") nor the unflickering beacon of an ideal social design—Q, after all, is ready to adjust its early views on both of these things—but the experience of alienation from those outside and increasingly deliberate and noisier efforts in Q2 to arouse and articulate grounds for a compensating attachment to the group that feels that way. Thus, the "treasure" (Q 12:34) is the group itself and its survival in *some form*, and the campaign of Q is to win "hearts"—the "sentiment" of "affinity," in Bruce Lincoln's terms (1989: 8–11)—to this treasure (the group, rather than a fixed vision of the group) and keep them devoted to it at all costs. This is a part of how social formation works.[42] Note especially Q 9:57–60, which in the context of final Q works as a trope for pleading to its members, "stick with us, folks!"

Notes

1 I use "socio-mythic invention" not to coin a neologism, but as my shorthand tag for the dynamic and dialectical process of collective identity construction highlighted by the coeval activities of "mythmaking" (word) and "social formation" (deed) which Mack has persuasively introduced as analytic and explanatory categories (1996, 2000). My usage of "social formation" and "mythmaking" is of course indebted to Mack.

2 As Wright's "biography" of the concept of "class" shows: "Concepts are produced. The categories that are used in social theories, whether they be the relatively simple descriptive categories employed in making observations, or the very complex and abstract concepts used in the construction of 'grand theory', are all produced by human beings. ... They are never simply given by the real world as such but are always produced through some sort of intellectual process of concept formation" (Wright 1985: 20).

3 Brown on the later Christian attraction to the older model of the διδασκαλεῖον: "Small study-circles were the powerhouses of the Christian culture of the second and third centuries. The extraordinary intellectual ferment of the period is unthinkable without them" (Brown 1988: 104).

4 Recent work on Greco-Roman voluntary associations demonstrates how "school" and "voluntary association" converge as venues of scholastic activities. See, in general,

Kloppenborg and Wilson (1996); especially Mason's argument for considering the *philosophiai* as voluntary associations (1996). On "wissenschaftliche Vereine" see Ziebarth (1969 [1896]: 69–74); on early Christian groups as a hybrid of "philosophical school" and "association" see Wilken (1971a: 287); for a good survey of scholarly discussions of "school" and "voluntary association" see Ascough (1998: 19–49, 71–94).

5 See, for example, Bremmer (1995: 29–38); Stowers (1984: 59–82); Lynch (1972); Townsend (1971: 139–163).
6 See Kloppenborg (1991: 77–102).
7 I trust that my use of the words "strategic" and "analytic" make it clear that I am not trying to slip in some notion of "intellectual" that is itself not fundamentally social, that is, recursively dependent on the contextuality of common (shared) motivations, interests, and the various means of articulating these interests which makes thought and communication among people possible in the first place. Nor am I suggesting sympathy for a "top down" conception of social structuration dynamics which renders the common person as a passive, ineffectual "inarticulate dolt" (ἰδιώτης τῷ λόγῳ; 2 Cor. 11:6) who is dependent on the intellectual specialist as an external provider of discursive goods on the assumption that the common person has neither the cognitive diagnostic wherewithal to be a "sociologist" nor the ability to be an intentional actor in the social arena. Nor, finally, am I representing an idealist/intellectualist theory of social emergence and formation, in contrast to a materialist theory. Neither the term "intellectual" nor so-called intellectual competencies and modes of communication and influence need entail an idealist or intellectualist theoretical stance; rather, "intellectual" is a category subject to materialist conditions and analysis. See further Arnal and Braun (2004: 459–469). There is no need to hold to a disjunctive model of social emergence, formation, change, and so forth, that gives agentive priority to intellectual activities over non-intellectual activities, or vice versa.
8 Although Judge himself does not do so, he could just as well have directed his criticism of the "proletarian origins" theory also against the Bultmannian form-critical view of the history of the synoptic tradition (the Jesus traditions textualized in the first three canonical gospels) and its mysterious "law" of *Kleinliteratur* in which a folk process, itself notoriously conceived as a process without intentionally active folk contesting real social and material interests, displaced the role of a schooled intelligence.
9 See the demonstrations in Mack and Robbins (1989).
10 Readers should now consult the magisterial fruition of scholarship on Q in Kloppenborg Verbin (2000).
11 See his argument concerning the literary history of Q (Kloppenborg 1987).
12 See my criticism of the form critics' "author" (Braun 1995: 134–136).
13 Although studies on Q have not been inattentive to the topic of time in Q itself (see, for example, Mack's comments (1995: 53) on Q's effort to place itself within a cosmic *Urzeit-Endzeit* teleology by means of combining in its Jesus the retrospective knowledge of wisdom and the prospective knowledge of the apocalyptic prophet), or to the issue of Q's real time span in the first century, a school hypothesis might require additional consideration of Q and time, both in terms of duration (how long does it require to set up the disciplinary apparatus?) and use of time (how was "study" time designated and located, that is, temporally, physically and socially emplaced?) to promote and make possible scholarly *askesis*. See Giddens (1984: 110–161) for a discussion of "time" as both environment and instrument of social formation—a discussion culminating in a conversation with Foucault's argument (in *Discipline and Punish*) that time is a mechanism of confinement which makes discipline possible.

14 While Kloppenborg's observation of scribal values and techniques in Q allows him to bring Q into a school orbit, he also notes that "Q does not show the same sort of self-conscious and studied composition expected in the products of the elite scribal establishment" (1991: 84-85).
15 See, for example, Piper (1982: 411-418), Cameron (1990: 35-69) and Douglas (1995: 116-131).
16 For more on the distinction see Harris (1989: 7-8).
17 Issues of training, function and status pertaining to the *grammaticus* are analysed by Kaster (1988).
18 Mack makes an additional move that is relevant. Informed by his expertise in ancient rhetoric he observed that the blocks of material in Q1 are built upon an "aphoristic core" (1993: 110). On the logic that aphorism precedes both clustering and argumentative elaboration, he suggests that Q1 had its origins in "aphoristic discourse" which then allows him to get "in touch" with the earliest stage of Q's social history. Supposing Mack is right on his demarcation of an aphoristic beginning as the "documentary" foundation for literary Q (at least Q1), the tradition-invention distinction is about collapsed. Earliest Q invents the "tradition" that later Q will comment on, elaborate and revise for years to come. This is possible, perhaps even likely. On the oxymoron of the "invention of tradition," and discussion of modern examples, see Hobsbawm and Ranger (1983).
19 On the dating of Q strata, see Arnal (2001: 172). Arnal's estimates (Q1 in the 30s or 40s; Q2 in the 40s or 50s) are based on his analysis of Q's knowledge of and reaction to "the long-term and structural effects of Galilee's gradual incorporation into the Roman-Herodian orbit ... [which] were beginning to be felt with a vengeance" in the times noted above.
20 On the relationship of authority, power, class-emplacement, and the discursive instruments for establishing or corroding authority, see also Lincoln (1989, 1994).
21 Note the ritualized recognition of this in a child's prayer: "Lord, give me the grace of good understanding, that I might learn letters and gain the upper hand over my fellows" (*Vita Eutychii* 8; cited by Kaster 1988: 11).
22 For example, Paul or the *Gospel of Thomas*; see Mason (1996: 48).
23 Cf. Billault (1993: 231), who characterizes Apollonius' discourse as a "rhetoric of sovereign speech."
24 For example, Antisthenes: "Excellence is a matter of actions, not of discoursing or learning" (D.L. 6.11; cf. Crates, *Ep.* 21).
25 The notion of "novelty" in relation to "new" social movements is a slippery and contested concept among social theorists; see Melucci (1995). How easily some notion of "novelty" can be converted into a mystified and inscrutable "origin," effected by a *deus ex machina*, is exemplified in the historiography determined by the Lukan-Eusebian myth of Christian beginnings; see Cameron (1994); cf. Wilken (1971b); on the fascination for absolute origins even among modern historians of religion, see Masuzawa (2004). If, however, "novelty" is revalued, as Mack, Cameron and others have begun to do, as a term that focalizes attention on the social and intellectual moves in the emergent moment of social formation, a redescribed use of novelty may help us alight on disciplined (learnt and learned) Hellenistic-Roman means of "track laying" to enable "switches" in social-religious formations. (The metaphor of "track laying, and converting to a new gauge" is used by Mann (1986), adjusting Weber's image of "switchmen," to talk about the importance of manipulating ideas to potentialize, especially in times of socioeconomic and political instability, the emergence of new

arrangements out of social interstices.) For helpful conceptualizing by social historians and theorists on emergent moments of social formations and practices, see Hobsbawm and Ranger (1983) and Anderson (1983); and on comparative studies of working-class formations, see Katznelson (1986) and Perrot (1986).

26 The idea of "recursive reproduction" is argued complexly by Giddens (1984). Its key point is that social action, even in times of high degrees of social change, is bounded by and dependent on the structures (material, economic, political, etc.) and resources (means of communication, mythmaking, etc.). The full package of a society's constitution thus is both means and outcome of social actions and practices. Analogy: even a "novel" sentence is a reproduction of the rules of grammar and the bounded vocabulary of the language in which the sentence is uttered. For an instructive application of Giddens' structuration theory to the formation of theological ideologies in a post-Pauline Christian circle, see Hornell (1995).

27 See especially Bourdieu (1997: 168) for a reflection on how the "natural" truth of a society is exposed as artificial when "objective crises" (such as class divisions) generate the practical destruction of the self-evidence of a society's social facts. Once these facts are no longer factual, either by rationale of law (*nomos*) or nature (*physis*), the possibility of refabrication is in place.

28 On these interlinked moments of historical production see Trouillot (1995: 1–30, especially 26).

29 One might note that Vaage makes this metaphoric move in a note where he acknowledges the criticisms of Theissen's "itinerants," then decides to "pick up and play off" Theissen's idea in such a way that itinerancy is now a trope for "an alternate 'type' of 'intelligence' characterized by its 'itinerant' (or in postmodern speak, disseminating) logic, comparable, e.g., to the account of *metis* or Détienne and Vernant" (Vaage 1994: 185 n. 5, citing Détienne and Vernant 1991 [1978]).

30 Kloppenborg's suggestion of "'petit bourgeois' in the lower administrative sector in the cities and villages" (1991: 85) in the upper Galilee, suggested by Q's "mapping" of its geographical location, of course begged the question if one could postulate a sufficient number of people in the mid- to lower-level administrative and scribal class in the region. His own initial positive answer, based on examination of evidence concerning administrative infrastructures, receives further support from Arnal (2001), however with a view toward describing their circumstances that could support plausible theorizing of real deracination as the motive for responding to those circumstances in the manner that Q does.

31 Several of the usual cautions against analogizing apply here: Kaster's evidence is drawn from late antiquity (his prosopographical survey covers 250 to 565 CE), though he reaches into earlier data when he can find it. His focus is specifically on the *grammaticus* and thus may not offer a reliable typical profile of other lower-level functionaries in the civic or provincial administrative apparatus. Nevertheless, as a social type (rather than a narrowly defined professional type) the grammarian perhaps may help us to think about the scribal mediators that are imagined as the authorial figures behind Q. The type thus allows for a metaphorical analogizing. On the difference between metaphoric and metonymic comparison, see Smith (1996: 275).

32 Representation from both extreme ends of the social hierarchy are exceptional. Kaster found few people from among the *humiliori* and only one example of a grammarian of equestrian background (1988: 108).

33 Kaster describes the grammarian as "the man whose function set him amid many vital spheres of activity [but who] most often was without a place at the center of any of them" (1988: 7).

34 Cf. the analysis of a particular case from Oxyrhynchus by Parsons (1976).
35 I am uncertain about how one locates Q's research and writing beyond pointing out that Q *is* a product of such activity. In part the question is one of physical placement and one of time allocation. In part, however, it concerns valuation of both place and time and the intersection of textual and communal formation in ritual practice. I am here mindful of Jonathan Z. Smith's comment on the Greek Magical Papyri as representing "a displacement of ritual practice into writing, analogous, in important respects, to the displacement of sacrifice into speech in the emergent Judaisms and Christianities" (1995: 26-27). On the intersection of texts, group formation, and ritual see Boyarin (1992) and Long (1992).
36 *Thessalos* 22; text in Friedrich (1968: 53); on the importance of Thessalos of Tralles see Smith (1993: 172-189).
37 On μῆτις in Greek traditions see Détienne and Vernant (1991 [1978]); see also Mack (1989: 47-50).
38 See Katznelson (1986), for example, for criticism of this tendency in comparisons of working-class formations in France, Germany and the United States.
39 Charting the evolution of Q as a recursive process of intended action and unintended consequences undoubtedly needs more thought that should also include factors of power exercised within the group itself and the possibility of sectoral ideological moves within the group to "take over" the group's interest and motivations. Note, for example, Kloppenborg's suggestion that at its later stages "the group succeeded in attracting scholars, perhaps only a handful, for whom the institutions of Torah and Temple had essential and positive meaning" (1991: 100). This infusion of Pharisaic talent and interest seems as unthinkable for earliest Q as it was consequential for later Q, perhaps effecting a shift from broader social movement to a more circumscribed Pharisaic-like club or διδασκαλεῖον. Arnal's observation (2001: 153-54) on the "gradual transformation" of the pre-war synagogues from local political assemblies "into self-consciously and explicitly religious bodies" whose revised primary function was "the affirmation of communal identity made in religious worship" may also be significant, if, speculatively speaking, this allows us to envision Q's decision at some point to locate (move?) its contest for itself as "Israel" within the Galilean synagogue(s).
40 Bruce Malina's attempt to use "small group formation theory to explain Christian organizations" may be cited as an example. Apart from the fact that his model, characterized by stages of "forming, storming, norming, performing, adjourning," is frustrated by its application to poorly described early Christian groups, its weakness is its disinterest in the question of difference and how to account for it (1995: 103-106). A similar demurring arises against Victor Turner's well-known liminality-communitas-structure cycle which Kloppenborg (1991) uses to elucidate stages in the social history of Q. The problem is not that Turner's categories do not fit Q, for they do; rather, the problem is that the categories tend to homogenize rather than differentiate social formations in that they would also fit the *Gospel of Thomas* and, as Frischer points out (1982: 69), also the formation of the Epicurean fraternities, or any other group whose emergence is driven by anti-structural sentiments.
41 Cf. Lightstone (1997: 286): "Through this exercise [mishnaic textual and rhetorical practices] an ordered, fictive and ideal world is defined, in which (in the text) the Jerusalem Temple yet stands, and Temple-based judiciary and legislative institutions still operate."
42 This is not say that things cannot go the other way, that sentiments of estrangement can lead to disidentification with members of the same group.

References

Anderson, Benedict (1983). *Imagined Communities: Reflections on the Origin and Spread of Nationalism*. London: Verso.

Arnal, William E. (1995a). "Redactional Fabrication and Group Legitimation: The Baptist's Preaching in Q 3:7–9, 16–17." In John S. Kloppenborg (ed.), *Conflict and Invention: Literary, Rhetorical, and Social Studies on the Sayings Gospel Q*, 168–180. Valley Forge, PA: Trinity Press International.

—— (1995b). "The Rhetoric of Marginality: Apocalypticism, Gnosticism, and Sayings Gospels," *Harvard Theological Review* 88: 471–494. https://doi.org/10.1017/S0017816000031722

—— (1996). "The Rhetorical Use of Gentiles in Q and Group Self-definition." Unpublished paper.

—— (2001). *Jesus and the Village Scribes: Galilean Conflicts and the Setting of Q*. Minneapolis, MN: Fortress Press.

Arnal, William E. and Willi Braun (2004). "Social Formation and Mythmaking: Theses on Key Terms." In Ron Cameron and Merrill P. Miller (eds.), *Redescribing Christian Origins*, 459–468. Atlanta, GA: Society for Biblical Literature.

Ascough, Richard (1988). *What Are They Saying about the Formation of the Pauline Churches?* New York: Paulist Press.

Bilault, A. (1993). "The Rhetoric of a 'Divine Man': Apollonius of Tyana as Critic of Oratory and as Orator According to Philostratus," *Philosophy & Rhetoric* 26(3): 227–235.

Bourdieu, Pierre (1997). *Outline of a Theory of Practice*. Richard Nice (trans.). Cambridge Studies in Social Anthropology 16. Cambridge, Cambridge University Press.

Boyarin, Jonathan (1992). "Voices Around the Text: The Ethnography of Reading at Mesivta Tifereth Jerusalem." In Jonathan Boyarin (ed.), *The Ethnography of Reading*, 212–237. Berkeley, CA: University of California Press. https://doi.org/10.1525/california/9780520079557.003.0010

Braun, Willi (1995). *Feasting and Social Rhetoric in Luke 14*. Society for New Testament Studies Monograph Series 85. Cambridge: Cambridge University Press.

—— (1997). "Argumentation and the Problem of Authority: Synoptic Rhetoric of Pronouncement in Cultural Context." In Thomas H. Olbicht and Stanley E. Porter (eds.), *The Rhetorical Analysis of Scripture: Essays from the 1995 London Conference*, 185–199. Journal for the Study of the New Testament Supplement 146. Sheffield: Sheffield Academic Press.

—— (1999). "Amnesia in the Production of (Christian) History," *Bulletin of the Council of Societies for the Study of Religion* 28: 3–8.

Bremmer, Jan N. (1995). "The Family and Other Centers of Religious Learning in Antiquity." In Jan Willem Drijvers and Alsadair A. MacDonald (eds.), *Centers of Learning: Learning and Location in Pre-Modern Europe and the Near East*, 29–38. Leiden: Brill.

Brown, Peter (1988). *The Body and Society: Men, Women, and Sexual Renunciation in Early Christianity*. Lectures on the History of Religions NS 13. New York: Columbia University Press.

Bryant, Joseph M. (1996). *Moral Codes and Social Structure in Ancient Greece: A Sociology of Greek Ethics from Homer to the Epicureans and Stoics*. The State University of New York Series in the Sociology of Culture. New York: University of New York Press.

Cameron, Ron (1990). "'What Have You Come out to See?' Characterizations of John and Jesus in the Gospels." In Ron Cameron (ed.), *The Apocryphal Jesus and Christian Origins*, 35–69. Semeia 49. Atlanta, GA: Scholarly Press.

—— (1994). "Alternate Beginnings—Different Ends: Eusebius, Thomas, and the Construction of Christian Origins." In Lukas Bormann, Kelly Del Tredici and Angela

Standhartinger (eds.), *Religious Propaganda and Missionary Competition in the New Testament World: Essays Honoring Dieter Georgi*, 501–525. Novum Testamentum Supplement 75. Leiden: Brill.

Carruth, Shawn (1995). "Strategies of Authority: A Rhetorical Study of the Character of the Speaker in Q 6:20–49." In John S. Kloppenborg (ed.), *Conflict and Invention: Literary, Rhetorical, and Social Studies on the Sayings Gospel Q*, 98–115. Valley Forge, PA: Trinity Press International.

Détienne, Marcel and Jean-Pierre Vernant (1991) [1978]. *Cunning Intelligence in Greek Culture and Society*. Janet Lloyd (trans.). Chicago, IL: University of Chicago Press.

Douglas, R. Conrad (1995). "'Love Your Enemies': Rhetoric, Tradents, and Ethos." In John S. Kloppenborg (ed.), *Conflict and Invention: Literary, Rhetorical, and Social Studies on the Sayings Gospel Q*, 116–131. Valley Forge, PA: Trinity Press International.

Friedrich, Hans-Viet (1968). *Thessalos von Tralles: griechisch und lateinisch*. Meisenheim am Glan: Anton Hein.

Frischer, Bernard (1982). *The Sculpted Word: Epicureanism and Philosophical Recruitment in Ancient Greece*. Berkeley, CA: University of California Press.

Geertz, Clifford (1993). "Thick Description: Toward an Interpretive Theory of Culture." In *The Interpretation of Cultures: Selected Essays*, 4–24. New York: Basic Books.

Giddens, Anthony (1984). *The Constitution of Society: Outline of the Theory of Structuration*. Cambridge: Polity.

Harris, William V. (1989). *Ancient Literacy*. Cambridge, MA: Harvard University Press.

Hobsbawm, Eric and Terence Ranger (eds.) (1983). *The Invention of Tradition*. Past and Present Publications. Cambridge: Cambridge University Press.

Horrell, David G. (1995). "The Development of Theological Ideology in Pauline Christianity: A Structuration Theory Perspective." In Philip F. Esler (ed.), *Modelling Early Christianity: Social-Scientific Studies of the New Testament in Its Context*, 224–236.

Judge, E. A. (1960–1961). "The Early Christians as a Scholastic Community," *Journal of Religious History* 1: 4–15, 125–137. https://doi.org/10.1111/j.1467-9809.1961.tb00766.x

Kaster, Robert A. (1988). *Guardians of Language: The Grammarian and Society in Late Antiquity*. Berkeley, CA: University of California Press.

Katznelson, Ira (1986). "Working-Class Formations: Constructing Cases and Comparisons." In Ira Katznelson and Aristide R. Zolberg (eds.), *Working-Class Formation: Nineteenth-Century Patterns in Western Europe and the United States*, 3–41. Princeton, NJ: Princeton University Press.

Kautsky, Karl (1925). *Foundations of Christianity*. Jacob W. Hartmann (trans.). New York: Monthly Review Press.

Kienle, Walter von (1961). *Die Berichte über die Sukzessionen der Philosophen in der hellenistischen und spätantiken Literatur*. Berlin: Ernst Reuter.

Kloppenborg, John S. (1987). *The Formation of Q: Trajectories in Ancient Wisdom*. Studies in Antiquity and Christianity. Philadelphia, PA: Fortress Press.

—— (1990). "City and Wasteland: Narrative World and the Beginning of the Sayings Gospel (Q)." In Dennis E. Smith (ed.), *How Gospels Begin*. Semeia 52. Atlanta, GA: Scholars Press.

—— (1991). "Literary Convention, Self-Evidence, and the Social History of the Q People." In John S. Kloppenborg and Leif E. Vaage (eds.), *Early Christianity, Q and Jesus*, 77–102. Semeia 55. Atlanta, GA: Scholars Press.

—— (1995). "Conflict and Invention: Recent Studies on Q." In John S. Kloppenborg (ed.), *Conflict and Invention: Literary, Rhetorical, and Social Studies on the Sayings Gospel Q*, 1–14. Valley Forge, PA: Trinity Press International.

—— (2006). "Beyond Tinkering and Apologetics." Paper presented at Society for Biblical Literature meetings in Washington DC, November.

Kloppenborg, John S. and Stephen G. Wilson (eds.) (1996). *Voluntary Associations in the Graeco-Roman World*. London: Routledge.

Kloppenborg Verbin, John S. (2000). *Excavating Q: The History and Setting of the Sayings Gospel*. Edinburgh: T. & T. Clark.

Lightstone, Jack N. (1994). *The Rhetoric of the Babylonian Talmud: Its Social Meaning and Context*. Studies in Christianity and Judaism 6. Waterloo: Wilfrid Laurier University Press.

—— (1997). "Whence the Rabbis? From Coherent Description to Fragmented Reconstruction," *Studies in Religion/Sciences Religieuses* 26: 275–295. https://doi.org/10.1177/000842989702600301

Lincoln, Bruce (1989). *Discourse and the Construction of Society: Comparative Studies of Myth, Ritual, and Classification*. New York: Oxford University Press.

—— (1994). *Authority: Construction and Erosion*. Chicago, IL: University of Chicago Press.

Long, Elizabeth (1992). "Textual Interpretation as Collective Action." In Jonathan Boyarin (ed.), *The Ethnography of Reading*, 180–211. Berkeley, CA: University of California Press. https://doi.org/10.1525/california/9780520079557.003.0009

Lynch, John Patrick (1972). *Aristotle's School: A Study of a Greek Educational Institution*. Berkeley, CA: University of California Press.

Mack, Burton L. (1989). "Elaboration of the Chreia in the Hellenistic School" In Mack, Burton L. and Vernon K. Robbins (eds.), *Patterns of Persuasion in the Gospels*, 30–68. Foundations and Facets/Literary Facets. Sonoma: Polebridge.

—— (1993). *The Lost Gospel: The Book of Q & Christian Origins*. San Francisco, CA: HarperSanFrancisco.

—— (1995). *Who Wrote the New Testament? The Making of the Christian Myth*. San Francisco, CA: Harper San Francisco.

—— (1996). "On Redescribing Christian Origins," *Method & Theory in the Study of Religion* 8: 247–269. https://doi.org/10.1163/157006896X00350

—— (2000). "Social Formation." In Willi Braun and Russell T. McCutcheon (eds.), *Guide to the Study of Religion*, 283–296. London: Cassell.

Mack, Burton L. and Vernon K. Robbins (1989) (eds.). *Patterns of Persuasion in the Gospels*. Foundations and Facets/Literary Facets. Sonoma: Polebridge.

Malina, Bruce (1995). "Early Christian Groups: Using Small Group Formation Theory to Explain Christian Organizations." In Philip Esler (ed.) *Modelling Early Christianity: Social Scientific Studies in the New Testament in Its Context*, 96–113.

Mann, Michael (1986). *The Sources of Social Power, Volume 1: A History of Power from the Beginning to AD 1760*. 3 volumes. Cambridge: Cambridge University Press. https://doi.org/10.1017/CBO9780511570896

Mason, Steve (1996). "*Philosophiai*: Graeco-Roman, Judean and Christian." In John S. Kloppenborg and Stephen G. Wilson (eds.), *Voluntary Associations in the Graeco-Roman World*, 31–58. London: Routledge.

Masuzawa, Tomoko (2000). "Origin." In Willi Braun and Russell T. McCutcheon (eds.), *Guide to the Study of Religion*, 209–224. London: Cassell.

Melucci, Alberto (1995). "The New Social Movements Revisited: Reflections on a Sociological Misunderstanding." In Louis Maheu (ed.), *Social Movements and Social Class: The Future of Collective Action*, 107–122. London: SAGE.

Parsons, P. J. (1976). "Petitions and a Letter: The Grammarian's Complaint, 250–60 A.D." In Ann Ellis Hanson (ed.), *Collectanea Papyrologica: Texts Published in Honor of H. C. Youtie*, 409–446. Papyrologische Texte und Abhandlungen 20. Bonn: Habelt.

Perrot, Michelle (1986). "On the Formation of the French Working Class." In Ira Katznelson and Aristide R. Zolberg (eds.), *Working-Class Formation: Nineteenth-Century Patterns in Western Europe and the United States*, 71-110. Princeton, NJ: Princeton University Press.

Piper, Ronald A. (1982). "Matthew 7,7-11 par. Lk 11,9-13: Evidence of Design and Argument in the Collection of Jesus' Sayings." In J Delobel (ed.), *Logia: Les paroles de Jésus— The Sayings of Jesus: Mémorial Joseph Coppens*, 411-418. Bibliotheca Ephemeridum Theologicarum Lovaniensium 59. Leuven: Peeters Publishing, Leuven University Press.

——— (1995). "The Language of Violence and the Aphoristic Sayings in Q: A Study of Q 6-27-36." In John S. Kloppenborg (ed.), *Conflict and Invention: Literary, Rhetorical, and Social Studies on the Sayings Gospel Q*, 53-72. Valley Forge, PA: Trinity Press International.

Reed, Jonathan J. (1995). "The Social Map of Q." In John S. Kloppenborg (ed.), *Conflict and Invention: Literary, Rhetorical, and Social Studies on the Sayings Gospel Q*, 17-36. Valley Forge, PA: Trinity Press International.

Robinson, James M. (1971) [1964]. "LOGOI SOPHŌN: On the Gattung of Q." (English trans.). In James M. Robinson and Helmut Koester (eds.), *Trajectories Through Early Christianity*, 71-113. Philadelphia, PA: Fortress Press.

Smith, Jonathan Z. (1990). *Drudgery Divine: On the Comparison of Early Christianities and the Religions of Late Antiquity*. Chicago, IL: University of Chicago Press.

——— (1993). "The Temple and the Magician." In *Map is not Territory: Studies in the History of Religions*, 172-189. Chicago, IL: University of Chicago Press.

——— (1995). "Trading Places." In Marvin Meyer and Paul Mirecki (eds.), *Ancient Magic and Ritual Power*, 11-27. Religions in the Graeco-Roman World 129. Leiden: Brill.

——— (1996). "Social Formation of Early Christianities: A Response to Ron Cameron and Burton Mack," *Method & Theory in the Study of Religion* 8: 271-278. https://doi.org/10.1163/157006896X00369

Stowers, Stanley K. (1984). "Social Status, Public Speaking and Private Teaching: The Circumstances of Paul's Preaching Activity," *Novum Testamentum* 26: 59-82. https://doi.org/10.2307/1560504

Theissen, Gerd (1973). "Wanderradikalismus: Literatursoziologische Aspekte der Überlieferung von Worten Jesu im Urchristentum," *Zeitschrift für Theologie* 70: 245-271.

Thompson, E. P. (1963). *The Making of the English Working Class*. London: Victor Gollancz.

Townsend, John T. (1971). "Ancient Education in the Time of the Early Roman Empire." In Stephen Benko and John J. O'Rourke, *The Catacombs and the Colosseum: The Roman Empire as the Setting of Primitive Christianity*, 139-163. Valley Forge, PA: Judson Press.

Trouillot, Michel-Rolph (1995). *Silencing the Past: Power and the Production of History*. Boston, MA: Beacon.

Vaage, Leif E. (1994). *Galilean Upstarts: Jesus' First Followers According to Q*. Valley Forge, PA: Trinity Press International.

Wilken, Robert (1971a). "Collegia, Philosophical Schools, and Theology." In Stephen Benko and John J. O'Rourke, *The Catacombs and the Colosseum: The Roman Empire as the Setting of Primitive Christianity*, 268-291. Valley Forge, PA: Judson Press.

——— (1971b). *The Myth of Christian Beginnings*. London: SCM.

Wright, Erik Olin (1985). *Classes*. London: Verso.

Zanker, Paul. *The Masks of Socrates: The Image of the Intellectual in Antiquity*. Alan Shapiro (trans.). Sather Classical Lectures 59. Berkeley, CA: University of California Press.

Ziebarth, Erich (1969) [1896]. *Das griechische Vereinswesen*. Wiesbaden: Martin Sändig.

7

In the Beginning Was Not the Word

> The Formalists ... are followers of St. John. They believe that "In the beginning was the Word." But we believe that in the beginning was the deed. The word followed, as its phonetic shadow.
>
> —Trotsky (1957 [1924]: 183)

Scholars of early Christianities and other Greco-Roman religious formations are predisposed to begin and end their studies within an envelope that is stuffed with words, word-oriented methods of explanation, logographic theories of persuasion, a "doctrinal" mode of rationality in the most general but thorough-going sense.[1] The reasons for this are easy to find. Foremost among them is the historical evidence itself. Whatever nonliterary traces of ancient societies and their religious worlds may have found their way into the archive, and however seriously and competently they are given evidentiary value, it is the ancient word-record, fossilized in textual form, that is the foundation for nearly all substantive scholarly conclusions about early Christianities and their contemporary ways of being religious (see especially Brett 1990). All the more so is this true for the study of the motives and manners of religious rhetoric in Greco-Roman antiquity. Because rhetorical critics have little other territory than the documents they interpret, the temptation to reduce the persuasions and persuasiveness of early Christianities to their textualized verbal discourses and arguments is great—and understandable[2]—despite the fact that at least prior to the first Christian scholasticism during the so-called Patristic period Christians were demonstrably skeptical toward the persuasive efficacy and reliability of words, especially the written word and rhetorical techniques of manipulating words (Alexander 1990; cf. Osborn 1959), and despite the fact that Greek and Roman religiosity was action-centered rather than word/text/doctrine-focused (Burkert 1985; Henrichs 1998, 2003) and, moreover, despite well-known scholarly reminders that Greco-Roman cultures generally preferred "live" performances and visual representations to written texts (Thomas 2003; Hedreen 2004), spirits to letters, and *sacra* and *auspicia* to sermons.

Second, "verbal art forms are so susceptible to treatment as self-contained, bounded objects separable from their social and cultural contexts of production and reception" (Bauman and Briggs 1990: 72). Grammatical structures, syntax, the logic of arrangement, style and other inner-textual features are among the most elemental trade interests of biblical scholars.[3] Aristotle, Cicero and Quintilian, along with other ancient rhetorical theorists and compilers of technical handbooks of the "art of rhetoric" provide not only evidence of the prominence of the formalities of rhetoric in the discourses of ancient Mediterranean cultures, but also determine the theoretical and methodological terms for the modern study of ancient procedures for crafting persuasions by the use and arrangement of words. The recent attempts to associate a good number of biblical texts with "school" settings (e.g., Braun 2004; Henderson 2004; Beavis 2000), where the core curricula stressed training in increasingly formalized grammatical and rhetorical arts, a very close association of persuasion with verbal arts, even textual arts, is given a further nod.

It is not, I hasten to add, that the trade practices of biblical and early Christian text-focused and rhetoric-attentive scholarship have little return to show for all the learned toil; on the contrary, we know more than ever before about the "patterns of persuasion" (Mack and Robbins 1989) in early Christian and other contemporary philosophical, moral and religious literature. Just the same, however, this knowledge is foremostly beholden to and in service of the assumption that persuasion is an effect of the convincing force of the right words placed in calculated, correct order and delivered with an appropriate style and tone of pleading.[4] This assumption and the temptation derived from it toward a hyper-value on words and texts as "self-contained, bounded objects" is surely in need of inspection when we try to come to grips with the old-but-perennial question of just how to account for early Christianities and other religious associations, for that matter, as compelling (persuasive) options for social, intellectual, emotional—in short, self-definitional—affiliation in the multi-cultural and colonial context of the Roman Mediterranean.

The first two reasons are firmly sustained by a third, one that I call to attention with an assist from Michel de Certeau's idea of the "scriptural economy" (1984: xiii–xvi, 131–153) by which modern disciplines constitute themselves, by whose laws disciplinary practices are governed and which, because of its hegemonic rule in the constitution of Western cultures generally, has been formative not only for a pervasively normative understanding of religion but also for conceptualizing persuasion of and to religion(s) as the result of logographic reasoning. De Certeau contends that the speech act "has been changed by three or four centuries of Western fashioning," a fashioning achieved by "the installation of the scriptural apparatus" that has "conquered" and "colonized" the human "voice" (1984: 131).[5] "Scriptural practice," he states,

> has acquired a mythical value over the past four centuries by gradually reorganizing all domains into which the Occidental ambition to compose its history, and thus to compose history itself, has been extended. ... Thus one can read above the portals of modernity such inscriptions as "Here, to work is to write," or "Here only what is written is understood." (De Certeau 1984: 133–134)

"Europe was alphabetized" (Bender and Wellbery 1990: 22). And this "alphabetical liftoff" (Debray 2004: 59–82) helped to ensure that *logos*, the communicative process in the widest sense, including its constitutive facets of cogency and persuasion, was re-posed as *logismos*, a textualized rationality. There is no need, here, for a remarking on all the contributing forces in this development,[6] only to note that the European alphabetization of knowledge and rationality as the superordinate register of what Kant and others called the "free public exercise of reason"[7] imposed itself focally on the rationalization of religious and religion's persuasion and the scholar of religion as a historian, critic and interpreter of texts (see Asad 1993: 79; LaMothe 2004).

This conception of the "exercise of reason" was locked to a further myth that emerged as a touchstone of Western modernity, the "notion of the unique, integrated, more-or-less consistent individual" (Sabean 1984: 208), or in the somewhat exaggerated synthetic terms of Clifford Geertz,

> the conception of the person as a bounded, unique, more or less integrated motivational and cognitive universe, a dynamic center of awareness, emotion, judgment, and action organized into a distinctive whole and set contrastively both against other such wholes and against its social and natural background. (Geertz 1976: 225)

When these two complementaries—(1) persuasion indexed with reference to the values of a scriptural reason, coupled, as it is, with an implicit theory of language as a stable, even static, system of logical semantic relations and stable language-referent relations and (2) the human subject as a self-aware, bounded, "rational" cognitive unit—took root as rather stubborn, incorrigible axioms by which knowledge and discourse came to be defined, we have a powerful set-up for restricting "rhetoric" to a science on the inter-mental influence of words, ideas, propositions, creeds, doctrines.[8]

My intention is to ambiguate the object defined as "rhetoric" that is (at least tacitly) interlinked with, even restrictively posed in terms of, a logographic formalism of the classical (Aristotelian) *ars rhetorica*. The aim is to put this kind of "rhetoric," and thus temptations to see the persuasion of and to early Greco-Roman Christianities as the effect of ideas, which one can put up for inspection and analyze on the model of a stationary, stable text, in motion by bouncing it first against an ancient theorist, Gorgias of Leontini, then over to a modern one, Harvey Whitehouse.

* * *

Gorgias of Leontini was a Sicilian who became one of the superstars of classical Athenian rhetoric in the heyday of the Greek Enlightenment (see Solmsen 1975). He is of special interest because, though he is usually considered the founder of rhetoric's most splashy, performative branch, namely epideictic,[9] he is clearly "predisciplinary" to the developments that resulted in the formalization and technicalization of rhetoric, as Edward Schiappa (1996) has demonstrated. And for this reason his perspective offers aid in re-posing the relation between words and persuasion as part of the larger question of how to theorize persuasion. His *Encomium of Helen*, devoted to a crafty defence of the notorious Helen of Greek mythology, who was persuaded to abandon her husband Menelaos, king of Sparta, and to elope with Paris of Troy, "is the earliest surviving extended discussion of *logos* and certainly the most sophisticated of its time" (Schiappa 1996: 81). Though this positions Gorgias as an early voice in a trend toward a perception of the "world as *logos*-textured" (Mourelatos 1973: 16)[10] persuasion by means of *logos* is only one facet in his theory of how to explain the movement of people to disaffiliate and reaffiliate themselves, whether the transfer of loyalty is in relation to ideas and beliefs or to social groups, a transfer that Gorgias equates with persuasion.

In Georgias's view speech is *logos* akin to a "living organism" (Süss 1910: 22) that, as such, asserts its persuasion by force of a psycho-physical imposition on the auditor's mind, in some respects apparently quite independently of a speaker's artful and tactical deployment of *logos*. Gorgias speaks of *logos* as "the persuader" and the mind as "the persuaded", and the power relation between speech and *psyche* as compeller and compelled (12), or as Segal puts it, as "the conquest of a weaker subject by a stronger force" (Segal 1962: 122). A range of other power-related terms underscore the compelling wallop of *logos* on the mind: it is god-like in its effects, so one must assume for it a superhuman potency (19); using a pharmacological analogy, Gorgias argues that "the power of *logos* has the same effect on the condition of the *psyche* as the power of drugs on the nature of bodies; for just as drugs dispel different humors from the body, and some stop it from being diseased and others stop it from living, so also in the case of *logos*—some cause pain, others pleasure, some cause fear, others instill courage in the hearers" (14);[11] *logos* acts with a violent force akin to that of a rapist overpowering his victim;[12] it stamps or molds the *psyche* as it wishes (13).[13]

When we ask why *logos* has such power, Gorgias opts for a set of quasi-scientific explanations that are correlated with different kinds of speech.[14] Poetry, which Gorgias simply stipulates as "speech with meter," impresses itself on the mind with aesthetic and emotive appeal: "into those who hear it enters fearful shuddering and tearful pity and mournful longing" (9). As importantly, it also performs persuasion in a social sense in that it locutes empathy, sympathy, inter-personal affective links, i.e., it effects and performs the contiguity of self and group, in a manner reminiscent of the Frazerian notion of the effects of contagious magic (see Tambiah 1968: 190): "the *psyche*, through [poetic], *logoi* fortune," writes Gorgias (9).

Gorgias's description of the effects of "speech with meter" evokes a more general theory of the power of metonymic speech. Unlike metaphoric speech, which uses "devices of purposive contrast" for the purpose of "development and extension of thought" and thus is constitutive of rhetorics of change by a sleight-of-hand trick of evoking similarity by drawing attention to difference (Paine 1981: 188),[15] metonym trades in "the already-known and accepted; its structure is 'closed' and always near tautology ... [W]here metonym prevails over metaphor it can be expected that symbols (needing explanation) will relinquish their place to *signs that do not need explanation*" (Paine 1981: 188–189; italics original). Metonymic speech—Gorgias's "speech with meter"—thus is persuasive *logos* without *logismos* (ratiocination, rational argument). It evokes shared "knowns" and stabilizes them with speech that is emotive, working its persuasion in a word spectacle—or ritual utterance—that relies on the properties of language for solidifying self-in-group recognition and thus the formation of the social body.[16] Metonymic rhetoric above all serves the purpose of enculturation; it is an ongoing "speech expressive of custom" (Aristotle, *Rhet.* 1.8)—the Trotskyan "phonetic shadow" (Trotsky 1957 [1924]: 183) of the native, local commonplace.

Not all speech is metonymic, however. A second kind of speech includes the disciplinary discourses of science, exemplified by the speeches of astronomers, compulsory speechifying contests in the courts, and philosophical debates (13). What interests Gorgias about these genres is not, as one would perhaps expect, to show that they have power to overcome mere opinion by the combination of statements of facts with reasoned arguments. Nor is it that they demonstrate a truth as a solid foundation for belief, for it is entirely possible—though not inevitable, of course—that these kinds of speeches are "not spoken with truth" (13); in fact, Gorgias implies that they, like nasty drugs and dazzling spells, have the capacity to achieve reprehensible effects, to "drug and bewitch the mind with an evil persuasion" (14).[17] What does interest him is to point out that these genres represent the addition of a technical reasoning to *logos* and that this addition directs and raises the power of speech's persuasion (13). Astronomers, Gorgias points out, are able to demolish one opinion and replace it with another by making "unbelievable and obscure things apparent"; court advocates are able to please and persuade juries with speeches that are "written with skill"; philosophers are able to change opinion and belief with "quick-wittedness."

Why technical *logos*, or any argumentative speech, has force inheres in the incompleteness and fluctuation of knowledge itself, which makes belief and opinion necessarily "unsteady and unreliable" (11) and, hence, subject to be toppled and replaced by the persuading influence of skilled (technically dazzling) speech. "If everyone, on every subject, possessed memory of the past and understanding of the present and foreknowledge of the future, speech would not be as powerful," Gorgias argues (11). Shift and slip in social knowledge may give speech a certain *force majeure* at a given time and situation, but its force is easier to measure or construe as success in hindsight than as a guarantee in foresight.

Despite the incredible power of speech that he has painstakingly argued, Gorgias concludes with an important ramifying hedge: if anyone—he refers to Helen specifically—is persuaded by *logos*, one must reckon that an element of chance, even misfortune, is involved. Moreover, speech, its power cleverly diminished by Gorgias in the course of his composition, is also *only one human mover among others*—and even then, given his metaphors of speech as drug that dulls sense, as rape that effects an endogenous violence on the mind, as a stamp that imprints external "knowledge" on a pliable psyche, *logos* in Gorgias may fall rather more in Whitehouse's imagistic category than the doctrinal category. Gorgias refers to three others, though these are not discussed with the same depth of interest as *logos*.

1 *Contingent persuasion.* People find themselves in places, situations, social relationships and affiliations, even assenting to doctrinal beliefs, by accident, that is, neither as foreseen or intended or planned—to translate into my terms Gorgias's transcendent causes,

such as Chance, Necessity, or the "purposes of the gods" (6), which are all rationalizations for the fact that many, if not most, human moves on noetic, moral or social planes are neither obviously nor necessarily outcomes of preconsideration, hence not the result of belief-making or action-producing speech. Georgias's "purposes of the gods" can and should be translated into demystified, non-transcendental terms, such as, for example, the variation of human signification of the same words or other semiotic entities, as we learned from Émile Benveniste and others. Georgian Chance thus is translatable into the problem of historical contingency and cultural locatedness in relation to the persuasion attached to semantic or ideational goods. Even if one does presuppose, already with Lévi-Strauss[18] and certainly with later cognitive theory, a panhuman set of neuro-noetic structures that function as a constant for concept formation, concept signification and concept belief, the variety of human "minding" nonetheless indicates the theoretical necessity for postulating persuasion in radically historicist and particularist terms *alongside* structuralist-cognitive terms.[19]

2   *Forced persuasion.* It is also the case, Gorgias observes further, that people end up in life situations and conditions quite involuntarily. He is not speaking of consequences of circumstances beyond an individual's control, though that would be a reasonable extension of his observation, but about the case of someone who has been seized by force, or who is the victim of unjust hubris (7) or more subtle forces. Here too Georgias dimly points to a feature that a cogent theory of persuasion must accommodate and account for: factors of power that complexly mediate the relations between material realities, behavioral performances, self-identity and mental schema, or "mentifacts," as Eric Wolf calls them (1997 [1982]: xiv).[20]

3   *Affective persuasion.* Finally, one must reckon with the possibility that people are persuaded not by *logos*, but moved by "compulsions of love" (19) or, now generalizing Gorgias's affective language, by an attraction that is driven by a sentimental affinity (Lincoln 1989).[21] As Bruce Lincoln argues, echoing the social theory of Raymond Williams (1977; see Filmer 2003), often "ideological persuasion has nothing and sentiment evocation everything to do with" attraction to someone or a group (Lincoln 1989: 10), hence with group formation even where the group may rationalize its groupness with an ideological rhetoric. I should immediately add that there is nothing cheesily sentimental about the idea of sentiment as a "mover" in social affiliation and group formation. For Williams, sentiments, or "structures of feelings," to use his terms, are "defined as social experiences *in solution*, as distinct from other social semantic formations which have been precipitated [by these experiences in solution] and are

more evidently and immediately available ... and it is primarily to emergent formations (though often in the form of modification or disturbance of older forms) that the structure of feeling, as solution, relates" (1977: 133–134, emphasis added). Williams is trying to get a conceptual grip on what he also calls the rather inchoate moment of "pre-emergence" (1984: 64–65) in the material-social formation process, a moment that hovers somewhere "between the privacy of subjective feeling and the publicity of linguistic utterance" (Filmer 2003: 209),[22] a moment in which people are dispositionally opened either to filiation or estrangement, and a moment that of course is fluid, on the way to linguistic publication, which is when it becomes visible both for public and scholarly observation—and then often, I would recommend especially with reference to biblical rhetoric, as verbal rhetorics that purport to persuade towards that person or group or stance to which one already has an affinitive affective bent. Although Gorgias insinuates a distaste for what he considers the deceptive, mind-incapacitating compulsion of *eros*,[23] he is surely on to something when he characterizes the persuading force of affect as "coming when it comes ... not through intentions of mind ... [nor through] contrivances of *techne*" (19). One should allow Gorgias this at least as a reasonable hypothesis that needs to be verified by modern investigational strategies and be given full weight in any full-fledged theory of persuasion.

When, in the light of this rather complex theory of persuasion that includes as its causal forces any or all or, likely, an inseparable combination of language arts/practices, chance, brute hubris and power as well as aeolian sentiment or "socio-gravitational forces of attraction and repulsion" (Lincoln 1989: 176 n. 9), Gorgias nonetheless apparently wagered on the efficacy of his speech-craft, it is with a sense—its face is an ironic smirk—that all bets are off on whether that efficacy can be controlled, directed or predicted in any way, much less on whether a persuasion achieved by verbal rhetorical means will be stable and enduring in the social theatre of competing rhetorics and influences. At most, it would seem, insofar as speech, in his view, has an immediate effect and insofar, too, as the *psyche* has an independent mind, so to speak, plastic and impressionable as it may be, the best the rhetor can do is to learn as much as he or she can about *logos* and *psyche* so as to be able shrewdly to manipulate the former with a view toward influencing the latter to *some* extent (Segal 1962: 106–107). This is not nothing, for it is respect for the power in the word and confidence in the efficacy of speechifying that allows Gorgias confidently to say near the beginning of the *Helen* that he intended "by adding reasoning to [his] speech, ... to demonstrate what is true" (2).

At the least (and possibly worst), even the most skillfully crafted speech might make no difference at all, either because its power is overrun by countermanding speeches or knowledge, or because its noise is hardly distinguishable from the babble on the broadband of social discourse, verbal and non-verbal.[24] Gorgias seems prepared for this possibility of the ambiguity and unreliability of the persuadability of *logos*, for in the very last words of his composition he states that he wrote the encomium to Helen as a little game, as a contrivance for self-amusement and, no doubt, as a (re)marking of himself as a member of the intellectual élite class by means of rhetorical skill—auguring what would become, during the next several centuries and on into the period of emergent Christianities, Judaisms and other socio-religious formations (such as Mithraism), a widely diffused Greco-Roman spectator sport in which rhetoric frequently became detached from the philosophical and moral aims of persuasion and was put to use as entertainment in the form of highly rule-bound "improv theatre" performances,[25] as a cultural commodity with some purchasing power on the market of social positionality, in other words.[26]

* * *

Most interesting, even if most befuddling for theorizing rhetoric and practising rhetorical analysis, is what we might call the "Gorgian middle," the neither-nor but also the both-and of rhetoric as *logismos* that is able to demonstrate truth and bring about persuasion and rhetoric as *paignion*, a word-play that amuses and marks social place but one that has been "amputated from [the] effective, pragmatic, or persuasive dimension" of language.[27] In this middle, between the view of speech as a controllable and predictable compeller and the view of speech as so unreliable that it might as well be reduced to a play-puppet, rhetoric is best conceived in the broadest term—as "rhetoricality," a neologism of whose value I have been persuaded by John Bender and David Wellbery (1990). Although they use the term rather restrictedly to characterize the discourse peculiar to modernism, their elaboration of the connotative features of rhetoricality, as distinct from rhetoric, helps to unfuddle the "Gorgian middle" for the purpose of thinking about the relation of rhetoric and the persuasions of and to early Christianities. Thus, using Bender and Wellbery as a rough guide but re-aiming their insights for clarifying the center of gravity of this volume's address, "rhetoricality" entails two general observations.

Most elementally, first, rhetoricality does not refer to a restricted canon of logographic techniques of argumentation, though such may be subsumed; it is, rather, a bid for an understanding of the general condition of human social life (25; cf. Borch-Jacobsen 1990), in which what counts as knowledge, where the value or "truth"—whether weighed in moral, aesthetic or pragmatic (beneficial, advantageous) terms—assigned to that knowledge, and where the more or less recognized modes of proving or authorizing that knowledge are all subject to fluctuating judgments that are worked out on the run, more often than not in agonistic, even antagonistic discursive improvisation in a given "local" social and cultural context.[28] Rhetoricality thus signals a general theoretical orientation on "the social" as an argumentative work in progress, as always subject to labors of persuasion and as a never-finally-stable effect of persuasion.[29] Rhetoricality does not admit a "rhetorical situation" (Bitzer 1968) in contrast to an implied non-rhetorical situation. Nor does it grant the distinction—as a long-standing dispute, going back at least to Plato's squabbles with the sophists, would have it—between *homo rhetoricus* and some other *homo* who is not *rhetoricus* (Fish 1995), for all discourse performances are spin performances.[30] No "speech situation" is "ideal" in the sense that, say, Habermas longs for: "No force except that of the better argument is exercised; ... all motives except that of the cooperative search for truth are excluded" (1975: 107–108).[31]

Second, within the rhetoricality of the social, rhetoric, now in the classical-technical sense familiar to biblical scholars, may then be thought of as one *particular* (among others) "art of positionality" (Bender and Wellbery 1990: 7) or "placement" (see Smith 1995), an art that, moreover, utilizes a *particular*, distinguishable form of verbal action—"rhetorolect," to use Vernon Robbins's term (1996b: 355–357; 2002: 65)—to perform its address whose aim is to stake out place and role vis-a-vis and within the local social whole. The procedural implication of this for the study of rhetoric, whether biblical or any other, is then not only to parse the rhetoric in the text so as to see its "discursive architecture and adornment" (Bender and Wellbery 1990: 4), something at which biblical rhetorical critics have been remarkably good. It also means to "see through" the rhetoric so as to situate its positionality with respect to what constitutes "proper" persuasiveness in a cultural context,[32] and also within the grid of give-and-take tussle over material and symbolic goods by which a social or socio-religious body strives to constitute itself—something that the general logographic, doctrinal, philological, and exegetical orientation of scholarship on early Christianities has pursued with lesser enthusiasm and results.

* * *

There is more, of course, in angling toward a theory of persuasion that helps us account for social and religious affiliations we call early Christianities. This means reckoning with a theory of cognition and an anthropology of knowledge that Gorgias perceptively but imprecisely articulated long ago and Harvey Whitehouse (2000, 2002, 2004) is persistently working out in our time. Required is, in part but first, an adjustment in what data for early Christianity are admitted as evidence and how some admitted evidence is read. What if were to take Jonathan Z. Smith's advice (1990: 113) and "set aside" a "doctrinal mode" of scholarship on early Christianities as "an essentially theological determination"[33] so as to let in some other data and explanatory models? I can here cite just a few teasers, in part because the preserved records of early Christianities leave us with no complete small-scale, local ethnographic field (like, say, the Mithraic data which Luther Martin has been able to reinterpret with assists from Whitehouse; see Martin 2005), in part also because of an as-yet incomplete inventory of fragments and glimpses for the purpose of imagining a theory of persuasion that does not cede *a priori* privilege to logographic modalities over ocular, auditory, or other diverse sensory "persuasion models" (Shore 1996: 66–67).

1   Graydon Snyder's remarkable book, *Ante Pacem: Archaeological Evidence of Church Life Before Constantine* (1985), now three decades old but

rarely read much less effectively assimilated in scholarship on early Christianities,[34] lays out an iconic parcel of data that simply refuses to support the totalizing stress in scholarship on early Christianities as organized in accordance with the principles and characteristics of a doctrinal mode of religiosity. Snyder alerted us to the "methodological error" of reconstructing early Christian associations from the "sacred" literature. This procedure assumes: that this literature is ethnographically reliable rather than "tendentious" in purpose; that the literature is the *solo voce* informing us of historical matters, when actually it demonstrates an interest in suppressing or assimilating other information; that the literature represents "popular religion" rather than standing in tension with it (Snyder 1985: 8). All three assumptions Snyder demonstrates to be incorrect. What his iconographical evidence shows is a religiosity tending toward the imagistic mode—i.e., highly localized, small-scale, emotively charged rituals, especially those that perform nocturnal commerce with the dead by means and in the context of refrigerium meals—that stands "in difference" with respect to the doctrinal mode of religiosity represented in the canonical literature (the New Testament) at the level of the doctrinal mode's "psychological features" (see Whitehouse 2002: 309 for convenient tabularies) and "in difference" to the doctrinal mode's "sociopolitical features" that mark the dominant Christianity of the late-third and fourth centuries. The relations of difference still need to be worked out and Harvey Whitehouse has available a shop full of assists for this.

2. The doctrinal/logographic mode of inquiry also may have shoe-horned textual material, that though textual, bespeaks a mode of religiosity in which texts were not used in a mode that Whitehouse calls "doctrinal" or that Gorgias might have called logistic. The Coptic *Gospel of Thomas* is arguably such an example, though scholars have persistently attempted to decode this text's enigmatic and cryptic utterances into a coherent, integrated ideational set—generating remarkably little agreement despite decades of persistent labor, one might add. Stevan Davies thus opts for a different hypothesis altogether: "The inadequacy of our scholarly attempts to decipher the *Gospel of Thomas* shows that it is some other sort of text than the coded but theoretically comprehensible set of ideological and theological teachings we have assumed it to be" (Davies 1994). He continues: "Scholars interested in Christian origins, and in the transmission of the sayings of Jesus of Nazareth, must take seriously into account the possibility that early compilations of the sayings of Jesus were oracle divination lists that were not written in order to promulgate social, ideological, or theological programs" (Davies 1994). He adduces evidence in antiquity[35] and points to modern

cross-cultural analogies[36] to make the argument that the sayings in the *Gospel of Thomas* were for the purpose of random oracular divinization and that one of the key words in this text, *hermeneia* (interpretation), is not to be understood as a deductive reasoning that leads to a coherent cognitive repertoire amenable to thetic or narrative discourse and memorizing strategies. That is, the outcome of the "hermeneutical" ritual[37] might be erratic, multivariate, and unpredictable in terms of the kind of knowledge it produces, though we might surmise a kind of stability in the divining ritual itself for social-formational effect[38]—apparently evincing imagistic rather than doctrinal modes of representing and organizing the "religion" of Thomas.[39]

3   If we stay with the work of Stevan Davies for a moment, one should point also to his provocative book, *Jesus the Healer: Possession, Trance, and the Origins of Christianity* (1995), received by scholars of early Christianity usually either with dumb-founded silence or smirking dismissal. Here he argues that the Jesus traditions, of course highly refracted in the various gospel literature, evinces early Christian experimentation with possession trances. Using cross-culturally and temporally ranging data sets for possession trances, and drawing widely on psychological and anthropological scholarship for a second-order analysis of these phenomena, he argues that Jesus was a shamanistic healer who may have specialized in the therapy of a "pathologically dissociative clientele"—in the language of early Christians, demon possession, impurity, etc.—who were cured by a "spirit-possessed" healer (Jesus), and who then spoke of their cured dissociative tendencies in terms of the experience of the "spirit" or "entering the Kingdom." Further, Davies links spirit-possessed healing to a theory of transmission of spirit and to a theory of persuasion that works its stamp on the mind through the induction of altered states of consciousness. What we have here is an attempt to dislodge from the kind of scholarship described above the Jesus traditions, especially their stress on spirits, spirit-possession, and interest in transferring spirit-possession to others, from their submerged assimilation into a doctrinal mode of religiosity and into a logographic kind of rationality.

The examples can be (and ought to be) multiplied. A tempting one has come to light in recent redescriptive efforts of a so-called Pauline Christ association in first-century Roman Corinth, an association whose procedures, practices and interests are highly imagistic, much to the persistent aggravation of the doctrinal interests of Paul (see Smith 2004; Winter 2001; briefly Martin 2005; see also Mount 2005; Parrish 2006). But for this occasion more examples are not necessary; a full inventory of evidence for imagistic modes of experimenting with the Jesus/Christ figure is a scholarly desideratum, in any case. If the "archival" record of early

Christianity is indexed in terms of models of persuasion (for which Gorgias gives us some assists) and Whitehouse's conceptual "modes of religiosity," it is clear that the religiosities of early Christianity have been distorted by the rather monothetic commitment to the logographic/doctrinal imagination of scholarship. With Whitehouse's ethnographic data as an analogistic field and his theoretical map as a conceptual aid we are poised for a redescription of early Christianities that does not pose early Christians part and parcel as merely followers of the Word, where the Word, and all the assumptions that sponsor it and poor (unreflectively idealist) theories of religion that are implied by it, is postulated as the sufficient lift-off power for these multivariate movements.

Notes

1. The first part of this essay takes up in revised form a portion of Braun (2005).
2. Cf. Loraux (2002: 60) for a similar temptation among historians and historical anthropologists to objectify ancient societies and city cultures as realities reduced to their depictions in literary remains.
3. Even when these textual crafts are re-aimed in the recent turn, in biblical studies especially, to rhetorical criticism, notably "socio-rhetorical" criticism that, under the productive tutelage of Vernon Robbins, has brought into robust relation text and context in rhetorical analysis, the temptation nonetheless to regard persuasion in terms of a complex inner- to inter-textual game of Scrabble has been compelling. "Socio-rhetorical," by now a familiar term in the lexicon of biblical scholars, was coined by Vernon Robbins (1994), who has also outlined its theoretical foundations (Robbins 1996a, 1996b; cf. Gowler 1994), applied it in countless textual, and inspired numerous socio-rhetorical studies by others, including a socio-rhetorical commentary series on the writings of the New Testament. The latter is somewhat indicative of this impressive *oeuvre*, in that a broad social theory of persuasion and the extra-textual realities, including the "social," the "ideological," or the conditions that contribute to the affectability or compliance of those to whom a persuasion is directed, are not at the focal center of socio-rhetorical criticism. Rather, these matters are infiltrated into texts and there are attended as "textures" of these texts that, at the end of day, are of interest for their classical "scholastic" patterns of argumentation as a way to arrest the meaning of the text. Risking distortive exaggeration, biblical rhetorical criticism for all its formalistic, even positivist modus operandi, is above all motivated by hermeneutic interests that have theological underpinnings.
4. In my mind reverberates the definition of textual practice by Michel de Certeau: "Linguistic fragments or materials are treated (factory-processed, one might say) in this space [the blank page] according to methods that can be made explicit and in such a way as to produce an order. A series of articulated operations (gestural or mental)—that is what writing *literally* is—traces on the page the trajectories that sketch out words, sentences, and finally a system. In other terms, on the blank page, an itinerant, and regulated practice ... composes the artefact of another 'world' that is not received but made" (de Certeau 1984: 134–135). He goes on to suggest that this "artefact" (text) has become the modern "model of a productive reason" that is "the fundamental and generalized utopia of the modern West" (1984: 135). For a similar argument, however focusing much more on the how (raw materials, implements, printing technologies, etc.) of writing than on its what, see Debray (2000, 2004).

5 De Certeau speaks of "voice" and "orality," but it is clear that he thinks not exclusively of oral verbal articulation, though that is included. Rather, with reference to the work of Émile Benveniste (*Problemes de linguistique générale*, 1966), he has in view the speech act in the widest sense that includes four characteristics: (1) "*construction* of individual sentences with an *established* vocabulary and syntax"; (2) it is, however, an act of "enunciation" that "is not reducible to a knowledge of the language"; (3) "appropriation, or reappropriation, of language by its speakers [that] establishes a *present* relative to time and place"; (4) "it posits a *contract with the other* (the interlocutor) in a network of places and relations" (de Certeau 1984: xiii, italics in the original).

6 Consider the following developments of early modernism that are inseparable from the take-over of cultural discourses by the scriptural apparatus: scriptural production was made possible by the technology of reproduction, the printing press (de Certeau 1984: 131–132; Bender and Wellbery 1990: 22); the emergence of science contributed to the enthronement of scribal discourse; the rise of the nation-state compelled the need for standardized national languages, hence the over-riding of a polyglottal state of affairs by scribal/scriptural means (see Bender and Wellbery 1990: 5–22) and by nation-state apparatuses whose bureaucratic, administrative and ideological interests are heavily reliant on scribal values, methods and corpora; all of these contributed to the "general social condition of the progress of reason" (Bourdieu 1975) that placed mythic value on logographic methods and theories of what is persuasive.

7 "By the public use of one's own *reason* I mean that use which anyone may make of it as a *man of learning* addressing the entire *reading public*" (Kant 1784: 488, my trans. and emphasis); not even "Caesar is above the grammarian" (*Caesar non est supra grammaticos*), quipped Kant (489). Cf. Luther's table-talk bit, roughly a century earlier, that "through it [the printing press] God is intent on making true religion known through the entire earth."

8 See the criticism of F. Barth (2002: 2): "Though it is experience-based, most knowledge [and, presumably, the criteria of validity that constitute what we know as knowledge] ... does not become private in any individual sense. ... Our academic prototype of 'knowledge' probably refers to the things that are contained in a textbook, an encyclopedia, a dictionary. Such sources lay out knowledge as if it were context-free—a mode that collapses historical time in acquiring knowledge, elaborates taxonomies, and prizes coherence. It simulates a knowledge without knowers."

9 "Gorgias's great contribution to Greece was this: he was the founder of artistic prose, and with him begins epideictic literature; or the rhetoric of display" (Van Hook 1930: 163); "Begründer und Meister der Epideiktik" (Buchheit 1960: 28); "Gorgias is ... the founder, according to tradition, of the epideictic mode of rhetoric, and in that sense he is the quintessentially rhetorical artist, the rhetorician's rhetorician" (Gumpert 2001: 72). Aristotle (*Rhet.* 1.3.3) would later sort rhetoric into three genres: deliberative, judicial and demonstrative. This classification became canonical in later rhetorical theory (see Kennedy 1997: 45), just as demonstrative, or encomiastic, rhetoric became, by some estimates, "the quasi-obligatory mode for all literary production" well into late antiquity (Fournet 2003: 103), though it reached its gaudiest heights in the Second Sophistic.

10 On the emerging *logos*-culture in the Greek Enlightenment see also Poulakos (1995). For example: "Sophistical rhetoric inaugurated a new aristocracy, crowning 'logos' as the new master of the polis ... Their message underscored neither the primacy of the world nor the primacy of human beings; rather, it emphasized the primacy of logos as

the medium circulating between human beings and constituting both human beings and the world. In this sense they can be said to have instituted a new regime whose sympathies and character were neither aristocratic nor democratic but logocratic" (15).

11 Gorgias may be the inventor of the speech-as-drug simile, which will become a trope that is used for various purposes by orators (e.g., Isocrates 8.39) and philosophers (e.g., Plato *Gorgias* 464b and elsewhere), then later by numerous Cynic and Stoic moralists (see Braun 1995: 32–33).

12 "So what reason is there against Helen's also having come under the influence of speech just as much against her will as if she had been seized by violence of violators? For persuasion expelled sense" (12). See Wardy (1996: 42–44) for a suggestion that in the *Encomium of Helen* "the successful orator performs psychic rape" (43). The *Encomium*, however, seems to ascribe this capacity to *logos*, not to the orator *per se*.

13 "'Moulding' both summons up a mechanical rather than rational model of persuasion and contributes further to the portrayal of the *psyche* as something entirely passive, since the word suggests that it is worked like wax or clay, taking the impress of *logoi* without resistance" (Wardy 1996: 44–45), noting also Gorgias's "wax-like *psyche* molded by *logos*" (1996: 48). For an impressive explication of Gorgias's theory of the *psyche* see Segal (1962).

14 By "quasi-scientific" I mean that Gorgias, despite his extravagant, even "magical" (de Romilly 1992) regard for the power of speech, does not identify this power in magical or theological terms, nor associate it with the inspiration of the Muses, as the poets of his day would have it and as was popularly thought in ancient Mediterranean societies (Graf 2004). Rather, *Helen* is remarkable for its description of the effects of speech and for its attempt to explain these effects in rational terms. See especially Schiappa (1996: 81–85): "In the case of Gorgias, the single most important theoretical contribution of the *Helen* is that it engaged in rational—i.e., systematic, secular, physical—explanation and description ... of the workings of logos and the mind" (81).

15 I am speaking generally, allowing for exceptions, that is, of the fact that metaphorical (comparative, analogic) speech often is supportive of the status quo, is about stability rather than change. For example, "the emperor is to his slaves as a father is to his son" by analogy extends the value of hierarchical status relation from one domain to another in what amounts to a plea for the stability and universality of such relations. See Tambiah (1973: 211–212; Paine 1981: 187–188).

16 Cf. J. L. Austin's notion of "constative utterances" that linguistically describe, but do not aim to change, a state of affairs (Austin 1962), a type of locution that is instructively glossed as "word rituals" by Finnegan (1969) and the "magic of words" by Tambiah (1968). On the power of ritual utterances in antiquity see Graf (2004), Versnel (2002) and Bäumer (1984). On the "culture of spectacle" in which sophistical rhetoric emerged and flourished see Poulakos (1995: 39–46, and the literature cited there).

17 Speech "not spoken with truth" implies that Gorgias believes in the opposite possibility, but he gives not a hint at what he means by "truth" nor at whether he thinks truth has some kind of *sui generis* persuading force or, if not, if he has thought about the relationship between speech, truth and persuasion. Speech in general is for Gorgias a tool of domination: to compel mind both to obey what is said and to approve what is done (12). And because of this he is more worried that speech's "intercourse with the opinion of the *psyche*" results in "deviations of the *psyche*" and "deceived views" (10). He laments: "How many have persuaded and do persuade how many, on how many subjects, by fabricating false speech!" (11). I am thus inclined to think that Gorgias

has his tongue pointedly in cheek when he states his aim in *Helen*: "I wish, by adding reasoning to my speech, ... to demonstrate what is true" (2).

18 A panhuman, hard-surface cognitive structure seems to be implied in Lévi-Strauss's "binary oppositions" that structure thought. See Lévi-Strauss (1962: 263–264), for instance.

19 A single case in point is Marshall Sahlins's (1985) instructive meditation on why and how Hawaiians transformed their local idea of *mana* into the value of conspicuous consumption of foreign import goods. Tantalizingly implied, but not developed here, is a postulated relationship between persuasion, i.e., strong affinity for and affiliation with groups and their ideas, and particular motivational structures in a given cultural totality that function contingently, by chance, akin to Gorgias's "necessity."

20 "Mentifacts" are "schemata of organized knowledge and symbolic operations learned and communicated among human beings." Wolf further argues, contrary to some universalist claims about human mental structures and operations, that mental schemata are not stable, universal neuropsychological forms; rather they are "variably distributed among men and women, young and old, wealthy and poor, homebodies and immigrants, powerful and powerless, people who speak with the spirits and those who do not." Variable repertoires and distributions of "mentifacts" also define who is who and who does what in a given social formation; they are deployed "to construct and accumulate some forms of power" (Wolf 1997 [1982]: xiv; see also Wolf 1999, where he puts into explanatory relation mentifacts/cognitive processes and power, either for domination or for resistance).

21 Lincoln uses "sentiment" with some trepidation, offering a disclaiming note that is itself instructive: "I am aware, of course, that use of the term *sentiment* is likely to cause some problems, given the almost insuperable difficulty of speaking with precision about the affective dimension of social life; at times I have considered coining a neologism to avoid talk of sentiment, for example, speaking of the *sociogravitational forces of attraction and repulsion that can be stimulated by discourse*" (1989: 176 n. 9, emphasis added). See now Kile (2005; 2006: chap. 2) on sentiment as an important phenomenon and analytic category in theorizing persuasion and, by extension, social formation.

22 The idea of the affective, pre-emergent moment in the process of group formation (or sentiments of affinity toward a group) has long fascinated social theorists concerned with explaining formative "moments" in the social formation of a group or society. See, for example, E. P. Thompson who, in *The Making of the English Working Class*, suggests that a class is "a very loosely defined body of people who share in the same congeries of interests, social experiences, traditions and value-system, *who have a disposition to behave as a class*, to define themselves ... in class ways ... [C]lass itself is not a thing, it is a happening" (1968: 939, emphasis added).

23 Gorgias struggles to explain the working of *eros* by means of several speculative options. He recommends that it transmits itself into the psyche by sight, rather than aurally. It may be a "god with a god's power," or it may be a "human malady" or a "mental ignorance." Whatever it is, it, like speech, imposes itself with irresistible force.

24 The inherent risk of communication generally is the possibility either of not coming to voice or not coming to audition. Cf. this timeless lament: "Everyone babbles the words, but few obtain thereby a stronger faith" (Johann Valentin Andreae 1622, in Sabean 1984: 1).

25 Paradoxically and understandably, it is this detachment of rhetoric from the aims of serious pleading on high-stakes issues, whether intellectual, moral, legal, political or religious, that would put the "serious" rhetoricians in the quandary of how to

distinguish their honorable and noble speech-crafts from those rhetoricians who had usurped the very same techniques for unabashed theatrical performance, for entertaining "spin" and unscrupulous deception that treated the audience as mere gulls. The solution to the quandary was the development of a fiction that consisted of a "spin on spin" or a "rhetoric of anti-rhetoric" (phrase from Valesio 1980: 41–60; on this phenomenon in antiquity see Hesk 1999 and 2000: 202–291). Its topoi were various delegitimating charges and antagonistic contrastives in the battle for trustworthiness: the defender in court charges the prosecutor with using dangerous "unholy arts of speech" to deceive the jury (Aeschines 2.56) and vice versa; highly skilled rhetors and intellectual élites present themselves as unskilled speakers in *faux*-derogatory contrast to the "skilled speaker," evidently exploiting popular mistrust of rhetorical speech (on this topos see especially Ober 1989: 170–177); pinning on each other the label "sophist," using characterizing terms from the semantic domain of magic and witchcraft, became common (see Hesk 1999: 211–214); many more examples of anti-rhetorical rhetorical strategies are remarked by Jon Hesk (1999, 2000). Note in this context Paul's use of this topos when he insists that though "we [Paul] persuade people" (2 Cor. 5:11), this persuasion is not by means of *logos* which is "of no account" (2 Cor. 10:10), a charge from his opponents that Paul seems to accept as a virtue. Note as well in early Christian discourses the common contrast between pagan intellectuals and their logographic learning and the plain and simple message of the Christians (see Braun 2004: 46–47), and the frequent transfer of the burden of persuadability from logographic technologies to the self-evident authority of the speaker, often posed as a manifestation of divine wisdom (see Mack and Robbins 1989: 203–208; Braun 1997): these moves belong to the same anti-rhetorical rhetorical set, which, as Valesio has rightly noted, has a "legion" of other examples from antiquity to modernity that have yet to be analyzed "as part of the future, general, critical history of rhetoric" (1980: 41).

26 It has long been an axiom of sociolinguistic theory that the manner of speaking (e.g., inflection, accent, lexical preferences, etc.)—and "rhetoric" is as much about manner of speaking as about its substance—is an important marker of social class and status. On this for the Hellenistic period see especially Swain (1996: 7–100), but also Morgan's study (1998) of Hellenistic literate education as in part motivated by the regulatory aims of the élite. Goldhill summarizes: "For the Greek citizen of the Roman Empire ... an engagement with culture also meant ... a heightened consciousness of linguistic performance as a key to élite identity. The protocols of proper speech are central to a politics of class and status" (1999a: 91). A magnificent modern analogy is presented in Mugglestone's study (1995) of "talking proper" as a class and status symbol in 18th- and 19th-century English class contests.

27 The cited phrase is Borch-Jacobsen's (1990: 130), who uses it in his criticism of "restricted rhetoric," that is, highly codified and formalized speech-crafting generally glossed as "classical rhetoric."

28 I do not much care how "local" is defined for the purpose of my point here: kin, group, village, town, regional or transregional special-purpose or interest associations, such as early Christian or Mithraic clubs, may all be included in "local"—as opposed only to the "universal" and the ahistoricality toward which that term bends. My general point is both lexically and substantively indebted to David Warren Sabean's wonderfully instructive *exemplum* of "rhetoricality" in 18th-century Beutelsbach, a village in the Württembach District of Schorndorf, where, when its cattle stock was decimated by hoof and mouth disease, the villagers were launched into a complex, multi-layered

process of assigning blame, staking out interests, and using a crisis for entrenching or re-placing one's position in a web of social power relationships. See "The Sins of Belief: A Village Remedy for Hoof and Mouth Disease (1796)" (in Sabean 1984: 174–198). I thank Johannes C. Wolfart (Carleton University) for drawing Sabean's work to my attention.

29 Recall Gorgias's insinuated worry that the most spectacularly contrived *logos* may fall flat, prove untrue in this sense, in the face of a countermanding affect-generated persuasion, or in the face of resistance enabled by brute hubristic power, or in encounter with an auditor whose life reality is sharply disjunctive to the argued point of *logos*—for example, an argument, however clever, for the inalienability of human agency and freedom is likely to be taken quite correctly as "mere spin" by those whose agentive possibilities are restricted by various types of physical, social and political incarceration.

30 (Readers who wish to see in this statement a boomerang that will return to whack its author are welcome to do so, though they are advised that the author has already seen it.) A note on the term "performance" and my insinuation of rhetoric *as* performance: Why *as*? The simplest—at once most general and fundamental—reason is paradigmatically announced by Erving Goffman: "All the world is not of course a stage, but the crucial ways in which it isn't are not easy to specify" (Goffman 1969: 78). This aphorism condenses Goffman's entire argument, in his classic *The Presentation of Self in Everyday Life*, of self-presentation, hence self-identification on the social stage—and when is self-identification not on the social stage?—as a "theatrical" or "performative" process, a process in which speech is both a production (invention, manipulation, methodical crafting, etc.) and an acting out, a performative, speech literally put into and to practice to vie for hearing, place, status, capital (real and symbolic) on the social stage in the cultural theatre. Although Goffman is speaking about modern Western self-presentation, his argument is incisively relevant to Christian self-presentation in the Greco-Roman period, and relevant to the question of how to think of Christian persuasive performances in the context of ancient Mediterranean "performance cultures" (Goldhill 1999a, 1999b). See especially Goldhill (1999b) on the emergence of "performance studies" as a heterogeneous discipline that coalesces around a shared view of the social, political functioning of language where speech, especially the art of rhetoric, was not infrequently glossed in visual terms (textual references in Braun 1995: 12 and n. 19; see Hedreen 2004 on the creation of a "visual narrative"), and where speech and speaker are understood as a unified entity consisting of speech itself and the speaker's character and physical deportment, the latter including a range of physical features, as well as postural and gestural strategies available for physiognomic scrutiny intended to help scope out the reliability and integrity of the speaker and speech (see Hesk 1999: 218–226; Goldhill 1999a: 91–100). On the concept of "discourse" and its relevance for religious language behaviors see profitably Murphy (2000, 2003).

31 Stanley Fish's wry comment on Habermas's desire for an "ideal speech situation" deserves to be repeated: "If only we could eliminate from our discourse-performances those intentions that reflect baser goals—the intentions to deceive, to manipulate, to persuade—the ideal speech situation could be approximated" (1995: 219).

32 Any rhetoric's aim in part is explicitly or insinuatively to establish within the rhetoricality of the domain of social discourse performances its own legitimacy and persuasiveness. Any rhetoric thus is in part more or less anxiously self-referential, and its persuasiveness will depend to a large measure on its success in garnering esteem

for its topical concerns, chief values—in the terms of classical rhetoric, the "chief categories" of the right, the honorable or beautiful and the expedient or useful—and argumentative styles and techniques. Anyone who has perused the corpora of classical rhetoric, for example, cannot help but notice how much labor is invested in establishing its own credibility. One might point to the current turn to self-referential, self-legitimating advocations in the disciplines of the "human sciences" in Canadian universities as a modern illustration of the point.

33 The full statement reads: "The commonplace limitation of inquiry to the canon, indeed to the notion of written documents at all, is an essentially theological determination which must be set aside by the scholar of religion" (Smith 1990: 113).

34 Most notable exceptions are Smith (1990), Crossan (1992) and Martin (2005).

35 For example, the "Homer Oracle" (PGM VII.1–148), oracular inscriptions in the shrine Herakles Buraikos, and others. Cf. Schroeder (2002) the use of the Platonic text as oracle, i.e., a non-textual reception of textual traditions.

36 For example, I Ching phrases, the Ifa myth, Tarot iconic sets, and others.

37 To speak of a hermeneutical ritual is imprecise both conceptually and with reference to the textual data of the *Gospel of Thomas*. If Davies is correct, the idea of divination ritual is worth more disciplined scrutiny, both at the level of the data and at the level of explanation. Long ago J. Z. Smith suggested that Saying 37—referring to undressing, being naked without shame, treading upon the garments, and being as little children—points to an origin of this saying "within archaic Christian baptismal practices" (1965: 218); if so, and given that no communal meal or other repeated social venue is in view, it may be that we should think of the oracular interests of the Thomas group as performed in a theatrical baptismal ritual that is falls well within Whitehouse's "imagistic mode."

38 Davies (1994): "This hypothesis accounts both for the cognitive incoherence of the Gospel of Thomas and for the random ordering of its sayings. Random oracular divination is, and has been, practised throughout the world and is known to have been practised in Greco-Roman Egypt at the time of the circulation of the Gospel of Thomas. The magical papyri prove that at that time, in that place, peasant interest in the attainment of oracular insights was extremely great and so it is highly likely that Christians would have used a list of oracles for an oracular purpose." Cf. Arnal's (2005) study of the anti-linguistic stance of the *Gospel of Thomas*, which he takes as a "reflection of social positioning" by means of a rejection of endogenous logographic taxonomies, rationalities, and social hierarchies.

39 Without implying that the *Gospel of Thomas* is Gnostic, one should take note of the fact that the various Sethian and Valentinian forms of early Christianity are replete with indications that quotidian, everyday activities, such as washing, applying salves and balms, changing clothes, eating and meals, and engaging in sexual intercourse, among others, were assimilated into a ritual practice for cognitive purposes, usually enigmatic and obscure to modern interpreters (see Turner 1994).

References

Alexander, Loveday (1990). "The Living Voice: Scepticism Towards the Written Word in Early Christian and Greco-Roman Texts." In David J. A. Clines, Stephen E. Fowl and Stanley E. Porter (eds.), *The Bible in Three Dimensions: Essays in Celebration of Forty Years of Biblical Studies in the University of Sheffield*, 221–247. Journal for the Study of the Old Testament Supplement Series 87. Sheffield: Sheffield Academic Press.

Arnal, William E. (2005). "The Rhetoric of Social Construction: Language and Society in the *Gospel of Thomas*." In Willi Braun (ed.), *Rhetoric and Reality in Early Christianities*, 27–47. Waterloo, Ontario: Wilfrid Laurier University Press.

Asad, Talal (1993). *Genealogies of Religion: Disciplines and Reasons of Power in Christianity and Islam*. Baltimore, MD: Johns Hopkins University Press.

Austin, J. L. (1962). *How to Do Things with Words*. London: Clarendon.

Barth, Fredrik (2002). "An Anthropology of Knowledge," *Current Anthropology* 43: 1–18. https://doi.org/10.1086/324131

Bauman, Richard and Charles L. Briggs (1990). "Poetics and Performance as Critical Perspectives on Language and Social Life," *Annual Review of Anthropology* 19: 59–88. https://doi.org/10.1146/annurev.an.19.100190.000423

Bäumer, Änne (1984). "Die Macht des Wortes in Religion und Magie (*Plinius*, Naturalis Historia 28, 4–29)," *Hermes* 112: 84–99.

Beavis, Mary Ann (2000). "'Pluck the Rose but Shun the Thorns': The Ancient School and Christian Origins," *Studies in Religion/Sciences Religieuses* 29: 411–423. https://doi.org/10.1177/000842980002900402

Bender, John and David E. Wellbery (1990). "Rhetoricality: On the Modernist Return of Rhetoric." In John Bender and David E. Wellbery (eds.), *The Ends of Rhetoric: History, Theory, Practice*, 3–39. Stanford, CA: Stanford University Press.

Benveniste, Émile (1966). *Problemes de linguistique générale*. Paris: Gallimard.

Bitzer, L. F. (1968). "The Rhetorical Situation," *Philosophy and Rhetoric* 1: 1–14.

Borch-Jabobsen, Mikkel (1990). "Analytic Speech: From Restricted to General Rhetoric." In John Bender and David E. Wellbery (eds.), *The Ends of Rhetoric: History, Theory, Practice*, 127–139. Stanford, CA: Stanford University Press.

Bourdieu, Pierre (1975). "The Specificity of the Scientific Field and the Social Condition of the Progress of Reason," *Social Science Information* 14: 19–47. https://doi.org/10.1177/053901847501400602

Braun, Willi (1995). *Feasting and Social Rhetoric in Luke 14*. Society for New Testament Studies Monograph Series, 85. Cambridge: Cambridge University Press. https://doi.org/10.1017/CBO9780511520303

—— (1997). "Argumentation and the Problem of Authority: Synoptic Rhetoric of Pronouncement in Cultural Context." In Thomas H. Olbricht and Stanley E. Porter (eds.), *The Rhetorical Analysis of Scripture: Essays from the 1995 London Conference*, 185–199. Journal for the Study of the New Testament Supplement Series 146. Sheffield: Sheffield Academic Press.

—— (2004). "The Schooling of a Galilean Jesus Association (The Sayings Gospel Q)." In Ron Cameron and Merrill Miller (eds.), *Redescribing Christian Origins*, 43–65. Leiden: Brill; Atlanta, GA: Society of Biblical Literature.

—— (2005). "Rhetoric, Rhetoricality, and Discourse Performances." In Willi Braun (ed.), *Rhetoric and Reality in Early Christianities*, 1–26. Waterloo, Ontario: Wilfrid Laurier University Press.

Brett, Mark G. (1990). "Four or Five Things to Do with Texts: A Taxonomy of Interpretive Interests." In David J. A. Clines, Stephen E. Fowl and Stanley E. Porter (eds.), *The Bible in Three Dimensions: Essays in Celebration of Forty Years of Biblical Studies in the University of Sheffield*, 357–377. Journal for the Study of the Old Testament Supplement Series 87. Sheffield: Sheffield Academic Press.

Buchheit, Vinzenz (1960). *Untersuchungen zur Theorie des Genos Epideiktikon von Gorgias bis Aristoteles*. Munich: Max Hueber.

Burkert, Walter (1985). *Greek Religion*. Cambridge, MA: Harvard University Press.

Crossan, John Dominic (1992). "Bias in Interpreting Earliest Christianity." *Numen* 39: 233–235. https://doi.org/10.1163/156852792X00078
Davies, Stevan L. (1994). "The Meaninglessness of the Gospel of Thomas." Unpublished paper, Gospel of Thomas Consultation, Society of Biblical Literature.
—— (1995). *Jesus the Healer: Possession, Trance, and the Origins of Christianity*. New York: Continuum.
Debray, Régis (2000). *Transmitting Culture*. Eric Rauth (trans.). New York: Columbia University Press.
—— (2004). *God: An Itinerary*. Jeffrey Mehlman (trans.). London: Verso.
De Certeau, Michel (1984). *The Practice of Everyday Life*. Steven Rendall (trans.). Berkeley, CA: University of California Press.
De Romilly, Jacqueline (1992). *The Great Sophists in Periclean Athens*. Janet Lloyd (trans.). Oxford: Clarendon.
Filmer, Paul (2003). "Structures of Feeling and Socio-Cultural Formations: The Significance of Literature and Experience to Raymond Williams's Sociology of Culture," *British Journal of Sociology* 54: 199–219. https://doi.org/10.1080/0007131032000080203
Finnegan, Ruth (1969). "How to Do Things with Words: Performative Utterances Among the Limba of Sierra Leone," *Man* NS 4: 537–552. https://doi.org/10.2307/2798194
Fish, Stanley (1995). "Rhetoric." In Frank Lentricchia and Thomas McLaughlin (eds.), *Critical Terms for Literary Studies*, 203–222. 2nd ed. Chicago, IL: University of Chicago Press.
Fournet, Jean-Luc (2003). "Between Literary Tradition and Cultural Change." In Alaisdair A. MacDonald et al. (eds.), *Learned Antiquity: Scholarship and Society in the Near-East, the Greco-Roman World, and the Early Medieval West*, 101–114. Groningen Studies in Cultural Change, 5. Leuven: Peeters.
Geertz, Clifford (1976). "'From the Native's Point of View': On the Nature of Anthropological Understanding." In Keith H. Basso and Henry A. Selby (eds.), *Meaning in Anthropology*, 221–237. Albuquerque, NM: University of New Mexico Press.
Goffman, Erving (1969). *The Presentation of Self in Everyday Life*. Harmondsworth: Penguin.
Goldhill, Simon (1999a). "Body/Politics: Is There a History of Reading?" In Thomas M. Falkner, Nancy Felson and David Konstan (eds.), *Contextualizing Classics: Ideology, Performance, Dialogue*, 89–120. Lanham, MD: Rowman & Littlefield.
—— (1999b). "Programme Notes." In Simon Goldhill and Robin Osborne (eds.), *Performance Culture and Athenian Democracy*, 1–29. Cambridge: Cambridge University Press.
Gowler, David B. (1994). "The Development of Socio-Rhetorical Criticism." In Vernon K. Robbins (ed.), *New Boundaries in Old Territory: Form and Social Rhetoric in Mark*, 1–36. Emory Studies in Early Christianity, 3. New York: Peter Lang.
Graf, Fritz (2004). "The Power of the Word in the Greco-Roman World." In Simone Beta (ed.), *La Potenza della Parola: Destinatari, Funzioni, Bersagli (Atti del convegno di studi Siena, 7–8 maggio 2002)*, 79–100. Florence: Cadmo.
Gumpert, Matthew (2001). *Grafting Helen: The Abduction of the Classical Past*. Madison, WI: University of Wisconsin Press.
Habermas, Jürgen (1975). *Legitimation Crisis*. Trans. Thomas McCarthy. Boston, MA: Beacon.
Hedreen, Guy Michael (2004). "The Return of Hephaistos: Dionysiac Procession Ritual and the Creation of a Visual Narrative." *Journal of Hellenic Studies* 124: 38–64. https://doi.org/10.2307/3246149
Henderson, Ian H. (2004). "Christians, 'Schools' and Greek Literacy." In Rory B. Egan and Mark Joyal (eds.), *Daimonopylai: Essays in Classics and the Classical Tradition Presented to Edmund G. Berry*, 199–208. Winnipeg, OH: University of Manitoba Centre for Hellenic Civilization.

Henrichs, Albert (1998). "Dromena und Legomena: Zum rituellen Selbstverständnis der Griechen." In Fritz Graf (ed.), *Ansichten griechischer Rituale: Geburtstags-Symposium für Walter Burkert*, 33–71. Leipzig: Teubner.

—— (2003). "Writing Religion: Inscribed Texts, Ritual Authority, and the Religious Discourse of the Polis." In Harvey Yunis (ed.), *Written Texts and the Rise of Literate Culture in Ancient Greece*, 38–58. Cambridge: Cambridge University Press. https://doi.org/10.1017/CBO9780511497803.004

Hesk, Jon (1999). "The Rhetoric of Anti-Rhetoric in Athenian Oratory." In Simon Goldhill and Robin Osborne, (eds.), *Performance Culture and Athenian Democracy*, 201–230. Cambridge: Cambridge University Press.

—— (2000). *Deception and Democracy in Classical Athens*. Cambridge: Cambridge University Press.

Kant, Immanuel (1784). "Beantwortung der Frage: Was ist Aufklärung?" *Berlinische Monatsschrift* (Dezember-Heft): 481–494.

Kennedy, George A. (1997). "The Genres of Rhetoric." In Stanley E. Porter (ed.), *Handbook of Classical Rhetoric in the Hellenistic Period (330 BC—AD 400)*, 43–50. Leiden: Brill.

Kile, Chad J. (2005). "Feeling Persuaded: Christianization as Social Formation." In Willi Braun (ed.), *Rhetoric and Reality in Early Christianities*, 219–248. Waterloo: Wilfrid Laurier University Press.

—— (2006). "Christianity, Christians, and Christianization: On the Affective Dimensions of Religious Formation." Unpublished thesis. Edmonton: University of Alberta.

LaMothe, Kimerer Lewis (2004). *Between Dancing and Writing: The Practice of Religious Studies*. New York: Fordham University Press. https://doi.org/10.5422/fso/9780823224036.001.0001

Lévi-Strauss, Claude (1962). *Le totémisme aujourd'hui*. Paris: Presses Universitaires de France.

Lincoln, Bruce (1989). *Discourse and the Construction of Society: Comparative Studies of Myth, Ritual, and Classification*. New York: Oxford University Press.

Loraux, Nicole (2002). *The Divided City: On Memory and Forgetting in Ancient Athens*. Corinne Pache with Jeff Fort (trans.). New York: Zone.

Mack, Burton L. and Vernon K. Robbins (1989). *Patterns of Persuasions in the Gospels*. Foundations & Facets: Literary Facets. Sonoma: Polebridge.

Martin, Luther H. (2005). "Performativity, Narrativity, and Cognition: 'Demythologizing' the Roman Cult of Mithras." In Willi Braun (ed.), *Rhetoric and Reality in Early Christianities*, 187–217. Waterloo, Ontario: Wilfrid Laurier University Press.

Morgan, Teresa (1998). *Literate Education in the Hellenistic and Roman Worlds*. Cambridge: Cambridge University Press.

Mount, Christopher (2005). "1 Corinthians 11:3-16: Spirit Possession and Authority in a Non-Pauline Interpolation," *Journal of Biblical Literature* 124: 313–340. https://doi.org/10.2307/30041015

Mourelatos, Alexander P. D. (1973). "Heraclitus, Parmenides, and the Naive Metaphysics of Things." In E. N. Lee, A. P. D. Mourelatos and R. M. Rorty (eds.), *Exegesis and Argument: Studies in Greek Philosophy Presented to Gregory Vlastos*, 16–48. Assen: Van Gorcum.

Mugglestone, Lynda (1995). *Talking Proper: The Rise of Accent as Social Symbol*. Oxford: Oxford University Press.

Murphy, Tim (2000). "Discourse." In Willi Braun and Russell T. McCutcheon (eds.), *Guide to the Study of Religion*, 396–408. London: Cassell.

—— (2003). "Elements of a Semiotic Theory of Religion." *Method & Theory in the Study of Religion* 15: 48–67. https://doi.org/10.1163/15700680360549411

Ober, Josiah (1989). *Mass and Elite in Democratic Athens: Rhetoric, Ideology, and the Power of the People*. Princeton, NJ: Princeton University Press.

Osborn, E. F. (1959). "Teaching and Writing in the First Chapter of the *Stromateis* of Clement of Alexandria." *Journal of Theological Studies* NS 10: 335–343. https://doi.org/10.1093/jts/X.2.335

Paine, Robert (1981). "The Political Uses of Metaphor and Metonym: An Exploratory Statement." In Robert Paine (ed.), *Politically Speaking: Cross-Cultural Studies of Rhetoric*, 187–200. Social and Economic Papers, 10. St. John's: Institute of Social and Economic Research, Memorial University of Newfoundland.

Parrish, John W. (2006). "'Carry Up My Bones From Here': Semiotics, the Ancestral Dead and a Redescription of 1 Corinthians." Unpublished thesis. Edmonton: University of Alberta.

Poulakos, John (1995). *Sophistical Rhetoric in Classical Greece*. Studies in Rhetoric/Communication. Columbia, SC: University of South Carolina Press. https://doi.org/10.2307/358732

Robbins, Vernon K. (1984). *Jesus the Teacher: A Socio-Rhetorical Interpretation of Mark*. Philadelphia, PA: Fortress.

—— (1996a). *Exploring the Texture of Texts: A Guide to Socio-Rhetorical Interpretation*. Valley Forge, PA: Trinity Press International.

—— (1996b). "The Dialectical Nature of Early Christian Discourse," *Scriptura* 59: 353–362.

—— (2002). "Argumentative Textures in Socio-Rhetorical Interpretation." In Anders Eriksson, Thomas H. Olbricht and Walter Übelacker (eds.), *Rhetorical Argumentation in Biblical Texts: Essays from the Lund 2000 Conference*, 27–65. Emory Studies in Early Christianity, 8. Harrisburg, PA: Trinity Press International.

Sabean, David Warren (1984). *Power in the Blood: Popular Culture and Village Discourse in Early Modern Germany*. Cambridge: Cambridge University Press.

Sahlins, Marshall (1985). *Islands of History*. Chicago, IL: University of Chicago Press.

Schiappa, Edward (1996). "Toward a Predisciplinary Analysis of Gorgias' *Helen*." In Christopher L. Johnstone (ed.), *Theory, Text, Context: Issues in Greek Rhetoric and Oratory*, 65–86. Albany, NY: State University of New York Press.

Schroeder, Frederic M. (2002). "The Platonic Text as Oracle in Plotinus." In Theo Kobusch und Michael Erler (eds.), Metaphysik und Religion: Zur Signatur des spätantiken Denkens. Akten des Internationalen Kongresses vom 13.–17. März 2001 in Würzburg, 23–37. Beiträge zur Altertumskunde, 160. Munich: Saur. https://doi.org/10.1515/9783110975529.23

Segal, Charles P. (1962). "Gorgias and the Psychology of the Logos," *Harvard Studies in Classical Philology* 66: 99–155. https://doi.org/10.2307/310738

Shore, Bradd (1996). *Culture in Mind: Cognition, Culture, and the Problem of Meaning*. New York: Oxford University Press.

Smith, Jonathan Z. (1965). "The Garments of Shame," *History of Religions* 5: 217–238. https://doi.org/10.1086/462523

—— (1990). *Drudgery Divine: On the Comparison of Early Christianities with the Religions of Late Antiquity*. Chicago, IL: Chicago University Press.

—— (1995). "Trading Places." In Marvin Meyer and Paul Mirecki (eds.), *Ancient Magic and Ritual Power*, 13–27. Religions in the Greco-Roman World 129. Leiden: Brill.

—— (2004). "Re: Corinthians." In Smith, *Relating Religion: Essays in the Study of Religion*, 340–361. Chicago, IL: University of Chicago Press.

Snyder, Graydon (1985). *Ante Pacem: Archaeological Evidence of Church Life Before Constantine*

Solmsen, Friedrich (1975). *Intellectual Experiments of the Greek Enlightenment*. Princeton, NJ: Princeton University Press.
Süss, Wilhelm (1910). *Ethos: Studien zur älteren griechischen Rhetorik*. Leipzig: Druck Von B. G. Teubner.
Swain, Simon (1996). *Hellenism and Empire: Language, Classicism and Power in the Greek World, AD 50-250*. Oxford: Clarendon.
Tambiah, S. J. (1968). "The Magical Power of Words," *Man* NS 3: 175-208. https://doi.org/10.2307/2798500
—— (1973). "Form and Meaning in Magical Arts: A Point of View." In Robin Horton and Ruth Finnegan (eds.), *Modes of Thought: Essays on Thinking in Western and Non-Western Societies*. London: Faber & Faber.
Thomas, Rosalind (2003). "Prose Performance Texts: *Epideixis* and Written Publication in the Late Fifth and Early Fourth Centuries." In Harvey Yunis (ed.), *Written Texts and the Rise of Literate Culture in Ancient Greece*, 162-188. Cambridge: Cambridge University Press. https://doi.org/10.1017/CBO9780511497803.010
Thompson, E. P. (1968). *The Making of the English Working Class*. Harmondsworth: Penguin.
Trotsky, Leon (1957) [1924]. *Literature and Revolution*. New York: Russell & Russell.
Turner, John D. (1994). "Ritual in Gnosticism." In Eugene H. Lovering (ed.), *Society of Biblical Literature 1994 Seminar Papers*, 136-181. Atlanta, GA: Scholars Press.
Valesio, Paolo (1980). *Novantiqua: Rhetorics as Contemporary Theory*. Advances in Semiotics. Bloomington, IN: Indiana University Press.
Van Hook, Larue (1930). *Greek Life and Thought: A Portrayal of Greek Civilization*. New York: Columbia University Press. https://doi.org/10.7312/hook91352
Versnel, Hank S. (2002). "The Poetics of Magical Charm: An Essay on the Power of Words." In Paul Mirecki and Marvin Meyer (eds.), *Magic and Ritual in the Ancient World*, 105-158. Religions in the Greco-Roman World 141. Leiden: Brill. https://doi.org/10.1163/9789047400400_008
Wardy, Robert (1996). *The Birth of Rhetoric: Gorgias, Plato and Their Successors*. London: Routledge.
Whitehouse, Harvey (2000). *Arguments and Icons: Divergent Modes of Religiosity*. Oxford: Oxford University Press.
—— (2002). "Modes of Religiosity: Towards a Cognitive Explanation of the Sociopolitical Dynamics of Religion," *Method & Theory in the Study of Religion* 14: 293-315. https://doi.org/10.1163/157006802320909738
—— (2004). *Modes of Religiosity: A Cognitive Theory of Religious Transmission*. Walnut Creek, CA: AltaMira.
Williams, Raymond (1977). *Marxism and Literature*. London: Oxford University Press.
—— (1984). *Writing in Society*. London: Verso.
Winter, Bruce W. (2001). *After Paul Left Corinth: The Influence of Secular Ethics and Social Change*. Grand Rapids, MI: Eerdmans.
Wolf, Eric R. (1997) [1982]. *Europe and the People without History*. Berkeley, CA: University of California Press.
—— (1999). *Envisioning Power: Ideologies of Dominance and Crisis*. Berkeley, CA: University of California Press.

8

Sex, Gender and Empire: Virgins and Eunuchs in the Ancient Mediterranean World

What follows is an argument that the oft-supposed centrality and stability of "the family" in Greco-Roman antiquity belongs as much to the realm of ancient and modern desire and mythmaking as to historical reality. The centrality of the family as the keystone of Greco-Roman societies and the stability of this keystone will be questioned in light of the anti-familial margins, metonymically represented by the figure of the eunuch-priest and the vestal virgin, both spectacular investments in celibacy. Both figures, the argument goes, are simultaneously symptoms and signs of empire: the vestal virgin a totemic emblem of the fantasy for an inviolable, eternal Rome, but also its sacrificial scapegoat that reasserted Rome and *Romanitas* by expiating its failures; the eunuch a creaking announcement of empire's more fundamental fissures, an exposure of the hegemony of empire as a contestable ideology of stability that could not hold up against a disquieting sense of its frailty that was as frail as its people's gender vestures and "family values" that Greeks and Romans often lethargically regarded as natural, fixed, stable.

The title of the colloquium where this essay was presented–"the family as strategy"–brings to mind Michel Foucault's idea of the "complex strategical situation" (Foucault 1978: 93), a situation that is complex because of the intricate and ambiguous power relations that render equally ambiguous, even opaque, strategies for exercising power and for resisting power. Among these ambiguities is the relationship of those who hold power and those who heed it. This relationship, Foucault suggests, is miscast when it is posed in binary oppositional forms: powerful vs. powerless, oppressor vs. oppressed, and the like. Not only are those who ostensibly hold and wield power and those who comply with power in a mutually enabling relationship to each other, but also are those ostensibly powerful often rather hapless hostages to the ideologies and apparatuses that produce and allocate power, just as the ostensibly powerless have at their disposal surprising potential for agency that may be both semiotic (signaling the fissures and flaws of regnant ideologies and power structures) and emancipatory (producing alternate forms of knowledge and social vision). Power, states Foucault, thus "needs to be considered as a productive network which runs through the whole social body, much more than as a negative instance whose function is depression" (Foucault 1980: 199).

In this kind of strategic situation where power relations are ambiguous we should expect that "the family as strategy" too will be ambiguous, even ironic.

What follows suggests that precisely this is the case when we approach the Roman family through perspectives opened up by the idiomatically diverse discourse on celibacy, most spectacularly represented by the Roman vestal virgin and the eunuch-priests of the Magna Mater.

* * *

Preliminarily: using "celibacy" to isolate a list of phenomena in ancient Greek or Roman or post-ancient Greco-Roman societies depends almost entirely on how we define the term that in Western usage has been deeply impregnated with the Christian *imaginaire*. The Greek language speaks of the "unwed" (*agamos*), but it is not an equivalent term. The Latin *caelebs*, etymological ancestor to "celibate," refers to a man or woman unwed, either in preference or by circumstance, which may, but commonly does not, imply abstinence from sexual activity.[1] If we constrict celibacy to mean, say, "deliberate abstinence from sexual activity" (Gold 2005: 1474), we may be scooping water from the Tiber with a sieve, so to speak, retrieving from the various classes of ancient sources a few isolated solid bits that are for that reason not given to generalizations about celibate practices in ancient Mediterranean societies as a whole, perhaps not even at all.[2] In the cultural pools of the ancient Mediterranean deliberate sexual continence was hardly a commonplace in practice, although always a topic of conversation, proscription and varied worry from ancient periods until well into the period of Christianity for which celibacy became a defining bodily and rhetorical mark to which Christians staked their difference (Brown 1988, 1990; MacMullen 1986: 242–243).

The Greek mythic corpus displays some fascination for renunciation of marriage and sex. Among its female deities, Athena (Roman Minerva), known both as *Athena Parthenos* (Virgin Athena) and *Athena Polias* (Athena of the City), is born without a mother, a lover of man and manliness but renouncer of marriage, yet defender of patrilineality and patriarchy, the touchstones of ancient Greek social structure.[3] Artemis (Roman Diana), as aggressively virginal and unmarried as Athena, is the patron of untamed nature, where she is *primus inter alia* of "the countless anonymous nymphs of forests, rivers, and mountains, who are all pictured as virginal creatures of the wild" (Versnel 1992: 49). Hestia (Roman Vesta), goddess of hearth and home, is the sexually inactive, the stable, immovable, female element in patrilocal marriage in which women were movable goods. Thus she is, paradoxically, the promoter of patrilineal descent and, as Vernant (1983) shows, the divine warrant for the patriarchal fantasial desire for producing offspring and securing patrimony without the help of women.

Outside the club of the Olympian gods, we might note the widely popular Anatolian Attis myth complex, variously narrated but widely disseminated in iconography and cults throughout the Greco-Roman regions. Attis, often thought to be the eponymous inspiration for the familiar emasculated eunuch-priests in the Greco-Roman goddess cults (see below), was, as everyone knew, the demi-god "whose genitals had been harvested by a potsherd" (Min. Fel. *Oct.* 24.12), either in a fit of madness or in remorse over a horny lapse in his chaste devotion to Cybele.[4] The Pythia, Apollo's priestess, who occupied the bronze oracular tripod at Delphi, was a complexly ambiguous virgin (Plut. *De Pyth. or*; Pind. *Pyth.*), closed to male penetration, but vaginally open to divine possession and thought to be in a hierogamous relationship with the god (Sissa 1990).[5]

Dire consequences of lost virginity are among the matters for thought also in the tale of the Danaides in the demogonic myth of the Mycenaean city of Argos (exhaustively studied by Bonner 1902). Here the fifty daughters of King Danaus of Argos were forced to marry on a single occasion the fifty sons of Aegyptus. Instructed by their father, all but one of them killed her newly-wed man on the wedding bed. As a result, the women were condemned to an afterlife of endless and futile chores, carrying water from the Styx in perforated jars or sieves, thus displaying in their fruitless bodies and pointless activity who they really were: no longer virgins, never to be mothers, hence "mythological prototypes" of all unproductive *agamoi* (Sissa 1990: 130, citing E. Rohde), and understandably also associated with the uninitiated in the Eleusinian mysteries. In another version of the Danaides's crime, their infernal banishment to eternal unproductive labor is replaced with a restoration of the Danaides to remarriage and motherhood. It is this version, perhaps, that makes it possible for Herodotus (Herod. 2.171) and others to credit the Danaides with bringing the *Thesmophoria* to Greece that appeared also in Rome at the festival of the Bona Dea—a festival, honoring Demeter, where participation was limited to married women who prepared themselves for the rituals by temporary sexual abstinence.

These are mere tidbits from the ancient myths, legends and commentaries on them. They are replete with divine, quasi-divine and heroic figures that are remarked in terms of their sexual activities or renunciation thereof, their ambiguously gendered bodies and "unnatural" sexual proclivities and preferences.

But gods, like heroes and ancestral prototypes, are not necessarily role models nor paradigms of human gender identity and behavior; in Greco-Roman societies these mythological figures were not normally revered by emulation but tended by placation. In resistance to one long scholarly tradition, once ought not hasten to interpret the meaning of myths and mythemes as symbolic images of a society that hosts these myths, much less as a coded charter for that society or for human behavior generally (Penner 2008). Certainly, celibacy of varying kinds and linked to diverse motives and effects is a recurring motif in the mythological and ritual repertoire. Although it is possible, with a dash of interpretive daring, to presume that celibacy in myth and ritual is a means for thought about gender, sex, division of labor, the viability of communal identities, and the ideals of household and civic organization, "good for thought" is not equivalent to "good in practice."

Greco-Roman philosophical discourses too are replete with worries about sex and/or the renunciation of it. Although the philosophers did not fear sex, they agreed on the deleterious effects of unregulated passions in their pursuit of a rational, temperate, self-controlled moral character. In matters of sex, thus, as in other bodily appetites, philosophers from Plato and Aristotle to the Pythagoreans, Stoics, Cynics and later Platonists, an ascetic impulse, a countermanding *egkrateia* (self-mastery) was to be cultivated as the foundation for the virtue of *autarkeia* (self-determination) that marks the man of reason who is fit for intellectual or political callings. With the exception of a few elite "holy men" (e.g., Apollonius of Tyana), however, *egkrateia* in sexual matters did not entail the renunciation of sex altogether. Legitimate marriage and decent, restrained sexual union was, after all, requisite for reproduction, a civic duty. Sexual intercourse in accordance with "natural love," the human procreative mandate, was entirely compatible with an ascetically cultivated human dignity. Nothing is wrong with sex as such, the philosophers agreed. Rather than qualms about sex itself, the philosophers wanted to regulate it so as to align it to their imagined, ideal, self-reliant, rational man. The aim was not abstinence from sex, but a therapeutic regime (Nussbaum 1994) aimed at the higher cultural value of a robustly masculine character (Moxnes 1997) uninfected by corrosive desires and passions, character-consuming appetites, effeminate affectations, and animalistic lust. That is, celibate tendencies in philosophic thought were contemplated, occasionally practiced, not so much as a way of avoiding sexual activities, but as a way of "making men" (Gleason 1995; cf. Gleason 1990), which, in late Hellenistic antiquity, was among the most anxiously pursued forms of self-care.

To this philosophical preoccupation with the pursuit of self-mastery (*egkrateia*) and a nothing-in-excess moral sanity (*sophrosyne*) medical-gynecological "science" would add additional impetus with its theories on the relationship between the spilling of seed and the loss of vital spirit, a relationship that entailed moderation in sexual activity or, occasionally and eccentrically, even giving up sexual intercourse entirely, as Soranus advises (Sor. *Gyn.* 1.7.32). All this, however, does not amount to sufficient evidence of celibacy that is more than exceptional in Greco-Roman practice, although one is surely obliged to agree with Peter Brown that these cultural discourses gave sexual continence "a firm foothold in the folk wisdom of the world in which Christian celibacy would soon be preached" (Brown 1988: 19).

From the general chatter on the celibate on the Greco-Roman broadband, I now turn to two spectacular displays of celibacy, the Roman Vestal Virgins and the eunuch-priests of the Cybele and her various avatars.

* * *

The Vestal Virgins have been among the most scrutinized Roman celibates, for reasons that are easily generalized.[6] The virginal priesthood of Vesta (Greek *Hestia*), goddess of the domestic and "public hearth" (Cic. *Leg.* 2.20), was closely associated with the mythic origins of the Roman state and its evolution at least from the time of the early Republic to the end of the fourth century CE when it, along with so many other pagan cults, was terminated by the Christian emperor Theodotius I (394 CE). Aetiological and historical source materials have lent themselves to reconstructing a thousand-year evolutionary genealogy of a particular *cultus* and the history of religion generally, such that the cult of Vesta offered itself as an ideal example for a "'paleontological' approach to the study of religion" (H. Parker 2004: 565), an approach that is associated with the nineteenth-century interest in the evolutionary tracking of religious phenomena, an interest that conceded expository power, often in terms of authentic meaning, to origins (see

Masuzawa 2000). So, in theory we should expect to find, as we do in fact, that ancestral repertoires (myths, rituals, treasured texts) are not stable, but subject to various re-signifying and re-using strategies under new conditions and circumstances in the Greco-Roman worlds.

As E. R. Wolf (1982: 387) puts it:

> In the rough-and-tumble of social interaction, groups are known to exploit the ambiguity of inherited forms, to impart new evaluations or valences on them, to borrow forms more expressive of their interest, or to create wholly new forms to answer to changed circumstances ... A "culture" is thus better seen as a series of processes that construct, reconstruct, and dismantle cultural materials, in response to identifiable determinants.

So too the modern take on Vestal Virgins has been dyed in the hues of the centuries-old high-brow Western *imaginaire* of noble Rome and its "spinster dons" or in admiration, surely spun out of the fantasia of Christian mariology, for "the pagan nuns of the Roman forum—Christian holiness and self-denial *avant la lettre*" (Beard 1995: 166).[7] All this complements the sense that there is "something queer" (Versnel 1992: 269) about the *virgo vestalis* phenomenon, something "most extraordinary" (Staples 1998: 129) and "weird" (Beard 1995: 166).

This consternation is due in part to the peculiar features of Vesta's priesthood. The six Vestals constituted the only female priesthood at Rome and, although the internal supervision of the College—which had eighteen members, but only six cult-performing Vestals at any given time—fell to a superior Vestal, the *virgo vestalis maxima*, she and her colleagues carried on their duties under ultimate jurisdiction of the *pontifex maximus*, that is, the emperor himself. Selection for service as a Vestal was done by the emperor by means of a legal kidnapping, by capturing (*capere*) a prepubescent girl between the age of six and ten, who had no bodily defects and came from a patrician family, with both parents alive, i.e., not orphaned (Staples 1998: 138–139).[8] The *captio* ceremony, with similarities to Roman marriage rituals, released the initiate from the legal entity of the "power of the father" (*patria potestas*) and the authority of her agnatic family generally and transferred her to the *potestas* of the Roman state and to the Roman collectivity as her substitute agnates (Staples 1998: 144). The girl was taken to the Vestal house (*atrium Vestae*) adjacent to the Temple of Vesta, itself located near Rome's Forum and the Regia, the emperor's precinct. Here the Vestal was committed to a thirty-year term of service during which she was subject to an iron-clad vow of chastity. As Plutarch summarizes: "It was ordained by the king that the sacred virgins should vow themselves to chastity for thirty years; during the first decade they are to learn their duties, during the second to perform the duties they have learned, and during the third to teach others these duties" (Plut. *Num.* 10.1). "Then, the thirty years having passed," Plutarch continues, "any one who wishes is free to marry and adopt a different mode of life, after laying down her sacred office. We are told, however, that few have welcomed the allowance, and that those who did so were not happy, but were a prey to repentance and dejection for the rest of their lives, thereby inspiring the rest with superstitious fears, so that until old age and death they remained steadfast in their virginity" (Plut. *Num.* 10.2; see Martini 1997: 259–262). Hence, for most Vestals "their association with the cult remained a lifelong commitment" (Thompson 2005: 31) to celibacy and chastity, first by legal imposition, then objectively imposed by long corporeal practice and post-vestal life-stage circumstances.[9]

Virgo is in fact the *sine qua non* of the Vestal's status, implying perpetual (pre-pubescent) maidenhood, physical virginity, and chastity. As Ariadne Staples has rightly underscored, "[v]irginity was not merely a necessary attribute of the Vestals, it was reified" (1998: 129, see also 147). Physiologically it was ensured by pre-sexual induction into the Vestal college. While in office the Vestals' virginity was guarded by the Roman surveillance apparatus, including escort by a *lictor*, a ceremonial attendant and bodyguard (Plut. *Num.* 10.3).[10] Harsh punishment for *crimen incesti*, that is failure to preserve actual and perceived chastity, was severely punished, most drastically in a ritual execution by being buried alive, a spectacle, Plutarch notes, that is "more appalling and brings more gloom to the city than any other" (Plut. *Num.* 10.5; see Mustakallio 1992; Staples 1998: 131–132; H. Parker 2004: 575–578). The gloom, though surely commenting on the brutality of the Vestal's execution, is all the weightier because trials and penalization of Vestals occurred during times of political instability, civil unrest and military defeat, such that transgression of a Vestal was associated with a failure of the state itself and her punishment thus "was intended as expiation for the Roman state as a whole" (Thompson 2005: 35). Not least, lifelong celibacy was assured by the thirty-year hiatus between pre-sexual girlhood and the Vestal's retirement, as span of time that about corresponded to the period of a woman's child-bearing capacity. The term of conscription, that is, largely suppressed the possibility of productive sex and the natural physiological and status progression from virgin (*virgo*) to woman (*matrona*) (Beard 1980: 14 n. 21; Staples 1998: 147).

Her virginal status is confounded, however, by the fact that the Vestals' chief symbolic and ritual functions were matronal in nature. They had to perform various duties associated with Vesta's role as guardian of "the hearth of the city," chief among which was tending the sacred fire burning in the Temple of Vesta. They prepared the *mola salsa* (salt cakes) used in the sacrificial rites during the annual Vestalia. They performed the annual ritual cleaning of the temple on the last day of the Vestalia. Tending hearth, preparing food, cleaning: all core household duties of the Roman married woman. Additional ambiguity is imposed by the peculiar privileges of the Vestals. A *lictor*, the right to give testimony in court, ability to make their own wills, exemption from *tutela* in bequeathing their property, as crucial examples, usually were granted only to men.

The Vestal thus was an ambiguous figure; she was in a "position of perpetual *rite de passage*," as Mary Beard has influentially argued. She was suspended between several sexual and gender categories, "perpetually on the brink, perpetually fixed at the moment of transition from one category to another" (Beard 1980: 21). She belonged to several classes but to none surely and unambiguously. She partook symbolically and legally in any and all conventional sex, gender and status classifications but could not be fully assigned to a single one of them. She was every significant Roman, but not definitively a single type of Roman. In Holt Parker's concise summary:

> A Roman woman existed legally only in relation to a man. ... The act of freeing a Vestal from any man so that she was free to incarnate all men removed her from all conventional classifications, including the fundamental distinction between the living and the dead.[11] Thus she was unmarried and so not a wife; a virgin and so not a mother; she was outside *patria potestas* and so not a daughter; she underwent no *emancipatio*, no *coemptio* and so not a ward. (H. Parker 2004: 573)

Hence her representational value was metonymic: the Vestal was Rome and *Romanitas* (Staples 1998: 143). She was the totem of Rome in Durkheim's definition of a thing that represents the social whole, including its genealogical foundation, the ancestral spirits of dead Romans (Durkheim 1915: 123; H. Parker 2004: 574).

It should be stressed, however, that virginity was not just another aspect of the Vestal's totemic value. She served the ideology of the impenetrability of the Roman state. Her perfection and purity, along with her unclassifiability, made her the perfect sacrificial victim, a scapegoat, when Rome found itself in what R. Girard calls a "sacrificial crisis" (1977: 39).[12] The representational value of the Vestal, her categorically liminal status, her ritual duties, and the possibility, occasionally the reality, of her victimization by the very State she represented and embodied must be seen as a dense metonymic cluster of idealized *Romanitas*. Their virginity was not, after all, "a matter of free choice to them. No heroic freedom of the individual will was made plain" in their celibacy (Brown 1988: 8). Rome captured them, set them apart, inscribed itself ideologically and ritually on the physiological and symbolic body of the female virgins.

* * *

In 1925 Arthur Darby Nock wrote that since religious castration is Oriental in origin, "eunuchs have no place in purely Greek and Roman cults" (Nock 1925: 20). Let's allow that he was correct on the question of provenance. Eunuchs were a fixture in the royal establishments of the ancient Near East (see Riquet 1948). The eunuch priests, the Galli of the Anatolian mother goddess, variously called Kybele, Agditis, Rhea, Magna Mater, Cybele, Artemis, and other names over time (but depicted with a consistent iconography) are of neolithic central Anatolian origin. The Sumerian *gala*, castrated priests in the service of the Sumerian goddess Inanna and Akkadian Ishtar are documented in Mesopotamian temple records of the third millennium. And, the analogous *hijra* associated with the Indian mother goddess Bahuchara Mata may have roots as old as the Anatolian Galli (Roscoe 1996: 198, 206, 213). Be that as it may—"origin" and "purity" are by now discredited explanatory concepts in the study of cultural phenomena—the figure of the eunuch was well known from archaic to late antiquity, from Assyria to Rome and Byzantium, both as an important figure in the monarchic palaces and bureaucracies, in the cults of Attis and Cybele which entered Rome in the late third century BCE,[13] in the cults of the Syrian goddess (Lightfoot 2002), Ephesian Artemis (Sanders 1972: 996) and other avatars of the Anatolian *Magna Mater*, in popular imagination as reflected in its cultural productions, both literary (Lucian of Samosata, Terence, Apuleius) and iconographic (Hales 2002). By the first and second centuries CE the figure of the eunuch—the Gallus of course, but also a human gender classification problem—was a stock figure in the social and representational landscapes of the Greco-Roman world, as Greek and Roman as anything else, even though Romans contemptuously regarded the Cybelian eunuch-priests as alien Phrygian freaks and promptly outlawed castration for Romans.[14]

Lucius Apuleius, the second-century CE author of the romping, risqué novel *Metamorphoses*, draws a picture that permits us to appreciate the flaunted presence and cultural perception of the eunuch.[15]

> They [the *chorus cinaedorum*, "band of homosexual prostitutes" (8.26)] put on vari-coloured garments and beautified themselves hideously (*deformiter quisque formati*) by daubing clay pigment on their faces and outlining their eyes with greasepaint. Then they set out, wearing turbans and saffron-coloured robes and vestments of linen and silk. Some had white tunics decorated with purple lance-shaped designs flowing in every direction, gathered up into a girdle, and on their feet they wore yellow shoes. They wrapped the [Syrian] goddess in a silken mantle and put her on my [Lucius the ass's] back to carry, while they, with arms bared to the shoulders and brandishing frightful swords and axes, chanted and danced, excited by the frenzied beat of the music. ... [T]hey came to the country-house of a rich land-owner. As soon as they reached the entrance-way they frantically flung themselves forward, filling the place with the sound of their discordant shrieks. For a long time they dropped their heads and rotated their necks in writhing motions, swinging their hanging locks in a circle. Sometimes they bit their own flesh with their teeth, and finally they all began slashing their arms with the two-edged blades they were carrying. ... One of them started to rave more wildly than the rest, and producing rapid gasps from deep down in his chest, as though he had been filled with the heavenly inspiration of some deity (*divino spiritu repletus*), he simulated a fit of madness (*vecordiam*). ... Shouting like a prophet, he began to attack and accuse himself with a fabricated lie about how he had perpetrated some sin against the laws of holy religion (*sanctae religionis*); and he went on to demand just punishment for his guilty deed from his own hands. He snatched up the utensil which is the distinctive attribute of these half-men (*semiviris*), a whip with long tassels made of twisted strips of wooly hide studded with numerous sheep's knuckle-bones, and he scourged himself hard .... You could see the ground growing wet with the filthy, effeminate blood (*sanguinis effeminati*) from all this slashing of swords and lashing of whips. ... When they had grown tired, or at least sated with self-laceration, they ceased their butchery and took up a collection [i.e., resumed begging]. (Apul. *Met.* 8.27–29; trans. Hanson, LCL)

Even if we discount the Monty Pythonesque excesses in Apuleius's description of these devotees of the Syrian goddess, the tone of derision and language of scorn—half-men, effeminates, mad, hideous offenders of the laws of proper religion—is drawn from a standard thesaurus of slurs by which to hurl contempt at these figures. In Lucian of Samosata's *The Eunuch* Lycinus describes the eunuch as "neither man nor woman but something composite, hybrid, and monstrous, alien to human nature." He was regarded as "one whom the male sex has discarded and the female will not adopt" (Claud. *CLE* 1.468). Or, as Augustine would quip, upon emasculation "neither is he changed into a woman nor does he remain a man" (*De civ. D.* 7.24). Indeed, ancient authors had to invent a new category of person for the eunuch; he became a member of the *tertium genus hominum*, "third type of human," or *tertium sexus*, the "third sex" (SHA *Sev.* 23.7; Prud. *Perist.* 10.1071; see Cordier 2002; Roscoe 1996: 203). "Third" also designates their place in the hierarchy of human species: man on top, then woman, then eunuch, such that the aspersion "weaker than a eunuch" could be used to remark on human strength and virtue that registered at the feeblest end of the scale (Dio Chrys. *Or.* 3.35; see Brower 1996:162). David Hester (2005: 21–22) summarizes the suspicious and contemptuous character profile:

> Generally, they were viewed as soft (*mollis, eviratus, malakos*), effeminate (*semivir, semimas, effeminatus, androgynos*), sexually passive (*kinaidos*), unkind, immodest (*impudicitia*), ... weak, impotent, deceitful, cowardly and incapable of virtue. Popular novels depicted them as power-seeking, unscrupulous, greedy, untrustworthy and undependable. ... Dream interpretation, popular sayings, fables, even popular superstitions, all viewed the eunuch as an object of scorn, bad luck and deception. The eunuch, by definition, was not (could not be) a morally upright and virtuous figure, but was always suspicious.[16]

Of course, Hester assembles a mélange that contributes to the stereotype "eunuch" simply by combining bits and pieces of ancient stereotypes. And indeed, the Greco-Roman eunuch was in fact not just a man without testicles or a man unable to procreate; his additional burden was precisely "eunuch-as-stereotype" (Brower 1996: 151–153).[17] One looks in vain for approving nods or commentary on the eunuch in ancient sources,[18] even though they had traditionally enjoyed status as functionaries in high places, and continued into late antiquity to be employed as attendants in women's quarters—which earned them their appellation as "keeper of the bed" (discussion in Lieber 1996).

Were eunuchs celibate, both in the sense of refraining from sexual activity and in the (often) associated sense of chastity? A long Christian commentary tradition on the eunuch saying in the Gospel of Matthew 19:12 has posed the eunuch as "an emblem of extreme chastity" (Caner 1997: 399; also Hester 2005: 13),[19] a view that has bled into scholarship on eunuchism in Greek and Roman cultures generally. Prominently, Nock, rightly arguing against a favored then-*du jure* explanation of castration as the means of assimilating the priest to the goddess, suggests that the motives for the "self-mutilation" by the priests of Cybele, Dea Syria and other goddesses were to ensure for themselves ritual purity (Nock 1925: 28–32). This he understood as a "negative chastity," negative because "chastity in cultus was commonly regarded as something negative and as an abstention" (Nock 1925: 30). Equating castration with sexual disablement, he understood the practice as a way of cutting off the source of "the impurity involved in sexual intercourse" rather than motivated by "peculiar powers resting in the pure" (Nock 1925: 30). Purity and chastity are not, however, associated with eunuchism in the ancient sources, nor was castration a technique for de-sexualization that was known or believed to entail loss of sexual desire and, therefore, abstinence from sexual activity, as A. Rousselle has shown on historical evidence and medical science (1988: 121-127).[20] Although the eunuchs' sterility was taken for granted in the ancient sources, their sexual ability was debated (could he maintain an erection and be a penetrator or could he only be penetrated?), but rarely doubted,[21] both for the kind of sex they had and the excess of their lust. If sexual contact was considered a source of pollution that disqualified the devotee from servitude to the deity, the eunuch was hardly qualified "to serve through his whole life the object of his devotion" (Nock 1925: 31). But serve he did.

Rather than offering a motive for ritual castration or ablation, much less a "religious" one,[22] I should ask why the eunuch was universally disdained and ridiculed, but why, nevertheless, he was accorded some esteem, why, that is, the figure of the eunuch persisted robustly in the Greco-Roman world of all periods and even increased in popularity once the native palaces, temples and city-state bureaucracies that had provided the eunuch with function and status were overridden by the colonization and "globalization" of Greek and Roman imperial formations (see L. Martin and Pachis 2004).

The despicable and dangerous eunuch was culturally sustained by the regnant Greco-Roman gender ideology, which idealized maleness and pathologized femaleness at many levels (see especially Föllinger 1996, but also Katz 1995; Lloyd 1964; D. Martin 1995, 1997). In archaic and classical periods male gender identity was firmly linked to citizenship and the public (male) pursuit of civic virtues, including patrilineal and patriarchal household and civic structures. This gender ideology was not displaced under the conditions of imperial and colonial realities in the Mediterranean regions during late Hellenistic period, but it was inflected in more general, even cosmic terms. First, at the level of conceptualizing and remodeling the architecture of the cosmos in the late Hellenistic period, precisely when eunuchs assume an increase in social and literary profile, two interlinked problems emerge (see L. Martin 1987). One concerns the perceived emigration of the gods, once resident among humans in earthly temple and sacred place, to the super-lunar regions of the cosmic sphere. Not only did this leave humans to fend for themselves in the chancy muck of life under the moon, but it left them vulnerable to the *Stoicheia*, the demonic powers that patrolled the sub-lunar regions. The other is the recasting of the older concept of *Agatha tyche*—a notion that sees Fate at worst as benign and at best as a principle of sympathetic providential care—into *Heimarmene*, an understanding of Fate as a capricious, oppressive feminine principle that manifested itself especially in the incarcerating malevolence and maliciousness of the sub-lunar powers that separated earthy humanity from the ethereal gods. It is in this intellectual matrix that we see the emergence of the various theologies of male saviors, theologies which incipiently understand "salvation" in gendered terms: "maleness," physiologically complete and properly functioning man, represents the *telos* on the path to salvation. "Femaleness" represents the highest abstraction of the tyranny of this-worldly, material human existence. The eunuch does not, cannot, belong to either category. It is not a huge leap from imagining the perceived cosmic conflict as a gender war to identifying gender ambiguity as part of the parcel of human deficiencies that are beyond the natural, moral, civic pale.

A second theoretical base undergirding Greco-Roman gender ideology was constructed in the laboratories of research and philosophical thought on human physiology (for elaboration see Braun 2003). Ancient physiological and medical thought was based on a theory of monosexuality—Laqueur calls it the "one-sex" model—"in which men and women were arrayed according to their degree of metaphysical perfection, their vital heat, along an axis whose telos was male" (Laqueur 1990: 5–6). Physiological dimorphism, that is, was not converted into ontological gender dimorphism, into an anthropology in which man and woman are distinct categories of human being that, conceivably, could be valued as physiologically different but equal on scales of virtue, value, nobility, or just plain humanity. On the contrary, human bodies were understood in terms of a continuum running between poles of masculinity and femininity; each body was thought to contain both male and female aspects and "every human body, male or female, occupies some position on the spectrum male-female" (D. Martin 1995: 33). The position of bodies on the physiognomic spectrum corresponded to their embodiments of core Mediterranean values of virtue, honor and nobility, just as body types corresponded to a person's location on the social and political spectrum of power and influence. On this spectrum a range of "blessings" (education, rationality, virtue) that qualified people to be custodians (saviors) of the family, city and state (Dio Chrys. Or. 32.3) were firmly associated with the masculine ideal (Moxnes 1997: 273). Now, in theory the model of monosexuality allowed for, indeed expected, to mold persons so as raise the level of maleness (Gal. De sperm. 1; Rousselle 1992: 328; Gleason 1990: 402–406), though within the firm limits set by physiology. Although there was not complete agreement among the ancient physiologists on exactly how to take measure of a person's level of maleness or femaleness by means of temperature, humors and density of body mass (see Lloyd 1964), they did agree that the material apparatus of the body presents a measuring gauge and sets the limits (D. Martin 1995: 32). An impaired male body, a eunuchized effeminate body, thus blocked access to full manly excellence.

Further supporting the eunuch's access to manhood is found in the theory of commensurability of physiological body surface and inner quality of character, a theory that had its applied side in the "science" of physiognomy, the art of deducing character from physiology, of determining from physiological shape, gestures, deportment and so forth, which of the sexes prevailed in any given person.[23] The second-century physiognomist Polemon states the principle succinctly:

> You may obtain physiognomic signs of masculinity and femininity from your subject's glance, movement and voice. Then, taking these signs, compare one with another until you are able to satisfy yourself on which of the two sexes prevails. For in the masculine something feminine will be found, and in the feminine something masculine, but the designation "masculine" or "feminine" should be used in accordance with which of the two (sexes) prevails. (Polemon, Phgn 2 [vol. 1: 192; ed. Förster, Leipzig 1893])

According to this logic persons with "effeminate" body markings, accompanied by other ambiguous gender and sex displays, would be hard-pressed to convince anyone that their true or "prevailing" character was anything other than commensurate with their physiognomic signs. Eunuchs would always signal that they were deficient precisely in those character qualities that would most identify them as quintessential human beings because those character qualities were precisely those qualities which were physiologically represented in complete, male bodies, with properly (that is, reproductively) functioning genitals. Not all men, that is, were males.

This whole theoretical package, entirely committed to *andreia* (manliness) as the divinely and naturally ordained high nobility of human being, was forcefully represented and reproduced in a host of everyday practices and conventions—from schooling, to public discourse and rhetoric, to philosophy, to all kinds of gender-coded and gender-signifying domestic and public spaces and proprieties. The totality of Greco-Roman culture was univocal: humans have effeminate qualities and affectations, for which the female body and femaleness is the lowest limit, represented humans of deficient personhood. It is this whole cultural kit that explains why the eunuch was such an itch for all Greeks and Romans who worried about gender and sex and how these were related to character, virtue, ethnic, civic and imperial identity.[24] The eunuch, neither fully male nor entirely female, incapable of (re)productive sex but perceived to be enslaved to sexual desire and unconstrained in indulging this desire, a powerful yet feared interstitial figure, threatened to rupture the hegemony of *andreia* and by his very presence exposed *andreia* as an ideology that was contestable.[25]

It is perhaps for this reason that the eunuchs were not only detested, but also had supporters and clients. Apuleius, for example, remarks that people "vied in offering" copper and silver coins and various alimentary goods (wine, milk, cheese, grains) to the band of mendicant eunuch goddess devotees at whom he otherwise sneers (*Met.* 8.28). In an "important town" one of the "leading men (*vir principalis*) there, who besides a general religious disposition showed a special reverence for the goddess (*eximie deam reverens*)," took in "the goddess with devout hospitality," and provided lodging for the troop of *galli* "within the walls of his extensive *domus* while striving to win the goddess's favor with the utmost veneration (*summa veneratione*) and sumptuous sacrifices" (*Met.* 8.30). In another hill-town, a farmer, fearing what Apuleius construes as a "false prognostication" (*fictae vaticinationis*) performed by the *galli*, donated "his fattest ram for a sacrifice to satisfy the hungry Syrian goddess" (*Met.* 8.29). Assuming Apuleius's ethnographic reliability, more than simple charity for beggarly priests is at work here (Brower 1996: 142). Fear of the goddess and her priests is a motive for placating her; hence reverence is demonstrated by votive offerings. Other sources indicate that the emasculated beggar-priests were sought out for their skill in conducting contagious magic to ward off calamity for twelve months (Juv. 6.511–515); they were known for interpreting omens, both avian (Cic. *Div.* 1.41) and astral (Plin. *HN* 2.37). All this wants to say that the goddess priests were feared and revered not because of their purity, certainly not because of their continence, nor because they were considered exemplary models of honoring the gods, but because they performed various divinatory and magical rites to achieve quotidian benefits for people who subscribed to their services.[26] Horror and clientage-inspiring awe were the cross-eyed gazes directed at the eunuch.

* * *

As an unchaste and polluted of body, a metonym for Greco-Roman anxieties about gender, which is itself a trope for working on worries about identity—self, civic, imperial—the eunuch-priest is both kin and alter-ego to the Vestal Virgin. Both are simultaneously symptoms and signs of empire: one a totemic matronal emblem of the fantasy for an inviolable, eternal Rome, and its sacrificial scapegoat that reasserted Rome and *Romanitas* by expiating its (temporary) failures; the other a creaking announcement of empire's more fundamental fissures, an exposure of the hegemony of empire as a contestable ideology of stability that could not hold up against a disquieting sense of its frailty that was as frail as its people's gender vesture and "family values" that Greeks and Romans often lethargically regarded as natural, fixed, stable. Both figures destabilized gender categories and normalized, "natural" family structures. And when gender identity and familial norms wobble, a strategic situation for producing alternate familial models, gender modes and visions is in place.

Notes

1 The Greek term *agamos* means unwed, which may, but need not, imply sexual abstinence. For the Latin, see for example, Ov. *Met.* 10: "Pygmalion saw ... women waste their lives in wretched shame, and critical of flaws that nature had so deeply planted in their female hearts, he lived in preference, for many years unmarried (*caelebs*)." Pygmalion did not, however, abstain from sexual activity, illustrating a more general observation that in antiquity renunciation of marriage does not usually entail renunciation of sexual activity. He sculpted an ivory statue of a perfect virgin and took her as an artificial sex object, even impregnating her with an assist from Venus.
2 The metaphor of the sieve appears in Valerius Maximus's story of the vestal virgin, Tuccia, who, when accused of the crime of unchastity, "boldly and rashly" offered to prove her innocence by carrying water from the Tiber to the temple in a sieve, a dare to which "the Nature of Things gave way" (Val. Max, 8.1.absol. 5; see Richlin 1997).
3 "No mother gave me birth. I honour the male, in all things but marriage. Yes, with all my heart I am my Fathers child" (Aesch. *Eum.* 751–753).
4 The Attis/Cybele material has been subject to immense scholarly labor, classically by J. G. Frazer (1906), but see especially Vermaseren (1977), Roller (1999) and Lancellotti (2002).
5 The Pythia's ambiguous virginity mirrors real-life prenuptial virginity. As Giulia Sissa has shown in her programmatic study, in Greek cultures virginity and sexual intercourse were not incompatible once one looks beneath the surface of custom, law and dissimulating rhetoric. Hence nubile virgins were known to have given birth without losing their virginal status: "In literature countless children born to 'virgins' bear witness to a conception of virginity that had nothing to do with the body or sex ... The word *bastard* makes it clear that the Greeks did not expect of their *parthenoi* the

absolute, unwavering chastity that defines virginity in the Christian ethos" (Sissa 1990: 78, 83).

6 Among numerous remarks in the ancient sources on the putative origin, history, features and function of the cult of Vesta, see especially Plut. *Num.* 9–10; Gell. *NA* 1.12; and Dion. Hal. *Ant. Rom.* 2.66.1. Cf. the late comparison of the Vestals with Christian virgins in Ambrose's letters (*Ep.* 17 and 18) to the Western emperor Valentinian in 384 CE. Among modern studies note Worsfold (1932), Koch (1958), Prowse (1967), Hommel (1972), Rawson (1974), Pomeroy (1975: 210–214), Cancik-Lindemaier (1996, 1997), Abbott (1999: 29–33) and, with sharp focus on the virginal status of the Vestas, thus most useful to our topic, especially Dumézil (1970, vol. 1: 311–326), Beard (1980, 1995), Staples (1998: 129–156), Wildfang (1999), H. Parker (2004) and Thompson (2005: 29–39).

7 "In modern days the sisterhoods of the nuns of the Church of Rome, themselves of great antiquity, offer the closest resemblance" (Worsfold 1932: 11).

8 Rules of eligibility changed over time; from the fourth century BCE, girls of plebeian rank could be chosen; from Augustus and onward daughters of freedmen could be selected (Cass. Dio. 55.22.5–12; Suet. *Aug.* 31.3; Thompson 2005: 31 n. 32). The "capturing" of the Vestal is described by Gellius in *NA* 1.12.13–14. On the significance of the *captio* ceremony, including required language ("thus I take you, loved one"), the young initiate's bridal coiffure, see Thompson (2005: 32–33), who reviews and criticizes the view that the ceremony "would suggest that the Vestal entered into a kind of 'marriage' with the *pontifex maximus*" (Thompson 2005: 33). See also Staples (1998: 138–143) for a perceptive discussion of the peculiar legal exceptions applied in the Vestals' release from *patria postestas*.

9 Let's translate Plutarch's remarks on the retired Vestal's "dejection" and "superstitious fears" into Bourdieu's evocation of the Greek term *hexis*, a permanent condition, state of being, brought about, incorporated, through practice: "L'hexis corporelle est la mythologie politique réalisée, incorporée, devenue disposition permanente, manière durable" (Bourdieu 1980: 117).

10 Since *lictores* also accompanied men of imperial rank, some have suggested that assignment of this privilege to a Vestal contributed to the attribution of a male dimension to the symbolics of the Vestal (Dumézil 1970 vol. 2: 587, Beard 1980: 17). Others think the attendant is a visual symbol of the prestige and set-apart ritual status of the Vestal (Staples 1998: 145).

11 My note added: In a provocative argument, singularly ignored in subsequent scholarship on the Vestals, K. R. Prowse (1967) argues that the temple of Vesta shares attributes with other "homes" of Rome's ancestors and that, therefore, "the temple of Vesta guarded within its sacred circle the nameless ancestors upon whose power rested the power of Rome itself" (187). The Vestals' duties were in part to look after the needs of the spirits of the dead. Prowse's argument could be extended with the notice that the highly regulated ritual of live burial of a transgressive Vestal in a subterranean tomb outfitted with minimal furniture and a limited food supply (a scene itself analogous to the ancient hearth-centered house and the Temple of Vesta) takes her beyond the living *and* the dead so as both to join and to placate the powerful spirits of the dead.

12 Girard's theory of sacrifice is smartly applied to the ritual killing of the Vestal, and by extension to the sacrifice of women, by H. Parker (2004: 575–578).

13 "Nobles in their togas bare their feet before the car at the rites of the Idaean Mother [epithet for Cybele]" (Prudent. *Perist.* 10.154–55).

14 The scholarly literature is immense. Key older and recent works include Cumont (1910), Nock (1925), Browe (1936), Guyot (1980), Rousselle (1988: 107–128), Scholten

(1995), Stevenson (1995), Brower (1996: 93–144), Roscoe (1996), Tougher (2002), Casadio (2003), Mayhew (2004) and Hester (2005: 18–24). There is also much to be learnt in Riquet (1948), Brown (1988), Caner (1997), Taylor (2000), Keufler (2001) and Scholz (2001).

15 Eunuchs occupied various social positions, ranging from professional administrative assistants in royal and political administrative offices to the roving bands, likely attached to local shrines of Cybele or the Syrian Goddess, who "ventured to prowl the streets and countryside begging for alms and performing spectacular religious rites" (Roscoe 1996: 202). That eunuchs generally belonged to the slave classes is taken as a given (see Spencer 1992). I use the term here without respect either to subtypes or to the distinctions based on the how a male became a eunuch. Ancients did distinguish eunuchic types, even in law: "The name eunuch (*spadonum*) is general; it subsumes who are natural eunuchs (*qui natura spadones sunt*), those who were made eunuchs (*item thlibiae thlasiae*), and any other kind of eunuch" (Ulp. *Dig.* 50.16.128; discussion in Brower 1996: 155 and n. 27).

16 For the fullest survey of the ancient sources, see Guyot (1980: 42–44, 174–176) on which Hester relies.

17 To wit, "eunuchs, neither woman nor man, lustful, envious, ill-bribed, passionate, effeminate, slaves of the belly, mad for gold, ruthless, grumbling about their dinner, inconstant, stingy, greedy, insatiable, savage, jealous. What more need I say? At their very birth they were condemned to the knife. How can their mind be right when their feet are awry? They are chaste because of the knife, and it is no credit to them. They are lecherous to no purpose, of their own natural vileness" (Basil of Ancyra, *Ep.* CXV [To the heretic Simplicia]).

18 Hester (2005: 19 n. 13): "With respect to eunuchs, during the period under question I have found very few examples in which a eunuch was praised." The examples he did find (Amm. Marc. 16.7; Polyb. 22.22.1) cite eunuchs approvingly for outstanding compensating qualities rather than their emasculated state. Cf. the grudging comment by Sextus Empiricus: "The Mother of the Gods also accepts effeminates and the goddess would not judge so, if by nature unmanliness were a trivial matter" (*Pyr.* 3.217).

19 The early Christian practice of castration, for which there is evidence from mid-second century onward, demonstrates a mixture of approval and censure (Caner 1997).

20 See also Casadio (2003: 242) on Nock's views as "anachronistic and ethnocentric. (As it seems to me the British scholar was influenced above all by the model of celibacy laid down for Catholic Priests)." On purity issues in Greek religion see the standard work of R. Parker (1983).

21 A good collection of evidence is in Brower (1996: 174–178). Apollonius of Tyana, himself a famous sex-renouncer, instructs his companion Damis, who assumes castration means inability to have sexual intercourse, by pointing out that eunuchs too "feel desire" and, therefore, that castration is not a physical short-cut to moral sanity which is a matter of "not giving in to sexual intercourse when fueled with desire, but in abstinence and appearing superior to this madness" (Philostr. *VA* 1.33).

22 Positing of motives other than the eunuch as an impurity-avoiding celibate are available. For example, see Burkert's functionalist argument that coherence between the Antis myth and the ritual castration of the priest suggests cogently that "[c]astration puts a man outside archaic society in an absolutely irrevocable way; being neither man nor woman, but 'nothing,' he has no place to go." This displacement, less cogently, gives him (like Attis's complex dependency on the *Magna Mater*), "no choice but to adhere to his goddess; ... the mere act [of castration] makes apostasy impossible"

(Burkert 1979: 105). See Casadio (2003: 235–248) for a survey of other explanations of the motives behind castration and devotion to the goddess.

23 Physiognomical writings are collected in Förster (1893). On Polemon's *Physiognomy* see now Swain (2007). On the relations between physiognomy and anthropological engineering see Sassi (2001) and Gleason (1995).

24 Cf. Hester (2005: 20): "eunuchs were the nightmare embodiment of men's worst fears. Eunuchs had lost their masculinity." The weight of this increases when one recognises an insinuated further contrastive pair: the *pater familias*, embodying the ancestral *gens* and caring for the *sacra familiae*, and the slave without gens and *familia*, hence strategically positioned to imagine and experiment with a different micro-sociality.

25 Following Antonio Gramsci I use "hegemony" and "ideology" as related but not identical concepts. Hegemony refers to mass consent, as a matter of course, to a specifiable established order of thinking about everything (from anthropology to cosmology and back again) and ordering oneself morally, socially, and politically in accordance with that order of thought. Transgressions of hegemonic orders, typically first in practice rather than by argument, expose their ideological foundations, thus rendering them debatable, arguable, and contestable. See Braun (2003: 325–326 n. 32).

26 Roscoe (1996: 202–203) suggests, plausibly, that the *galli* were analogous to the Corybantes and Curetes, groups of ritual specialists who were considered dubious in terms of their piety but proficient as mental health specialists who were able to induce a temporary healing form of madness (*mania*) as a means of driving out deleterious psychological distresses.

References

Abbot, Elizabeth (1999). *A History of Celibacy*. Toronto: HarperCollins.

Beard, Mary (1980). "The Sexual Status of Vestal Virgins," *Journal of Roman Studies* 70: 12–27. https://doi.org/10.2307/299553

—— (1995). "Re-reading (Vestal) Virginity." In Richard Hawley and Barbara Levick (eds.), *Women in Antiquity: New Assessments*, 166–177. London: Routledge.

Bonner, Campbell (1902). "A Study of the Danaid Myth," *Harvard Studies in Classical Philology* 13: 129–173. https://doi.org/10.2307/310344

Bourdieu, Pierre (1980). *Le sens pratique*. Paris: Minuit.

Braun, Willi (2003). "Fugitives from Femininity: Greco-Roman Gender Ideology and the Limits of Early Christian Women's Emancipation." In D. B. Gowler et al. (eds.), *Fabrics of Discourse: Essays in Honor of Vernon K. Robbins*, 317–332. Harrisburg, PA: Trinity Press International.

Browe, Peter (1936). *Zur Geschichte der Entmannung. Eine religions- und rechtsgeschichtliche Studie*. Breslaw: Muller & Seiffert.

Brower, Gary R. (1996). "Ambivalent Bodies: Making Christian Eunuchs." Doctoral dissertation, Duke University, North Carolina.

Brown, Peter (1988). *The Body and Society: Men, Women and Sexual Renunciation in Early Christianity*. New York: Columbia University Press.

—— (1990). "Bodies and Minds: Sexuality and Renunciation in Early Christianity." In David M. Halperin, John J. Winkler and Froma I. Zeitlin (eds.), *Before Sexuality: The Construction of Erotic Experience in the Ancient Greek World*, 479–493. Princeton, NJ: Princeton University Press.

Burkert, Walter (1979). *Structure and History in Greek Mythology and Ritual*. Berkeley, CA: University of California Press.

Cancik-Lindemaier, H. (1996). "Priestly and Female Role in Roman Religion: The *Uirgines Vestae*," *Hyperboreus* 2: 138–150.

—— (1997). "Die Priesterinnen der Vesta." In Richard Faber and Susanne Lanwerd (eds.), *Kybele—Prophetin—Hexe: Religiöse Frauenbilder und Weiblichkeitskonzeptionen*, 109–125. Würzburg: Königshausen & Neumann.

Caner, Daniel F. (1997). "The Practice and Prohibition of Self-Castration in Early Christianity," *Vigiliae Christianae* 51: 396–415. https://doi.org/10.1163/157007297X00291

Casadio, Giovanni (2003). "The Failing Male God: Emasculation, Death, and Other Accidents in the Ancient Mediterranean World," *Numen* 50: 231–268. https://doi.org/10.1163/156852703322192400

Cordier, Pierre (2002). "*Tertium genus hominum*: L'étrange sexualité des castrats dans l'empire romain." In Philippe Moreau (ed.), *Corps romains*, 61–75. Grenoble: Jérôme Millon.

Cumont, Franz (1910). "Gallos," *RE* 13: 674–682.

Dumézil, Georges (1970). *Archaic Roman Religion*, 2 vols. Cambridge: Cambridge University.

Durkheim, Émile. (1915). *Elementary Forms of the Religious Life*. Joseph Ward Swain (trans.). London: Allen & Unwin. https://doi.org/10.2307/3405938

Föllinger, Sabine (1996). *Differenz und Gleichheit. Das Geschlechterverhältnis in der Sicht griechischer Philosophen des 4. bis 1. Jahrhunderts v. Chr*. Hermes Einzelschriften 74. Stuttgart: Franz Steiner.

Förster, Richard (ed.). (1893). *Scriptores physiognomonici Graeci et Latini*, 2 vols. Leipzig: Teubner.

Foucault, Michel (1978). *The History of Sexuality*, vol. 1. Robert Hurley (trans.). New York: Pantheon.

—— (1980). *Power/Knowledge: Selected Interviews & Other Writings 1972–1977*. C. Gordon (ed.). New York: Pantheon.

Frazer, James George (1906). *Adonis, Attis, Osiris: Studies in the History of Oriental Religion*. London: Macmillan.

Girard, René (1977). *Violence and the Sacred*. Baltimore, MD: Johns Hopkins University Press.

Gleason, Maud W. (1990). "The Semiotics of Gender: Physiognomy and Self-Fashioning in the Second Century CE." In David M. Halperin, John J. Winkler and Froma I. Zeitlin (eds.), *Before Sexuality: The Construction of Erotic Experience in the Ancient Greek World*, 389–415. Princeton, NJ: Princeton University Press.

—— (1995). *Making Men: Sophists and Self-Presentation in Ancient Rome*. Princeton, NJ: Princeton University Press.

Gold, Daniel (2005). "Celibacy." In Lindsay Jones (ed.), *Encyclopedia of Religion*, 2nd ed., 1474–1478. Detroit, MI: Macmillan.

Guyot, Peter (1980). *Eunuchen als Sklaven und Freigelassenen in der griechisch-römischen Antike*. Stuttgarter Beiträge zur Geschichte und Politik 14. Stuttgart: Klett-Cotta.

Hales, Shelley (2002). "Looking for Eunuchs: The Galli and Attis in Roman Art." In Shaun Tougher (ed.), *Eunuchs in Antiquity and Beyond*, 87–102. London: Classical Press of Wales and Duckworth.

Hester, J. D. (2005). "Eunuchs and the Postgender Jesus: Matthew 19 and Transgressive Sexualities," *Journal for the Study of the New Testament* 28: 13–40. https://doi.org/10.1177/0142064X05057772

Hommel, Hildebrecht (1972). "Vesta und die frührömische Religion," *Aufstieg und Niedergang der römischen Welt* 1.2: 397–427. https://doi.org/10.1515/9783110836417-018

Katz, Marilyn A. (1995). "Ideology and 'the Status of Women' in Ancient Greece." In Richard Hawley and Barbara Levick (eds.), *Women in Antiquity: New Assessments*, 21–43. New York & London: Routledge.

Keufler, Mathew (2001). *The Manly Eunuch: Masculinity, Gender Ambiguity, and Christian Ideology in Late Antiquity*. Chicago, IL: University of Chicago Press.

Koch, C. (1958). "Vesta," *RE* 16A: 1717–1776.

Lancellotti, Maria Grazia (2002). *Attis between Myth and History: King, Priest and God*. Religions in the Graeco-Roman World 149. Leiden: Brill.

Laqueur, Thomas (1990). *Making Sex: Body and Gender from the Greeks to Freud*. Cambridge, MA: Harvard University Press.

Lieber, Elinor (1996). "The Hippocratic *Airs, Waters, Places* on Cross-Dressing Eunuchs: 'Natural' yet also 'Divine'." In Renate Wittern and Pierre Pellegrin (eds.), *Medizin der Antike*, Bd. 1: *Hippokratische Medizin und antike Philosophie*, 451–476. Olms: Hildesheim.

Lightfoot, J. L. (2002). "Sacred Eunuchism in the Cult of the Syrian Goddess." In Shaun Tougher (ed.), *Eunuchs in Antiquity and Beyond*, 71–86. London: Classical Press of Wales and Duckworth.

Lloyd, G. E. R. (1964). "The Hot and the Cold, the Dry and the Wet in Greek Philosophy," *The Journal of Hellenic Studies* 84: 92–106. https://doi.org/10.2307/627697

MacMullen, Ramsay (1986). "What Difference Did Christianity Make?" *Historia* 35: 322–343.

Martin, Dale B. (1995). *The Corinthian Body*. New Haven, CT: Yale University Press.

—— (1997). "Paul without Passion: On Paul's Rejection of Desire in Sex and Marriage." In H. Moxnes (ed.), *Constructing Early Christian Families: Family as Social Reality and Metaphor*, 201–215. New York: Routledge.

Martin, Luther H. (1987). *Hellenistic Religions: An Introduction*. New York: Oxford University Press.

Martin, Luther H. and Panayotis Pachis (eds.). (2004). *Hellenisation, Empire and Globalisation: Lessons from Antiquity*. Thessaloniki: Vanias.

Martini, Maria Cristina (1997). "Charattere e struttura del sacerdozio delle Vestali: un approccio storico-religioso. Prima parte," *Latomus* 56: 246–263.

Masuzawa, Tomoko (2000). "Origin." In Willi Braun and Russell T. McCutcheon (eds.), *Guide to the Study of Religion*, 209–224. London: Cassell.

Mayhew, Robert (2004). *The Female in Aristotle's Biology: Reason or Rationalization*. Chicago, IL: University of Chicago Press. https://doi.org/10.7208/chicago/9780226512020.001.0001

Moxnes, Halvor (1997). "Conventional Values in the Hellenistic World: Masculinity." In Per Bilde et al. (eds.), *Conventional Values of the Hellenistic Greeks*, 263–284. Aarhus: Aarhus University Press.

Mustakallio, Katariina (1992). "The *crimen incesti* of the Vestal Virgins and the Prodigious Pestilence." In Tovio Viljamaa *et al.* (eds.), *Crudelitas: The Politics of Cruelty in the Ancient and Medieval World*, 56–62. MAev Sonderband 2. Krems.

Nock, Arthur Darby (1925). "Eunuchs in Ancient Religion," *Archiv für Religionswissenschaft* 23: 25–33.

Nussbaum, Martha C. (1994). *The Therapy of Desire: Theory and Practice in Hellenistic Ethics*. Princeton, NJ: Princeton University Press.

Parker, H. N. (2004). "Why Were the Vestals Virgins? On the Chastity of Women and the Safety of the Roman State," *American Journal of Philology* 125: 563–601. https://doi.org/10.1353/ajp.2005.0009

Parker, Robert (1983). *Miasma: Pollution and Purification in Early Greek Religion*. Oxford: Oxford University Press.

Penner, Hans H. (2008). "What a Difference Theory Makes." In Willi Braun and Russell T. McCutcheon (eds.), *Introducing Religion: Essays in Honor of Jonathan Z. Smith*, 418–433. London: Equinox.

Pomeroy, Sarah B. (1975). *Goddesses, Whores, Wives, and Slaves: Women in Classical Antiquity.* New York: Schocken.

Prowse, K. R. (1967). "The Vestal Circle," *Greece & Rome* 14: 174–187. https://doi.org/10.1017/S0017383500017228

Rawson, Elizabeth (1974). "Religion and Politics in the Late Second Century BC at Rome," *Phoenix* 28: 193–212. https://doi.org/10.2307/1087418

Richlin, Amy (1997). "Carrying Water in a Sieve: Class and the Body in Roman Women's Religion." In Karen Leigh King (ed.), *Women and Goddess Traditions in Antiquity and Today*, 330–375. Studies in Antiquity and Christianity. Minneapolis, MN: Fortress Press.

Riquet, Michel (1948). *La castration.* Paris: P. Lethielleux.

Roller, Lynn E. (1999). *In Search of God the Mother: The Cult of Anatolian Cybele.* Berkeley, CA: University of California Press.

Roscoe, Will (1996). "Priests of the Goddess: Gender Transgression in Ancient Religion," *History of Religions* 35: 195–230. https://doi.org/10.1086/463425

Rousselle, Aline (1988). *Porneia: On Desire and the Body in Antiquity.* F. Pheasant (trans.). Oxford: Blackwell.

—— (1992). "Body Politics in Ancient Rome." In Pauline Schmitt Pantel (ed.), *A History of Women in the West*, vol. 1: *From Ancient Goddesses to Christian Saints*, 296–336, 514–522. Cambridge, MA: Belnap Press of Harvard University Press.

Sanders, G. M. (1972). "Gallos," *Reallexikon für Antike und Christentum* 8: 984–1034.

Sassi, Maria Michela (2001). *The Science of Man in Ancient Greece.* Paul Tucker (trans.) Chicago, IL: University of Chicago Press.

Scholten, Helga (1995). *Der Eunuch in Kaisernähe: Zur politischen und sozialen Bedeutung des praepositus sacri cubiculi im 4. und 5. Jahrhundert n. Chr.* Frankfurt: P. Lang.

Scholz, Piotr O. (2001). *Eunuchs and Castrati: A Cultural History.* Shelley Frisch and John A. Broadwin (trans.). Princeton, NJ: Markus Wiener.

Sissa, Giulia (1990). *Greek Virginity.* Arthur Goldhammer (trans.). Cambridge, MA: Harvard University Press.

Spencer, F. Scott (1992). "The Ethiopian Eunuch and his Bible: A Social-Science Analysis," *Biblical Theology Bulletin: Journal of Bible and Culture* 22: 155–165. https://doi.org/10.1177/014610799202200403

Staples, Ariadne (1998). *From Good Goddess to Vestal Virgin: Sex and Category in Roman Religion.* London: Routledge.

Stevenson, Walter (1995). "The Rise of Eunuchs in Greco-Roman Antiquity," *Journal of the History of Sexuality* 5: 495–511.

Swain, Simon (ed.). (2007). *Seeing the Face, Seeing the Soul: Polemon's Physiognomy from Classical Antiquity to Medieval Islam.* New York: Oxford University Press.

Taylor, Gary (2000). *Castration: An Abbreviated History of Western Manhood.* London: Routledge.

Thompson, Joanne Elizabeth (2005). "Images of Vesta and the Vestal Virgins in Roman State Religion and Imperial Policy of the First and Second Centuries A.D." Doctoral dissertation, Yale University.

Tougher, Shaun (ed.). (2002). *Eunuchs in Antiquity and Beyond.* London: Classical Press of Wales & Duckworth.

Vermaseren, Maarten Jozef (1977). *Cybele and Attis, the Myth and the Cult.* London: Thames & Hudson.

Vernant, Jean-Pierre (1983). "Hestia—Hermes: The Religious Expression of Space and Movement in Ancient Greece." In Jean-Pierre Vernant, *Myth and Thought among the Greeks*, 127–175. London: Routledge.

Versnel, H. S. (1992). "The Festival for Bona Dea and the Thesmophoria," *Greece & Rome* 39: 31–55. https://doi.org/10.1017/S0017383500023974

Wildfang, Robin Lorsch (1999). "The Vestal Virgins' Ritual Function in Roman Religion," *Classica et Mediaevalia* 50: 227–234.

Wolf, Eric R. (1982). *Europe and the People Without History*. Berkeley, CA: University of California Press.

Worsfold, Thomas C. (1932). *The History of the Vestal Virgins of Rome*. London: Ride.

9

Physiotherapy of Femininity in Early Christianity: Ideology and Practice

> When it comes to history there is no quick fix. Not everything in the past can be redeemed.
> —Richard Kearney (2003: 189)

Prior to strong feminist readings of the early Christian writings we might say, with David Noble (1992), that these texts presented a "world without women." Although the presence of women, perhaps in great numbers, in early Christian associations and their writings was a matter of gratuitous recognition, this presence was not a subject of great interest and, therefore, not posed as a scholarly datum worth close scrutiny. Feminist criticism and historiography exposed the patriarchal ideological foundations of this scholarly disinterest and, upon returning to the archives of early Christianity with illumination from a searchlight powered by a "hermeneutic of suspicion," announced both a "eureka!" and an "alas!" The presumed discovery was that at least in their earliest stages the most progressive Jesus and Christ associations were excited over egalitarian social experiments, and, in keeping with experimental gender egalitarianism, did not merely tolerate women but assigned them status and function that were not derived from dominant Greco-Roman values and conventions concerning sex and gender (see the ground-breaking work of Schüssler Fiorenza 1984). Women were not just there; they were there creatively, effectively, and consequentially—and as women (see Jensen 1996: 5–30). Unfortunately, this discovery turned out to be but a sliver of silver lining on a dark androcentric cloud. And so the song of discovery was of course followed by a dirge of lament. The lament bemoaned the fact that the supposed originary golden moment of the recognition of women as full persons *qua* women was a marvelous, though an aberrant moment, at best an anomalous emancipatory blip that would be duly "corrected" in early Christian assimilating (re)turns toward dominant Greco-Roman gender ideologies and women-management practices.

One wonders, however, if some feminists' claim to have found in the cracks and beneath the early Christian textual corpus moments of women's liberation is, in the final analysis, not wishful thinking, a discovery that is not historical as much as mythographical, grounded in a desire for authoritative and authorizing precedents, for foremothers to contemporary women's struggles. For the purpose of provoking historiographical thought and meditation on early Christian liberationist rhetoric, I shall argue just so.

In doing so, however, I am both mindful of and grateful for feminist criticism, for it cogently and unignorably puts before us gender-related categories as powerful analytic and historiographic tools. Without those categories I would have neither words nor motive to read the early Christian texts with attention to issues and problems related to gender, femininity, and bodies. If I am not particularly interested in the search for foremothers (or forefathers, for that matter)—an easy game, after all, for anyone to play—that is not to say I am not interested in forms of ideological captivity, ideology criticism and ideology subversion, including the ideology of androcentrism. If I nonetheless find, as I do, that early Christianity was nearly without exception a world without women, it is by no means a finding that delights. Unfortunately history does not always present us with gifts that are beneficial and delightful—though it is possible, of course, by means of hermeneutical imagination and ingenuity, to conflate "believed-in imaginings" (Sarbin 1998) with history so as to make the latter coherent with our modern desires.

* * *

In all early Christian textual discourses the root problem with women is that they are female. This goes without saying for the most (in)famous New Testament texts that place women under male control, such as Matthew's women-absent households (Saldarini 2001; contra Wainwright 1998), but especially the so-called "household management codes" (see most convincingly Wagner 1994). But I want to claim this also for those early texts that *apparently* are, or at least have been *read as*, women-friendly—or, in Vernon Robbins's terms, that seemingly promote a woman-liberative ideology "in text" and "in interpretation" (Robbins 1996: chap. 6).

Thus first, for example, the gospel of Luke, ostensibly most visibly including women among the *dramatis personae* of its narrative and, therefore, not surprisingly frequently read as a "feminist" gospel, shows itself, on closer inspection, not to be such at all, certainly not unequivocally (Fander 1989; Davies 1991: 187; Corley 1993: 144–146; Seim 1994; Braun 1995: 76–80; Setzer 1997; for dissenting views see Arlandson 1997; Bieberstein 1998). I also do not take the view that Luke's easily demonstrable tendencies toward "masculinisation" (Seim 1994: 259) represent a "frauenfeindliche Redaktion" of a "frauenfreundliche Tradition" (Fander 1989: 309), for neither the gospel of Mark (Corley 1993: 83–107) nor the Sayings Gospel Q (Arnal 1997; cf. Levine 1990) puts before Luke traditions that are at odds with his masculinizing penchant.

Second, part of the return to an undifferentiated *primordium* that comes to expression in the *Gospel of Thomas* includes erasure of gender dimorphism. In accordance with this primordial ideal, itself a feature of Thomas's protological orientation (Davies 1992), "when male and female [are made] into a single one ... then you will enter [the kingdom]" (G. Thom. 22). The "single one," however, should be taken neither as an androgynous blend (Castelli 1991: 30–33)—a blend that neither Christians nor anyone else in Greco-Roman antiquity valorized, at least not in social terms—nor as an entirely genderless or sexless "one," for, as saying 114 shows, the "one" is imagined as masculine and women's salvation is contingent on "becoming male." This is all the more remarkable in light of saying 22:

> Jesus said to them, "When you make the two into one ... and when you make male and female into a single one, so that the male will not be male nor the female be female ... then you will enter [the kingdom]."

William Arnal (2005), commenting on this saying, rightly observes that "Thomas ... offers us a taxonomic anomaly ... in the form of the androgyne. The male-female division—the social taxonomy *par excellence*—is here contrasted with the kingdom, which is represented by the taxonomic anomaly *par excellence*, androgyny." That Thomas's "single one" is an androgyne is not evident to me, but that Thomas is interested in subverting the bipartite and value-hierarchical gender classification of "male" and "female" by imagining a re-constituted, sexually undifferentiated (primordial) "single one" is clear. When the female in saying 114 nonetheless appears as a male-resembling "living spirit" Thomas *apparently* reverts to a human-as-masculine sensibility, thus demonstrating the limits of even Thomas's subversive gender imagination.¹

Contrary to some interpretations of Paul, I cite him as a third example, though this is surely controversial and ideally requires extended exegesis and argument. Take the famous Galatian gender unification formula (Gal. 3:28), which, with its announcement that male and female are "one" "in Christ," "has been celebrated with enthusiasm as the cornerstone of early Christian egalitarianism, particularly within feminist exegesis" (Lieu 1994: 369). Closer inspection, however, shows that this enthusiasm is not warranted. The formula's rhetoric of female-male equality is not taken up in the remaining rhetoric of Galatians, as Judith Lieu notes (1994: 369–370).² Moreover, the Pauline "one" is much like Thomas's "one," though in Paul not so much with reference to a *primordium* as with reference to an *eschaton*. As Dennis MacDonald has demonstrated, it is the Greek masculine *heis*, rather than the gender-neutral *hen*, that expresses the gender quality of the Pauline "one." Gender hierarchy is here not levelled and the value distinction between male and female remains intact, though concealed in a three-letter pronoun. If we would argue, as Wayne Meeks (1973) and other do, but I most definitely do not, that the Galatian gender-unification formula reflects an androgynous ideal, it only suggests, in agreement with the *Gospel of Thomas*, that the female will be subsumed, indeed erased, within a masculine human ideal.³ Dennis MacDonald is right: "the androgyne myth is not antiquity's answer to androcentrism; it is but one manifestation of it." Androgyny "is reconstituted masculinity: the female must become male" (D. MacDonald 1988: 285). It is not surprising that when women come to Paul's extended attention (1 Cor. 11 and 14) they confront him as a problem for which he recommends solutions that display standard Greco-Roman fears about the dangers of femininity and that call for conventional strategies of control and containment (D. Martin 1995).

In post-Pauline Christian groups manliness (*vertu virile* or *andreia*) would come into its own as a preached value and performance, enjoined by early Christian men and frequently pursued by women themselves. The idea of the masculinization of the female in Christian salvation myths comes to repeated expression in some early Christian circles where salvation is envisioned as a return to "the unchangeable unborn state" (*Zostrianus* 130.24, in Robinson 1977) of male perfection: "Flee from the madness and the bondage of femininity, and choose for yourselves the salvation of masculinity" (*Zostrianus* 131.5-9). The aim is not to set rules for a men's club which bars women; rather, femaleness "is something that can enslave everyone, and its opposite, masculinity, does not appear to be a natural quality of males but a state that all must seek in order to be saved" (Wisse 1988: 301). Similar injunctions to flee from the horror of femininity toward the redemption of masculinity are scattered across other writings (see R. Smith 1988; Wisse 1988; generally, the essays in King 1988), often describing the therapy of humanity's gynopathology in fantasies, myths and metaphors of a phallic big bang: "Gnostics are trapped in a woman's parts and rescue comes down out of the sky as a logos-penis-snake with its potent and perfecting semen of salvation" (R. Smith 1988: 358; cf. Castelli 1988: 366). The famous sayings in the *Gospel of Thomas* are not exceptional in that they advocate erasure of gender dimorphism in the "single one" (22), not, however, by blending male and female into an androgynous one (Castelli 1991: 30-33) but, as the much-discussed saying 114 has it (Buckley 1985; Meyer 1985), by "becoming male" (cf. *Gospel of Mary*; Hennecke 1965: 1.342).

This notion that the company of the transformed, including its women members, must become wholly male is not limited, however, to so-called Gnostic circles. The "works of the female" appear elsewhere as a feared sign of unredeemed creation and humanity (Clement, *Strom*. 3.6.45.3; 3.9.63.1-2; citing the *Gospel of the Egyptians*). Clement of Alexandria, whose ideas of femininity and masculinity appear to be thoroughly steeped in dominant Greek cultural traditions within whose scope he attempts to make some allowance for female achievement of philosophic virtues (Irwin 1994), nonetheless capitulates to an androcentric measure of humanity in suggesting that women put off their feminine flesh that limits "the knowledge of those who are spiritual." Though "souls" are neither male nor female in Clement's view, he *does* suggest that the soul will have its day after marriage ceases when the perfection of the soul will emerge in manliness and "woman (will be) translated into a man" (*Strom*. 6.12.100).

Working with a masculated notion of piety, Christian writers throughout the first few centuries grudgingly admire women who transcend their femaleness and become, as Palladius says, "more like men than nature would seem to allow" (Palladius, *Historica Lausiaca*, Intro. 5; cited by Cloke 1995: 214). The same writer, speaking of Melania the Elder, compliments her with the epithet, *he anthropos tou theou*, strikingly combining a masculine noun with a feminine article, perhaps best translated as "the female man of God" (Cloke 1995: 214). Other writers, such as Tertullian, famous for his shuddering paranoia when it came to femaleness, could promise women as a reward "the self-same sex as man" (*On the Apparel of Women* 1.2). Similar sentiments of admiration and applause for the manly woman are expressed by many other Christian writers, including Gregory of Nyssa, Gregory of Nazianzus, John Chrysostom, Augustine and Jerome (Miles 1989: 53-77; Cloke 1995: 214-216). As ideals of monasticism and monastic institutions imposed themselves with increasing force in late antiquity and pre-modern Europe, monastic theory did allow the robust, celibate, monastic female considerable room in the superior moral spaces of pious masculinity of which the male monk was the normative embodiment (McNamara 1994: 6).

If the marks of Christian commitment and piety were frequently, if not normatively, measured in properties of maleness, one would naturally expect some Christian women to "seek wisdom like men" (Clement of Alexandria, *Strom.* 8.1.275). The options for women's pursuit of Christian piety "like men" varied in real life, but the variation was not so much along a sliding scale connecting the poles of femininity and masculinity, as it was in different ways of negotiating the complex and tricky connections between a robust, manly subjectivity and the female body. That is, risking "an exaggeration in the direction of the truth" (Smith 1992: 7), the ideal of manly piety had as the greatest obstacle to its pursuit affectations associated with femininity and the female body. The female body and its significations became the locus for the suppression and rejection of femininity as well as the site on which to work out the desire to become more manly. Hence, the pursuit of the religious life "like men" offered, on one end of a gamut of possibilities, the escape of femininity through renunciation of sex, marriage and networks of male social relationships that defined woman's status and roles, and, on the other end, more proactive strategies of bodily therapy toward masculinization. The entire range, however, represents the same desire to shuck the millstone of femaleness, of "escaping the feminine via the masculine" (Cloke 1995: 214-216). That is, sexual renunciation, exemplified especially in the "virgin of God" (Elm 1994), is sponsored by and reinforces androcentrism and patriarchy and, though ostensibly disrupting both, is a symptom of rather than salvation from androcentrism—"chastity as autonomy" (Burrus 1987) is a coy slogan that may represent a moment of "slippage" (Castelli 1991: 47; cf. Castelli 1986) in dominant gender conventions, but not a critical blow to patriarchy's hegemony (on hegemony see below).

* * *

It should be useful to dwell at greater length on one example of masculinized femininity, with some side glances at analogous literature and cultural practices, and then comment on the construction of manly femaleness with reference to ways in which Greco-Roman cultures thought of and fashioned bodies as "ideograms" (Brown 1990: 490) for the true—always gendered—self. The example concerns the Thecla narrative contained in the apocryphal *Acts of Paul* (Greek text in Lipsius 1972: 235-272; citations refer to section numbers in Hennecke 1965: 2.353-64). The *Acts of Thecla* records the story of a well-born young woman who, upon listening to Paul preach on the blessedness of "the bodies of virgins" (6), renounces her engagement to a leading Iconian aristocrat, Thamyris, and her family for an ascetic missionary life that will end up in a situation of martyrdom from which she is miraculously delivered. Thecla of course became the matronymic warrant for female ascetics and martyrs (Castelli 1990: 268), indeed, an incredibly versatile "mouthpiece" for many of the church fathers' orthodoxies (Pesthy 1996).

My intention here, however, is not to survey how Thecla was fondled by later Christian bishops, but to stay within the story itself and propose that it presents Thecla's conversion as a process of altering her "gender temperature" (Gleason 1990: 392), of her transformation from female to male by means of an "incorporating practice" (Connerton 1989: 72–104) that effects a therapy of the malady of femininity so as to re-corporate oneself and establish a manly *hexis*, a bodily state indicative of a being-condition as produced by incorporational practice, which I take as the individualized counterpart to Pierre Bourdieu's notion of the social *habitus*. In Bourdieu's terms: "L'hexis corporelle est la mythologie politique réalisée, *incorporée*, devenue disposition permanente, manière durable de se tenir, de parler, de marcher, et, par là, de *sentir* et de *penser*" (1980: 117; also 1998: 71). And, in Talal Asad's elaboration of Bourdieu's point: The human body is ... the *self-developable* means for a range of human objects—from styles of physical movement (for example, walking), through modes of emotional being (for example, composure), to kinds of spiritual expression (for example, mystical states) (Asad 1997: 47–48).

The story renders the transformation of Thecla from feminine to masculine in three interlinked movements. First, Thecla is introduced expectedly and familiarly in terms of her proprietary relationship to men, a relationship that cedes to men custodial rights over women and assumes that the latter are transferable property (Braun 1995: 76–78). Her fiancé Thamyris refers to her as "my Thecla" (8) and her mother likewise acknowledges that she (contractually) belongs to Thamyris, hence "thy Thecla" (9). Her conversion breaks this proprietary relationship and in due course her independence from men is stressed. On her journey to Antioch Paul corrects a mistaken impression that she belongs to him by saying "she is not mine" (26). Stereotypically male sexual possession moves are forcefully resisted by Thecla, most dramatically when she publicly humiliates the prominent Antiochene townsman Alexander (26). Of course, the story does insinuate that Thecla's desire to follow Paul is motivated by a romantic, perhaps erotic, interest in Paul (40), but this *topos* of the romance novel is not exploited in such a way that it counters the plot of Thecla's masculinization. Paul does not baptize her—the story clearly describes autobaptism (34, 40)—and she carries on missionary work independent of Paul and earns his respect as a colleague in the evangelistic enterprise (41). Thecla becomes her own "man," so to speak, and, though fondly linked to Paul, she does not work under his sponsorship or command.

Second, she crosses over the spacial boundaries that separated the sexes in Mediterranean antiquity (see Pomeroy 1975: 79–84; Burrus 1987: 68, 89). Initially the story depicts her in terms of her premarried virginal status and as someone, therefore, who is excluded from the *andreion* (men's room) of the family house so that she must eaves-drop on Paul's instructions from a window (7–9). As Virginia Burrus notes (1987: 89), Thecla's "stationary location inside the house" is a point of some emphasis in the story, and the fact that she must use stealth to sneak away at night to visit Paul, by now in prison for his dangerous subversion of the normal marriage rules, is marked as a transgression which, when discovered, leads to public outrage and Thecla's need to flee. In due course, however, she moves from the traditional female habitat of the household ghetto into the public (read: male) sphere and engages ably in the very male sports of challenge and riposte (26, 37) and gladiatorial combat (27–36).

The combat is depicted by means of the *topos* of the "fight with the beasts," common in martyrologies and other popular narratives where it usually serves the "rescue from danger" theme (D. MacDonald 1983: 22–23). Such is the case here too, but "the friendly lion" signals more: of interest is the narrator's remark that a lioness, trained to kill, becomes Thecla's protector and partner-in-arms against other voracious beasts (33). In the Greco-Roman physiognomic handbooks animals were used as an important analogy in gender identification and separation. According to Pseudo-Aristotle and other physiognomic theorists, the lion exhibits the male type in its most perfect form (Ps.-Aristotle, *Physiognomics* 809b). Later writers provide lengthy lists of the manly traits of the lion, analogically transferable to the ideal male human being: "of freeborn temperament, fiery, restrained, intelligent, kingly, a natural leader, statesmanlike, proud" (Vettius Valens; cited by Gleason 1990: 405 n. 60). The Roman physiognomist, Polemo of Laodicea (88–145 CE), further specifies that the lion is the exemplar of a species in which masculine qualities predominate in both males and females (Förster 1893: 1.194–198). That is, the lioness is an exemplar of masculinity despite being anatomically feminine (Gleason 1990: 405; 1995: 28–29; Cox Miller 1994: 198). Taking a measure of permission from the popularity of the physiognomic art of taking the body as a semiotic chart of gender identity, a popularity, expressed both in the visual and in the literary arts, that reached its height in the second century (Evans 1941, 1969; Krien 1955; Opeku 1979; Mason 1984; Kiilerich 1988; Raina 1989; Moxnes 1997: 271–272), i.e., within temporal proximity to the appearance of the Thecla narrative—whose framer evidently knew well the physiognomic conventions of the time (Bollók 1996; Bremmer 1996: 38–39)—we might take the story's depiction of the kinship between the lioness and Thecla as a symbolic transfer by literary means of the manly qualities from the one to the other. Thecla becomes a leonine human being. This move from the domestic privacy of woman's space to the public arena of man's space is further secured when, upon her successful combat against the animals, she becomes the leader of a retinue that includes an unspecified number of males (40). When she does finally return home (42–43), she is in all respects the opposite of the person who initially left the house. Indeed, as Johannes Vorster notes, upon her return to the family home, "Thecla fulfills the role of a man by supporting her mother" (Vorster 1995: 12).

Third, the story indirectly assumes, in a manner typical of ancient romance novels (Petropoulos 1995), that Thecla embodies the ideals of seductive feminine beauty when it notes that a leading man of Antioch takes her for a courtesan and falls in love with her. Not only does she decisively rebuff the male advance, but she takes measures to efface her beauty: she cuts off her hair (25). This is a gesture full of physiognomic significance that can be appreciated with a reference to a remark in Ps.-Athanasius's *Life of Syncletica* (5th century CE), where the female saint asked an elder to witness her discarding all her cosmetics and cutting off her own hair as a symbolic renunciation of a cosmologically and naturally required sign of female adornment (Castelli 1990: 271; cf. Castelli 1986: 76). Thecla then further annihilates the image of the beautiful female by means of a gesture of transvestism: "she sowed her *chiton* into a cloak after the fashion of men" (40).

The usual interpretation of this scene of transvestism goes back at least as far as the fifth century CE (Anson 1974: 3) and considers this not as an act of gender-crossing, but as a disguise for reasons of safety on the road or convenience of travelling attire (McGinn 1994) or as a surface-level "travesty" to prevent suspicion that her motives for following Paul might be "of a sexual nature" (Bremmer 1996: 45) or, somewhat more plausibly, as the donning of a "habit" that "served symbolically to dissuade men from initiating sexual advances" (Davies 1986: 104). In this case, however, these interpretation miss what is more fundamental; the story itself resists the notion of disguise as a protective measure, for Thecla is not travelling alone but in company of followers (40) that provides the protection that travelling single women might normally seek by means of disguise in men's dress. Nor ought one too quickly pass over the transvestism motif as an innocuous adoption of the Hagnodice legend in which a woman took on male disguise to enter the all-male Athenian medical college and eventually forced the Athenians to open the medical profession to freeborn women (Grant 1960: 176; cf. D. MacDonald 1983: 18–21)—a modern version of the legend best played out by Barbara Streisand as the "male" rabbinical student in the film *Yentl*. Though not denying that the Thecla story is an exemplar of the courageous woman who covertly enters the forbidden male domain with subversive intent, I take it as more than that. We should rather take the notice of transvestiture as a symbolic indicator that Thecla has entered not only spatial and social spheres of maleness, but also the bodily dimension of maleness. Or, as John Anson has correctly seen, "sexual disguise ... signalized and effected a transformation of self, the birth of a new identity, not only in the name of Christ but in the body as well" (1974: 11). In contrast to what was perhaps the dominant tendency of female Christian asceticism, where "maleness" was "projected inwards" so that no "male qualities may find an external expression" (Elm 1994: ix; see also Chadwick 1968: 121; Miles 1989: 53), Thecla's body is both an important locus and manifestation of her conversion. Her manly vesture signals her conversion to "the male norm," the "metamorphosis of a woman into a man," as Robert Doran rightly notes (1995: 149). Such a view certainly is in keeping with ancient physiognomical arguments that each class of creatures is marked by natural and stable *semeia*, as Aristotle calls them in his *Physiognomics*, by which to judge character, including gender, from physical appearance, bodily gestures and vestiture, to mention just some of the signs (Evans 1969; Gleason 1990; see further below).

In sum, Thecla's conversion entails a transformed self-definition and public persona in which femininity increasingly fades out to reveal a masculinized self. The metamorphosis takes her from male custody and control to manly independence, from the womanly space of the household enclosure to the public arenas of male discourse and politics, from female bodiliness to male bodiliness.

Side-glancing for a moment, female quests for the ideal of manly piety by means of transvestism and other incorporations of male physicalities is a frequent literary *topos* in the hagiographies of female saints (Delcourt 1961; Anson 1974; Patlagean 1976; Brock and Harvey 1987: 24-25; Vogt 1995; Abbot 1999: 71-79). To what degree a literary motif can be taken as evidence of social practice is a tricky decision. Fortunately we have some documentary evidence which indicates that female practices of sexual disguise out of desire for masculinization were carried on with enough strength to warrant conciliar anathemas and prohibitive legislation. In the fourth century the Council of Gangra in Asia Minor convened to condemn female tonsure and cross-dressing practiced by the followers of Eustathius of Sebaste—see especially canons 13 and 17 of the Council of Gangra (Yarbrough 1990: 453). The later Theodosian code (12.2.17) similarly prohibits female tonsure, suggesting that the forbidden practice was carried on (Vogt 1995: 147). Jerome expresses disdain for women who "change their garb and assume the mien of men, being ashamed of being what they were born to be—women. They cut off their hair and are not ashamed to look like eunuchs" (*Ep.* 22). The dismantling of femininity as a strategy for achieving Christian "holiness" thus should be regarded not merely as an idealist wish expressed as a literary motif in Christian hagiography but as women's actual incorporation (materialization) of andreic desires.

* * *

A look into the Greco-Roman theories and values concerning the interrelated issues of character, gender and bodies should provide us with perspective from which to appreciate Thecla and the manly woman type that she represents.

Virtue, excellence and other qualities by which to measure the human being along an axis of perfection-imperfection were not unisex—that is, equally attainable in male and female bodies—in Mediterranean antiquity. Excellence of character was bound to class, often also to ethnicity, and certainly to gender. Aristotle's argument (*Politics* 1277b20-23) that the highest possible level of female virtue does not exceed the level of mediocrity of male virtue generally reflects the dominant Greco-Roman gender ideology. Thomas Laqueur summarizes the sensibilities behind this view: "*man* is the measure of all things, and woman does not exist as an ontologically distinct category" (1990: 62). The philosophical tradition, especially the Aristotelian and Stoic trajectories, provided the metaphysical theory which the biological and medical scientists confirmed with their detailed analysis of human physiology: woman was an imperfect or incomplete male (Hanson 1990; Martin 1995: 3-37; Brown 1988: passim), a tradition that also found its proponents within early Christianity (e.g. Clement, *Paedagogus* 3.3). Laqueur demonstrates that according to ancient thinkers from Aristotle to the Hippocratics to Galen and Soranus the operative theory of human sexuality was not based on the modern (post-Enlightenment) "two-sex" model of male-female "dimorphism or "biological divergence" where a stress on "an anatomy and physiology of incommensurability" (Laqueur 1990: 6) has laid the ground for an anthropology in which man and woman are distinct categories of human being. Rather, the ancient beliefs that man is the measure of the human and the concomitant notion that "the standard of the human body and its representations is the male body" (Laqueur 1990: 62) were based on a theory of monosexuality—Laqueur calls it the "one-sex" model—"in which men and women were arrayed according to their degree of metaphysical perfection, their vital heat, along an axis whose telos was male" (Laqueur 1990: 5-6). Human bodies thus were not understood in terms of an unbridgeable dichotomy between male and female but in terms of a continuum running between poles of masculinity and femininity; each body contains both male and female aspects and "every human body, male or female, occupies some position on the spectrum male-female" (D. Martin 1995: 33).

In theory, then, the "one-sex" model of human being would seem to make possible the masculinization of the female just as it was possible to mold men to achieve greater levels of maleness (Galen, *De spermate* 1; Rousselle 1992: 328; Gleason 1990: 402-406). But the theory runs squarely against another dimension of ancient gender ideology: the hierarchy of the male-female continuum and the problem of female physiology that set firm limits on her masculinity. Female bodies, according to Hippocratic philosophical-medical theories, lacked the needed levels of dryness, heat, activeness, strength and solidity to achieve a male level of masculinity (Lloyd 1964). Although there was not complete agreement among the ancient physiologists on exactly how to take measure of a person's level of maleness or femaleness by means of temperature, humors and density of body mass, they were agreed that women's inferiority is firmly and "naturally" fixed, in one way or another, in the material apparatus of the body (D. Martin 1995: 32). Female physiology thus was the trap of women who aspired to manly heights of virtue and excellence either in philosophy or Christian piety.

Greco-Roman physiognomic "science," which has to do with the art of interpreting character from physiology and bodily characteristics, sheds some light on this. The basic principle behind the "science" is stated by Ps.-Aristotle in his *Physiognomonika* where he argues that a person's inner character and dispositions (*dianoiai*) follow bodily characteristics (*tois somasi*) and, conversely, that bodily characteristics and affectations appear in harmony with the affectations of the soul (*psyche*). Thus "in the creations of nature ... one can see how body and soul interact with each other" (805a). "It seems to me that soul and body react on each other; when the character of the soul changes, it changes also the form of the body, and conversely, when the form of the body changes, it changes the character of the soul" (808b). Aristotle thus contends that there is evidence of "some identity" (*homoia*) between inner character and outer bodyscape, an identity that makes it possible to draw "inferences from human surfaces to human depths" (Gleason 1990: 389). To aid the art of body-reading, physiognomic practitioners produced handbooks (Förster 1893; André 1981) that elaborate the theory and prescribe guidelines for deciphering true character from physiological "signs" and bodily surfaces (see Armstrong 1958; Barton 1994: 95-131; Cox Miller 1994: 196-199; Evans 1941, 1969; Gleason 1990, 1995).

Physiognomics also presented "itself as a tool for decoding the signs of gender" (Gleason 1990: 390-392). The second-century physiognomist Polemo states the basic idea:

> You may obtain physiognomic signs of masculinity and femininity from your subject's glance, movement and voice. Then, taking these signs, compare one with another until you are able to satisfy yourself on which of the two sexes prevails. For in the masculine something feminine will be found, and in the feminine something masculine, but the designation "masculine" or "feminine" should be used in accordance with which of the two (sexes) prevails. (Polemo, *Physiognomics* 2; Förster 1893: 1.192)

Not only does Polemo take for granted that maleness and femaleness are not exclusively located in anatomical males and females, but he assumes that it is possible to decipher the predominant gender type in any person, male or female. He goes on to restate these two assumptions and to relate, with evident reliance on Ps.-Aristotle (*Physiognomics* 809b–810a), a detailed list of the "signs" by which to tell the difference (Polemo, *Physiognomics* 2; Förster 1893: 1.192–194). What we have here, in effect, is a recipe for bodybuilding and body-decipherment that is of course wholly committed to the ideology of androcentrism. The entire structure of the physiognomies is built on the principle of opposites and contrasts in order to lay out a spectrum of body types in which the opposite poles are brilliantly evident. The positive type is beautiful, balanced, well-proportioned, solid, strong, majestically poised—the leonine male. The negative type is unattractive, unbalanced, ill-proportioned, flabby, weak, of shifty pose—the pantherine effeminate type most clearly displayed in female shape and bearing.

The location of bodies on the physiognomic spectrum corresponds to their embodiments of core Mediterranean values of virtue, honor and nobility just as body types correspond to a person's location on the social and political spectrum of power and influence. On this spectrum a range of "blessings" (education, rationality, virtue) that qualified people to be custodians (saviors) of the state (Dio, *Orations* 32.3) were firmly associated with the masculine ideal (Moxnes 1997: 273), just as both the literary and iconographic record indicates that the ideal of femininity was associated with "indoor" virtues such as demur modesty, guarding private morality in the domestic sphere and generally desisting from any provocative public displays (Houby-Nielsen 1997: 224; generally, Turner 1996: 120–121, 133–134). Bodies thus are not merely an image of society, as Marcel Mauss (1979 [1936]) and Mary Douglas (1970: 93–112) suggest, not merely a blank slate on which ideological values are etched for social show. Bodies, rather, are a modality by which ideology becomes material and body-being is both *representational* and *generative* of subjectivity in social *situ*, as recent revisionist meditations on the complex reciprocal interactions between body-self, gendered subjective self, and the wider body politic show (for example, Scheper-Hughes and Lock 1987; Connerton 1989: 72–104; McGuire 1990; Comaroff and Comaroff 1992: 69–91; Lock 1993; Asad 1997; Turner 1996 [1984], 1997; Warne 2000). In ancient Mediterranean societies (as in all societies) bodies do not merely *behave* ideologically or *symbolize* the values of the body politic; they *are* ideological constructs and body-selves and body practices both express and effect belief and compliance with those beliefs (Althusser 1994 [1970]: 127–28; Žižek 1994: 12–13). Bodies thus "matter" much more awesomely than we are used to think (Butler 1993: 31–36). Greco-Romans knew this and the physiognomies are reflective of and in collusion with all aspects of cultural discourse that sought to shape its bodies in theoretical conception, fashion their development by means of the educational system, maintain and control them by rhetorical force of praise or blame, then to let them loose in public practices and display that then, boomerang-fashion, generated the ideological foundation for those very same body cultivating procedures.

A culture that places such heavy burden of value on masculinity and so carefully constructs its bodies to display masculinity generates both motive and pressure for "physiognomical deception" (Gleason 1990: 406), that is, for manipulating and managing one's semiotic bodyscape as a way of concealing or obscuring negative physiognomic traits as a means of evading negative public judgments about oneself. Ancient observers were well aware of the physiognomic impostor (Gleason 1990: 406-11), the dissimulator who was able to conceal his "true character" by assiduously practiced deception (*studia et conversationes satis humana ingenia obscurant*, Förster 1893: 2.144; Dio, *Orations* 33.53-54; Diogenes Laertius 7.173). Conversely, practicing and projecting those traits that would lead the public assembly of body readers to infer the character one wished or thought oneself to be was a common technique, practiced especially by the rhetoricians (Evans 1969: 39-46; D. Martin 1995: 35), but also by sophists (Gleason 1995) and specialists in various divining arts (Barton 1994). It is the logic behind this that would seem to sponsor female tonsure and other gestures of male impersonation. In a culture that judges kind and quality of (gendered) character from its physiological cover one would expect females with aspirations to manliness to fashion their exterior surface into an "ideogram" of the man inside.

* * *

Returning to Thecla, we are entitled to ask: Should Thecla, standing in for other Christian female "men of God," be regarded as an example of heroic femaleness, as a proto-feminist "transvestite virgin with a cause" (Petropoulos 1995)? Or should she be viewed as someone whose masculinized self-identity as indicated by her manly physiognomic gestures is perhaps a pathetic result of an efficient, coercive androcentric cultural force, the product of a misogynist-ideological sex-change operation? A sample opinion poll of recent commentators on the Thecla story indicates that Thecla tends to be seen as a heroic example of women's liberation from patriarchal constraints. For Rosemary Ruether, Thecla is "an audacious role model for sweeping disobedience to the established order of family and state" (1979: 75). Virginia Burrus considers Thecla among the "heroic and defiant foresisters," a rare example to "us" that early Christianity was not exclusively a "man's affair" (1987: 108-109). Dennis MacDonald calls her "the archetypal liberated Christian woman" (1988: 291; cf. 1983: 53). For Johannes Vorster she is an emblem of "alternate personhood" in which "the androcentric component of the person" has been dismantled and replaced by a personhood that asserts "the power of womanhood" (1995: 11-12). It is not difficult to accept the language of heroism, archetype and liberation—the early Christian female man of God was heroic all right. Nor am I disapproving of citing foremothers (even some forefathers) to authorize one's own present desires; a self-serving appeal to ancestors and history is a deep motive in most if not all historiographies (Braun 1999: 8). Encomiums of Thecla therefore are understandable, but they are not all that interesting, if the aim and end of an analysis of the Thecla narrative is to claim her for "us" or against "them." This kind of historical reclamation is history turned into self-serving rhetoric.

If my reading of Thecla as a female-to-male conversion story is plausible, she takes flight from femininity so that masculinity and all the positive values attached to masculinity would "prevail," to use Polemo's term. Her aspiration for masculine piety, requiring disguise if not erasure of femininity, would seem to be a testament to the power of androcentric ideology that generally kept women in their place by full force of a web of efficient placement devices. The forceful and determined Theclas of early Christianity who managed to upstage the culturally required gender script by staging a transgressional gender act (see Halberstam 1998 on an analogous modern phenomenon) did succeed in crashing the male club, but their determined agency only reinvigorated the rules of the dominant game in town. Thecla heroism thus can be understood as an attempt at therapeutic agency that is at the same time a symptom of the structural malady of an ideology that would not accommodate femaleness. The very tough and interesting question posed by Thecla and her many named and unnamed like is how we will understand the social power relations that permit an emancipatory women's agency—Stevan Davies's (1986) argument that the Thecla story is part of a cycle of narratives that is expressive and generative of a "revolt of the widows" is entirely plausible—that regenerated and reinscribed a Christian culture which David Noble (1992) has described with only a little exaggeration as "a world without women." Or, to state the matter in the form of a question, what are the social and material conditions and the operational dynamics of ideology that makes it possible to regress into the same ideology from which Thecla (or any of us) sought to step out by transgressing it (Žižek 1994: 13)?

In Mediterranean antiquity all major "solutions" to the "female problem" in the end merely demonstrate the problem more sharply. They proved not to be solutions at all, and even the most transgressional agitation by early Christian women proved to be not so much serious blow to the hegemony[4] of androcentrism as a fugitive move that, though subversively aimed, furtively collaborated with that hegemony.[5]

* * *

Implied in the statement concerning the hegemony of androcentrism is the claim that early Christianity reflects and participates, even further sanctifies, the regnant, therefore hegemonic, Greco-Roman gender ideology, which pathologized femaleness at many levels, and linked theories on the pathology (Warne 2000: 141) of femaleness to strategies of containing and controlling women. Let me briefly outline aspects at the level of theory (see also pp. 130–131 above):

At the level of conceptualizing and remodeling the architecture of the cosmos in the late Hellenistic period, two interlinked problems emerge (see L. Martin

1987). One concerns the perceived emigration of the gods, once resident among humans in earthly temple and sacred place, to the super-lunar regions of the cosmic sphere. Not only did this leave humans to fend for themselves in the chancy muck of life under the moon, but it left them vulnerable to the *stoicheia*, the demonic powers that patrolled the sub-lunar regions. The other is the recasting of the older concept of *Agatha Tyche*—a notion that sees Fate at worst as benign and at best as a principle of sympathetic providential care—into *Heimarmene*, an understanding of Fate as a capricious, oppressive feminine principle that manifested itself especially in the incarcerating malevolence and maliciousness of the sub-lunar powers that separated earthy humanity from the ethereal gods. It is in this intellectual matrix that we see the emergence of the various theologies of male saviors, theologies which incipiently understand "salvation" in gendered terms: "femaleness" represents the highest abstraction of the tyranny of this-worldly, material human existence; "maleness" represents the *telos* on the path to salvation. The Christian version of this view comes to exquisitely clear expression in the following:

> A strange and new star arose doing away with the old astral decree, shining with a new unearthly light, which revolved on a new path of salvation, as the Lord himself, men's guide, who came down to earth to transfer from Fate [*heimarmene*] to his providence those who believed in Christ. (Clement, *Ex.Theod.* 74.2)

It is not a huge leap from imagining the perceived cosmic conflict as a gender war to identifying femaleness as part of the parcel of human deficiencies that require divine cure and, pending that, placement in male sanitizing and sanitational custody.

A second theoretical pillar undergirding Greco-Roman gender ideology was constructed in the laboratories of research and thought on human physiology (elaborated above). It is not hard to see that, according to Polemo's logic, persons with a female physiology would be hard-pressed to convince anyone that their true or "prevailing" character was anything other than commensurate with their physiognomic signs. That is, the game was rigged. Women's bodies would always convey that they were deficient precisely in those character qualities that would most ennoble them as full human beings because those character qualities were precisely those qualities that were physiologically represented in male bodies.

This whole theoretical package, entirely committed to *andreia* (manliness) as the divinely and naturally ordained nobility of human being, was forcefully represented and reproduced in a host of everyday *arts de faire* and conventions—from schooling, to public discourse and rhetoric, to philosophy, to all kinds of gender-coded and gender-signifying domestic and public spaces and proprieties. The "totality" of Greco-Roman culture was univocal: humans with female bodies represented humans of deficient personhood. It is this "totality" which, in my view, easily explains Christian and other women's desire to achieve manliness of piety and character, just as it is entirely evident to me that the pursuit and occasional achievement of female manliness is, in the final instance, nothing but a poignant capitulation to the ideology of *andreia* rather than a fatal rupture of its hegemony.

* * *

If all this is cogent, our work has really only begun. Among the difficult questions that my provocation surely raises, I will simply identify two. The first is formulated in down-to-earth terms: if early Christian groups reflected, assimilated and "baptized" prevailing gender ideologies, how do we account for the claim (and, perhaps, the fact), as old as Celsus, that Christianity was particularly appealing to women? Allow me to answer this by means of two items of rhetorical mischief. One mischief: how do we *know*—or why do we *think*—that Christianity *was* appealing to women, that they joined Christian associations because they were *attractive to women*? How do we know that women joined Christian groups independently, as intentional agentive actors, with autonomous motives? Another mischief: I find all kinds of evidence that tells me Christian women wanted to "seek wisdom like men" (Clement, *Strom.* 8.1.275). I have yet to find even one example of a Christian man (or any Greco-Roman man) who set out to "seek wisdom like women."

The second question is a theoretical one that I will attempt to answer here in modest outline: how will we understand the social power relations that permit an emancipatory women's agency that in its very agency, and in the form that such agency took, regenerated and reinscribed a Christian culture "without women"? Or, what are the social and material conditions and the operational dynamics of ideology that make it possible to regress into the same ideology which one wants to oppose or escape by transgressing it? This is the true intellectual and political challenge that we owe to feminist criticism, a challenge that has not been frontally appreciated in scholarship on the "Frauenproblem" in early Christianities.

As I have noted, insomuch as early Christian women's "salvation" discourse troped women as men, its resistant mood, even its intentional stance, was in effect more fugitive than subversive, more flight from femininity than fight against androcentric conceptions of salvation and social structures. Though most evidently so in the case of the female ascetic superstar, "the female man of God," the male-managed superwife similarly conceded femininity as a pathology that must be, if not cured, contained by the protective embrace of a male-savior ideology. This should not be understood as a specious indictment of early Christian women's feeble or unimaginative emancipatory agency. Rather, it requires recognition of the systematic process of repression that sets (as it usually does—take global capitalism as the current example) the limits of emancipatory agency.

Thus, in opposition to some theories of agency that posit the person, conceptualized as an autonomous self with both knowledge of and access to its own mental states and free agentive motives (i.e., the myth of the "just do it" modern self), let's regard "person" as a bound(ed) actor. Persons "do act, but they do so under circumstances not of their own choosing. Actors do define, and redefine, situations, but there are structural limits on what can be accomplished and changed in this way" (Fuchs 2001b: 24).[6] In terms of power to compel the quality of the world-as-represented and the world-as-lived—one should reckon with incommensurateness between the two, *ceteris paribus*—the structural repressive forces of a given cultural totality will impair the determinative capacity of individual, even small-scale collectivities of actors whose moods and motives are contrary to the cultural totality. Agency is a variable, not a natural (or essential) opposite, in relation to the determinative capacities of the social structures in a given time and culture. This, as Stephan Fuchs argues, "suggests modesty about persons" (2001b: 29); it commends regarding "person" and "agent" as second-order attributions, as "the outcome, not the origin or source, of certain kinds of cultural work" (2001b: 30). With respect to gender (or any social construction), the potency and effect of emancipatory-liberative agency would expectedly diminish the more "total" the cultural constraints, supervisory regimes, conventions, values are in a specific historical, cultural complex.[7] The early Christian female fugitives from femininity are then not so much a puzzle as a transparent *exemplum* of a severely unbalanced power ratio on the agency/structure continuum, since, as I have argued, Greco-Roman gender structures indeed were a *hegemoneia* that allowed for little elbow room either for nonhierarchical gender ideologies and practices or for a nonpathological view of femininity.

This is not to say, of course, that there could not have been some micro-situations (spousal units, small households, for example) in early Christian circles in which nonhierarchical gender experiments were conducted, and in which women's femininity was a point of little worry (see the rich data in Jensen 1996), nor to deny that women "had enormous power in the construction of a new religious movement" (M. MacDonald 1996: 46; see also 2005). As a *prevailing generality*, however, the ostensibly emancipatory, liberative strand of discourse on women was assimilated into the rhetoric and social reality of manly piety, where it typically displayed herself, not in historically brilliantly-visible liberationist gender experiments, but in the genre of hagiography and martyrology of unwomanish heroism by which the emergent Christian androcracy consolidated itself more effectively (see especially Dupriez 1982). The emergent and increasingly consolidated Christian androcracy is the analytical ground zero for explaining the hegemonic context and limp effects of early Christian liberationist ideological rhetorics.

Notes

1. See Arnal (2005: 24 n. 34) for a demonstration of the peculiar gender-mixed grammar in saying 114, "where Mary has been transformed into a male even in the grammar of the sentence."
2. See also Cohen (1998: 142–143): "Paul did not really believe that there was no longer male and female in Christ. Paul believed that men and women had separate functions in the new order, as in the old, and that the place of women was decidedly below that of men ... 'There is no longer male and female' seems to have been a rhetorical outburst (or, as is usually argued, a pre-Pauline formula, nothing more." Cohen cites 1 Cor. 11:7, 14:34-35, Rom. 10:12 and 1 Cor. 12:13 (where the latter two passages make reference to the Jew-Greek and slave-free distinction without adding the male–female clause that appears—singularly in Paul—in Gal. 3:28).
3. Although the figure of the androgyne was used as an instrumental anomaly for thinking about, even agitating against, the bipartite classification of human beings

(see, for example, Plato, *Symposium* 189E-192E; commentary by Lincoln 1989: 166-167), it appears never to have become a "potent weapon" that "anomalous entities can become," if taken up by "the right hands ... and under the right circumstances" (Lincoln 1989: 170).

4   The use of "hegemony" is deliberate, and used in the general sense of Antonio Gramsci, who elaborated this old term, which he took over from early Russian Marxism (for a history of "hegemony" see Joseph 2002), into a key concept in his sociopolitical theory. Thus Gramsci's oft-cited formulation: "Previously germinated ideologies become 'party', come into conflict and confrontation, *until only one of them, or at least a single combination, tends to prevail*, gaining the upper hand and propagating itself throughout society. It thereby achieves not only a unison of economic and political aims, but also intellectual and moral unity, posing all questions over which the struggle rages not on a corporate but on a *universal plane*. It thus creates the hegemony of a foundational social group over a series of subordinate groups" (Gramsci 1971: 181-182; emphasis added). Since the term is not generally part of the lexicon of biblical scholars, several explicatory comments should be useful: "By 'hegemony' Gramsci seems to mean a sociopolitical situation ... in which the philosophy and practice of a society fuse or are in equilibrium; an order in which a certain way of life and thought is dominant, in which one concept of reality is diffused throughout society in all its institutional and private manifestations, informing with its spirit all taste, morality, customs, religious and social principles, and all social relations ... An element of direction and control, not necessarily conscious, is implied" (Williams 1960: 587). "[H]egemony is a ruling class's (or alliance's) domination of subordinate classes and groups through the elaboration and penetration of ideology (ideas and assumptions) into their common sense and everyday practice; it is the systematic ... engineering of mass consent to the established order. No hard and fast line can be drawn between the mechanisms of hegemony and the mechanisms of coercion" (Gitlin 1980: 253). For further exegesis and explication of the Gramscian concept of hegemony see, for example, Bates 1975; Femia 1975; Mouffe 1979; Buci-Glucksmann 1982; Sassoon 1982; Berlinerblau 2001: 339-341. The assist that Gramsci offers for my purposes is to differentiate between ideology and hegemony. The difference is not *in* their aims, for ideologies agonistically aim for *hegemoneia*, but in the *achievement* of their aims along a spectrum between relatively sectoral (discretely "corporate") interests and the diffusion of those interests so as to achieve domination "on a universal plane," a "plane" that consists of a unity of material, social, and ideational dimensions, a unity that "can and must" (Gramsci 1971: 181) extract the consent (see especially Buci-Glucksmann 1982), paradoxically, even of parties possessed of ideologies that are apparently contrary to the *imperium* of an hegemony. Hegemonies thus may be thought of as the universal (in a given sociopolitical formation) lexicon and grammar that sets the possibilities and rules for the ideological assertions of a particular group. Hegemony, when truly hegemonistic, works mutely and invisibly; ideology is audible (argued) and open to visible contestation (Comaroff and Comaroff 1992: 29).

5   The logic of this collaboration, even if displayed by an apparently non-collaborative, subversive ideological rhetoric, is entailed in Gramsci's view of the conditions of the possibility of an hegemony, namely the effect of the hegemonic process to persuade, by forcible and consensual mechanisms, groups dominated and victimized by the hegemony to become collaborators in their own domination (see Berlinerblau 2001: 339 and n. 59).

6   See also Fuchs (2001a: 103): "As opposed to essentialism and agency metaphysics, the sociological problem is not free will, but variable amounts of elbow room and

discretion granted by various structures." This statement represents a point on a Marxian trajectory in which the "subject" is not the individual self but society which is the individual's "precondition" and which the individual assimilates—though, as Marx grants, this constructed and constrained (or interpolated, in Althusserian terms) self may apprehend itself as outside "the totality" by means of a speculative attitude which, however, should not be regarded as convertible to an ability to change the world by dint of individualistic agency (see Marx 1972 [1932]; Althusser 1994 [1970]; Vilar 1985). On the relation between ideas and the material and social world-as-lived see Arnal and Braun (2003).

7   See also the characterization and comparison of power in the "agentive mode" (ideology) and power in the "nonagentive mode" (hegemony) proposed by John and Jean Comaroff (1992: 28–31). Agentive power "appears as the (relative) ability of human beings to shape the lives of others by exerting control of the production, circulation, and consumption of signs and objects, over the making of subjectivities and realities" (28). Nonagentive power "immerses itself in the forms of everyday life, forms the direct human perceptions and practices along conventional pathways ... [It] saturates such things as aesthetics and ethics, built form and bodily representation, medical knowledge and material production. And its effects are internalized—in their negative guise, as constraints; in their neutral guise, as conventions; in their positive guise, as values" (28). Nonagentive (structural) power is the largely mute and invisible envelope, the hegemonic totality, in which agentive power has some elbow room to display itself in audible and visible ideological contests and rhetorics. Cf. Duby (1985) for a programmatic proposal for studying ideologies social-historically.

References

Abbott, Elizabeth (1999). *A History of Celibacy*. Toronto: HarperCollins Canada.

Althusser, Louis (1994) [1970]. "Ideology and Ideological State Apparatuses (Notes Towards an Investigation)." In Slavoj Žižek (ed.), *Mapping Ideology*, 100–140. London: Verso.

André, Jacques (ed. and trans.) (1981). *Anonyme Latin: Traité de physiognomonie*. Paris: Collection des Universités de France.

Anson, John (1974). "The Female Transvestite in Early Monasticism: The Origin and Development of a Motif," *Viator* 5: 1–32. https://doi.org/10.1484/J.VIATOR.2.301617

Armstrong, A. MacC (1958). "The Methods of the Greek Physiognomists," *Greece & Rome* 5: 52–56.

Arnal, William E. (1997). "Gendered Couplets in Q and Legal Formulations: From Rhetoric to Social History," *Journal of Biblical Literature* 116: 75–94. https://doi.org/10.1017/S0017383500014996

—— (2005). "The Rhetoric of Social Construction: Language and Society in the Gospel of Thomas." In Willi Braun (ed.), *Persuasion and Performance: Rhetoric and Reality in Early Christian Discourses*, 27–47. Studies in Christianity and Judaism / Études sur le christianisme et le judaïsme. Waterloo: Wilfrid Laurier University Press.

Arnal William E. and Willi Braun (2003). "Social Formation and Mythmaking: Theses on Key Terms." In Ron Cameron and Merrill Miller (eds.), *Redescribing Christian Origins*, 459–468. SBL Symposium Series. Atlanta, GA: Society of Biblical Literature; Leiden: Brill.

Asad, Talal (1997). "Remarks on the Anthropology of the Body." In Sarah Coakley (ed.), *Religion and the Body*, 42–52. Cambridge Studies in Religious Traditions 8. Cambridge: Cambridge University Press.

Barton, Tamsyn S. (1994). *Power and Knowledge: Astrology, Physiognomics, and Medicine under the Roman Empire*. Ann Arbor, MI: University of Michigan Press. https://doi.org/10.3998/mpub.13320

Bates, Thomas R. (1975). "Gramsci and the Theory of Hegemony," *Journal of the History of Ideas* 36: 351–366. https://doi.org/10.2307/2708933

Berlinerblau, Jacques (2001). "Toward a Sociology of Heresy, Orthodoxy, and Doxa," *History of Religions* 40: 327–351. https://doi.org/10.1086/463647

Bieberstein, Sabine (1998). *Verschwiegene Jüngerinnen—Vergessene Zeuginnen. Gebrochene Konzepte im Lukasevangelium*. Novum Testamentum et Orbis Antiquus, 38. Göttingen: Vandenhoeck & Ruprecht. https://doi.org/10.13109/9783666539381

Bollók, János (1996). The Description of Paul in the Acta Pauli." In Jan N. Bremmer (ed.), *The Apocryphal Acts of Paul and Thecla*, 1–15. Studies on the Apocryphal Acts of the Apostles. Kampen: Kok Pharos.

Bourdieu, Pierre (1980). *Le sens pratique*. Paris: Minuit.

—— (1998). *La domination masculine*. Paris: Seuil.

Braun, Willi (1995). *Feasting and Social Rhetoric in Luke 14*. Society for New Testament Studies Monograph Series, 85. Cambridge: Cambridge University Press. https://doi.org/10.1017/CBO9780511520303

—— (1999). "Amnesia in the Production of (Christian) History," *Bulletin of the Council of Societies for the Study of Religion* 28(1): 3–8.

Bremmer, Jan N (1996). "Magic, Martyrdom and Women's Liberation in the Acts of Paul and Thecla." In Jan N. Bremmer (ed.), *The Apocryphal Acts of Paul and Thecla*, 36–59. Studies on the Apocryphal Acts of the Apostles. Kampen: Kok Pharos.

Brock, Sebastian P. and Susan Ashbrook Harvey (eds.) (1987). *Holy Women of the Syrian Orient*. Berkeley, CA: University of California Press.

Brown, Peter (1988). *The Body and Society: Men, Women, and Sexual Renunciation in Early Christianity*. New York: Columbian University Press.

—— (1990). "Bodies and Minds: Sexuality and Renunciation in early Christianity." In David M. Halperin, John J. Winkler and Froma I. Zeitlin (eds.), *Before Sexuality: The Construction of Erotic Experience in the Ancient Greek World*, 479–493. Princeton, NJ: Princeton University Press.

Buci-Glucksmann, Christine (1982). "Hegemony and Consent: A Political Strategy." In Anne Showstack Sassoon (ed.), *Approaches to Gramsci*, 116–126. London: Writers and Readers Publishing Cooperative.

Buckley, Jorunn Jacobsen (1985). "An Interpretation of Logion 114 in *The Gospel of Thomas*," *Novum Testamentum* 27: 245–272. https://doi.org/10.1163/156853685X00355

Burrus, Virginia (1987). *Chastity as Autonomy: Women in the Stories of the Apocryphal Acts*. Studies in Women and Religion 23. Lewiston, NY: Edwin Mellen.

Butler, Judith (1993). *Bodies that Matter: On the Discursive Limits of "Sex."* New York: Routledge.

Castelli, Elizabeth A. (1986). "Virginity and Its Meaning for Women's Sexuality in Early Christianity." *Journal of Feminist Studies in Religion* 2: 61–88.

—— (1988). "Response to 'Sex Education in Gnostic Schools' by Richard Smith." In Karen L. King (ed.), *Images of the Feminine in Gnosticism*, 361–66. Studies in Antiquity and Christianity. Philadelphia, PA: Fortress Press.

—— (1990). "Pseudo-Athanasius: The life and activity of the holy and blessed teacher of Syncletica." In Vincent L. Wimbush (ed.), *Ascetic Behavior in Greco-Roman Antiquity: A Sourcebook*, 265–311. Studies in Antiquity and Christianity. Minneapolis, MN: Fortress Press.

——— (1991). "'I Will Make Mary Male': Pieties of the Body and Gender Transformation of Christian Women in Late Antiquity." In Julia Epstein and Kristina Straub (eds.), *Body Guards: The Cultural Politics of Gender Ambiguity*, 29–49. New York: Routledge.
Chadwick, Owen (1968). *Western Asceticism*. Philadelphia, PA: Westminster.
Cloke, Gillian (1995). *"This Female Man of God": Women and Spiritual Power in the Patristic Age, AD 350–450*. London: Routledge. https://doi.org/10.4324/9780203422540
Cohen, Shaye J. D. (1998). "Why Aren't Jewish Women Circumcised?" In Maria Wyke (ed.), *Gender and the Body in the Ancient Mediterranean*, 136–154. London: Blackwell.
Comaroff, John and Jean Comaroff (1992). *Ethnography and the Historical Imagination*. Studies in the Ethnographic Imagination. Boulder, CO: Westview.
Connerton, Paul (1989). *How Societies Remember*. Themes in the Social Sciences. Cambridge: Cambridge University Press. https://doi.org/10.1017/CBO9780511628061
Corley, Kathleen E. (1993). *Private Women, Public Meals: Social Conflict in the Synoptic Tradition*. Peabody, MA: Hendrickson.
Cox Miller, Patricia (1994). *Dreams in Late Antiquity: Studies in the Imagination of a Culture*. Princeton, NJ: Princeton University Press.
Davies, Stevan L. (1986). *The Revolt of the Widows: The Social World of the Apocryphal Acts*. Carbondale, IL: Southern Illinois University Press.
——— (1991). "Women in the Third Gospel and the New Testament Apocrypha." In Amy-Jill Levine (ed.), *"Women Like This": New Perspectives on Jewish Women in the Greco-Roman World*, 185–198. Atlanta, GA: Scholars Press.
——— (1992). "The Christology and Protology of the Gospel of Thomas," *Journal of Biblical Literature* 111: 663–682. https://doi.org/10.2307/3267438
Delcourt, Marie (1961). "Female Saints in Masculine Clothing." In *Hermaphrodite: Myths and Rites of the Bisexual Figure in Classical Antiquity*, 84–102. Translated by Jennifer Nicholson. London: Studio Books.
Doran, Robert (1995). *Birth of a Worldview: Early Christianity in Its Jewish and Pagan Context*. Boulder, CO: Westview.
Douglas, Mary (1970). *Natural Symbols: Explorations in Cosmology*. Harmondsworth: Penguin.
Duby, Georges (1985). "Ideologies in Social History." David Denby (trans.). In Jacques Le Goff and Pierre Nora (eds.), *Constructing the Past: Essays in Historical Methodology*, 151–165. Cambridge: Cambridge University Press.
Dupriez, Flore (1982). *La condition féminine et les Pères de l'Église latine*. Montreal: Éditions Paulines.
Elm, Susanna (1994). *Virgins of God: The Making of Asceticism in Late Antiquity*. Oxford: Clarendon.
Evans, Elizabeth C. (1941). "The Study of Physiognomy in the Second Century AD," *Transactions of the American Philological Association* 72: 96–108. https://doi.org/10.2307/283044
——— (1969). *Physiognomics in the Ancient World*. Transactions of the American Philosophical Society, 59, 5. Philadelphia, PA: The American Philosophical Society. https://doi.org/10.2307/1006011
Fander, M. (1989). "Und ihnen kamen diese Worte vor wie leeres Geschwätz, und sie glaubten ihnen nicht" (Lk 24,11): feministische Bibellektüre des Neuen Testaments. Eine Reflektion. In C. Schaumberger and M. Maasssen (eds.), *Handbuch feministischer Theologie*, 299–311. 3rd ed. Münster: Aschendorff.
Femia, Joseph (1975). "Hegemony and Consciousness in the Thought of Antonio Gramsci," *Political Studies* 23: 29–48. https://doi.org/10.1111/j.1467-9248.1975.tb00044.x
Förster, Richard (ed.) (1893). *Scriptores physiognomonici Graeci et Latini*. 2 vols. Leipzig: Teubner.

Fuchs, Stephan. (2001a). *Against Essentialism: A Theory of Culture and Society*. Cambridge, MA: Harvard University Press. https://doi.org/10.1111/0735-2751.00126
—— (2001b). "Beyond Agency," *Sociological Theory* 19: 24–40.
Gitlin, Todd (1980). *The Whole World Is Watching: Mass Media in the Making and Unmaking of the New Left*. Berkeley, CA: University of California Press.
Gleason, Maud W. (1990). "The Semiotics of Gender: Physiognomy and Self-fashioning in the Second Century CE." In David M. Halperin, John J. Winkler and Froma I. Zeitlin (eds.), *Before Sexuality: The Construction of Erotic Experience in the Ancient Greek World*, 389–415. Princeton, NJ: Princeton University Press.
—— (1995). *Making Men: Sophists and Self-Presentation in Ancient Rome*. Princeton, NJ: Princeton University Press.
Gramsci, Antonio (1971). *Selections from the Prison Notebooks of Antonio Gramsci*. Quintin Hoare and Geoffrey Nowell Smith (ed. and trans.). New York: International Publishers.
Grant, Mary (ed. and trans.) (1960). *The Myths of Hyginus*. University of Kansas Humanistic Studies 34. Lawrence, KS: University of Kansas Press.
Halberstam, Judith (1998). *Female Masculinity*. Durham, NC: Duke University Press.
Hanson, Ann Ellis (1990). "The Medical Writers' Woman." In David M. Halperin, John J. Winkler and Froma I. Zeitlin (eds.), *Before Sexuality: The Construction of Erotic Experience in the Ancient Greek World*, 309–337. Princeton, NJ: Princeton University Press.
Hennecke, Edgar (1965). *The New Testament Apocrypha*, 2 vols. Wilhelm Schneemelcher (ed.) and R. McL. Wilson (trans.). Philadelphia, PA: Westminster.
Houby-Nielsen, Sanne (1997). "Grave Gifts, Women, and Conventional Values in Hellenistic Athens." In Per Bilde, Troels Engberg-Pedersen, Lise Hannestad and Jan Zahle (eds.), *Conventional Values of the Hellenistic Greeks*, 220–262. Studies in Hellenistic Civilization 8. Aarhus, Denmark: Aarhus University Press.
Irwin, Eleanor M. (1994). "Clement of Alexandria: Instructions on How Women Should Live." In Wendy E. Helleman (ed.), *Hellenization Revisited: Shaping a Christian Response Within the Greco-Roman World*, 395–407. New York: University Press of America.
Jensen, Anne (1996). *God's Confident Daughters: Early Christianity and the Liberation of Women*. O. C. Dean, Jr. (trans.). Kampen: Kok Pharos.
Joseph, Jonathan (2002). *Hegemony: A Realist Analysis*. New York: Routledge. https://doi.org/10.4324/9780203166529
Kearney, Richard (2003). *Strangers, Gods and Monsters: Interpreting Otherness*. New York: Routledge.
Kiilerich, Bente (1988). "Physiognomics and the Iconography of Alexander." *Symbolae Osloenses* 63: 5–28. https://doi.org/10.1080/00397678808590814
King, Karen L. (ed.) (1988). *Images of the Feminine in Gnosticism*. Studies in Antiquity and Christianity. Philadelphia, PA: Fortress Press.
Krien, G. (1955). "Der Ausdruck der antiken Theatermasken nach Angaben im Pollux-Katalog und in der pseudo-aristotelischen Physiognomik." *Jahreshefte*, 84–117. Vienna: Österreichisches archäologisches Institut.
Laqueur, Thomas W. (1990). *Making Sex: Body and Gender from the Greeks to Freud*. Cambridge, MA: Harvard University Press.
Levine, Amy-Jill (1990). "Who Is Catering the Q Affair? Feminist Observations on a Q Paranaesis," *Semeia* 50: 145–161.
Lieu, Judith (1994). "Circumcision, Women and Salvation," *New Testament Studies* 40: 358–370. https://doi.org/10.1017/S0028688500012613
Lincoln, Bruce (1989). *Discourse and the Construction of Society: Comparative Studies in Myth, Ritual, and Classification*. New York: Oxford University Press.

Lipsius, Richard A. (1972). *Acta Apostolorum Apocrypha*. Hildesheim and New York: Georg Olms.

Lloyd, G. E. R. (1964). "The Hot and the Cold, the Dry and the Wet in Greek Philosophy," *Journal of Hellenic Studies* 84: 92–106. https://doi.org/10.2307/627697

Lock, Margaret (1993). "Cultivating the Body: Anthropology and Epistemologies of Bodily Practice and Knowledge," *Annual Review of Anthropology* 22: 133–155. https://doi.org/10.1146/annurev.an.22.100193.001025

MacDonald, Dennis Ronald (1983). *The Legend and the Apostle: The Battle for Paul in Story and Canon*. Philadelphia, PA: Westminster.

—— (1988). "Corinthian Veils and Gnostic Androgynes." In Karen L. King (ed.), *Images of the Feminine in Gnosticism*, 276–296. Studies in Antiquity and Christianity. Philadelphia, PA: Fortress Press.

MacDonald, Margaret Y. (1996). *Early Christian Women and Pagan Opinion: The Power of the Hysterical Woman*. Cambridge: Cambridge University Press. https://doi.org/10.1017/CBO9780511520549

—— (2005). "Can Nympha Rule this House? The Rhetoric of Domesticity in Colossians." In Willi Braun (ed.), *Persuasion and Performance: Rhetoric and Reality in Early Christian Discourses*, 99–120. Studies in Christianity and Judaism / Études sur le christianisme et le judaïsme. Waterloo: Wilfrid Laurier University Press.

Martin, Dale B. (1995). *The Corinthian Body*. New Haven, CT: Yale University Press.

Martin, Luther H. (1987). *Hellenistic Religions: An Introduction*. New York: Oxford University Press.

Marx, Karl (1972) [1932]. "The German Ideology." In Robert C. Tucker (ed.), *The Marx-Engels Reader*, 146–200. New York: W. W. Norton.

Mason, Hugh J. (1984). "Physiognomy in Apuleius' *Metamorphoses* 2.2," *Classical Philology* 79: 307–309. https://doi.org/10.1086/366883

Mauss, Marcel (1979) [1936]. "Body Techniques." In *Sociology and Psychology: Essays*, 95–123. Ben Brewster (trans.). London: Routledge & Kegan Paul. https://doi.org/10.2307/3032558

McGinn, Sheila E. (1994). "The Acts of Thecla." In Elisabeth Schüssler Fiorenza (ed.) *Searching the Scriptures*, Vol. 2: *A Feminist Ecumenical Commentary and Translation*, 800–828. New York: Crossroads.

McGuire, Meredith B. (1990). "Religion and the Body: Rematerializing the Human Body in the Social Sciences of Religion," *Journal for the Scientific Study of Religion* 29: 283–296. https://doi.org/10.2307/1386459

McNamara, Jo Ann (1994). "The *Herrenfrage*: The Restructuring of the Gender System, 1050–1150." In Clare A. Lees (ed.), *Medieval Masculinities: Regarding Men in the Middle Ages*, 3–29. Minneapolis, MN: University of Minnesota Press.

Meeks, Wayne A. (1973). "The Image of the Androgyne: Some Uses of a Symbol in Earliest Christianity," *History of Religions* 13: 165–208. https://doi.org/10.1086/462701

Meyer, Marvin W. (1985). "Making Mary Male: The Categories of 'Male' and 'Female' in the Gospel of Thomas," *New Testament Studies* 31: 554–570. https://doi.org/10.1017/S002868850001208X

Miles, Margaret R. (1989). *Carnal Knowing: Female Nakedness and Religious Meaning in the Christian West*. Boston, MA: Beacon.

Mouffe, Chantal (1979). "Hegemony and Ideology in Gramsci." In Chantal Mouffe (ed.), *Gramsci and Marxist Theory*, 168–204. London: Routledge.

Moxnes, Halvor (1997). "Conventional Values in the Hellenistic World: Masculinity." In Per Bilde, Troels Engberg-Pedersen, Lise Hannestad and Jan Zahle (eds.), *Conventional*

Values of the Hellenistic Greeks, 263–284. Studies in Hellenistic Civilization 8. Aarhus, Denmark: Aarhus University Press.
Noble, David (1992). *A World Without Women: The Christian Clerical Culture of Western Science.* Oxford: Oxford University Press.
Opeku, F. (1979). "Physiognomy in Apuleius." In Carl Deroux (ed.), *Studies in Latin Literature and Roman History*. Brussels: Latomus revue d'études latines.
Patlagean, Evelyne (1976). "L'histoire de la femme déguisée en moine et l'évolution de la sainteté féminine à Byzance," *Studi Medievale* 3(17): 593–623.
Pesthy, Monika (1996). "Thecla Among the Fathers of the Church." In Jan N. Bremmer (ed.), *The Apocryphal Acts of Paul and Thecla*, 164–178. Studies on the Apocryphal Acts of the Apostles. Kampen: Kok Pharos.
Petropoulos, John C. B. (1995). "Transvestite Virgin With a Cause: The Acta Pauli and Theclae and Late Antique Proto-'Feminism'." In Brit Berggreen and Nanno Marinatos (eds.), *Greece & Gender*, 125–139. Papers from the Norwegian Institute at Athens 2. Bergen: Norwegian Institute at Athens.
Pomeroy, Sarah B. (1975). *Goddesses, Whores, Wives, and Slaves: Women in Classical Antiquity*. New York: Schocken.
Raina, G. (1989). "Il versimile in Menandro e nella fisiognomica." In Diego Lanza and Oddone Longo (eds.), *Il meraviglioso e il verisimile: Tra antichità e medioevo*, 173–185. Biblioteca dell'"Archivum Romanicum," I.221. Florence: L. S. Olschki.
Robbins, Vernon K. (1996). *The Tapestry of Early Christian Discourse: Rhetoric, Society and Ideology*. London and New York: Routledge.
Robinson, James M. (ed.) (1977). *The Nag Hammadi Library in English*. San Francisco, CA: Harper & Row.
Rousselle, Aline (1992). "Body Politics in Ancient Rome." In Pauline Schmitt Pantel (ed.), *A History of Women in the West*, vol. 1: *From Ancient Goddesses to Christian Saints*, 296–336, 514–22. Arthur Goldhammer (trans.). Cambridge, MA: Belnap Press of Harvard University Press.
Ruether, Rosemary Radford (1979). "Mothers of the Church: Ascetic Women in the Late Patristic Age." In Rosemary Radford Ruether and Eleanor McLaughlin (eds.), *Women of Spirit: Female Leadership in the Jewish and Christian Traditions*, 71–98. New York: Simon & Schuster.
Saldarini, Anthony J. (2001). "Absent Women in Matthew's Households." In Amy-Jill Levine (ed.), *A Feminist Companion to Matthew*, 157–70. Sheffield: Sheffield Academic Press.
Sarbin, T. H. (1998). "Believed-in Imaginings: A Narrative Approach." In J. de Rivera and T. H. Sarbin (eds.), *Believed-in Imaginings: The Narrative Construction of Reality*, 15–30. Washington, DC: American Psychological Association. https://doi.org/10.1037/10303-001
Sassoon, Anne Showstack (1982). "Hegemony, War of Position and Political Intervention." In Anne Showstack Sassoon (ed.), *Approaches to Gramsci*, 94–115. London: Writers and Readers Publishing Cooperative.
Scheper-Hughes, N. and Margaret M. Lock (1987). "The Mindful Body: A Prolegomena to Future Work in Medical Anthropology," *Medical Anthropology Quarterly* N.S. 1: 6–41. https://doi.org/10.1525/maq.1987.1.1.02a00020
Schüssler Fiorenza, Elizabeth (1984). *In Memory of Her: A Feminist Theological Reconstruction of Christian Origins*. New York: Crossroad. https://doi.org/10.1017/S0360966900033120
Seim, T. K. (1994). *The Double Message: Patterns of Gender in Luke-Acts*. Edinburgh: T. & T. Clark.
Setzer, C. (1997). "Excellent Women: Female Witnesses to the Resurrection," *Journal of Biblical Literature* 116: 259–272. https://doi.org/10.2307/3266223

Smith, Jonathan Z. (1992). Differential Equations: On Constructing the "Other." Thirteenth Annual University Lecture in Religion, Department of Religious Studies, Arizona State University.

Smith, Richard (1988). "Sex Education in Gnostic Schools." In Karen L. King (ed.), *Images of the Feminine in Gnosticism*, 345–360. Studies in Antiquity and Christianity. Philadelphia, PA: Fortress Press.

Turner, Bryan S. (1996) [1984]. *The Body and Society: Explorations in Social Theory*. 2nd ed. London: Sage.

—— (1997). "The Body in Western Society: Social Theory and Its Perspectives." In Sarah Coakley (ed.), *Religion and the Body*, 15–41. Cambridge Studies in Religious Traditions 8. Cambridge: Cambridge University Press.

Vilar, Pierre (1985). "Constructing Marxist History." Ian Patterson (trans.). In Jacques Le Goff and Pierre Nora (eds.), *Constructing the Past: Essays in Historical Methodology*, 47–80. Cambridge: Cambridge University Press.

Vogt, Kari (1995). "'The Woman Monk': A Theme in Byzantine Hagiography." In Brit Berggreen and Nanno Marinatos (eds.), *Greece & Gender*, 141–148. Papers from the Norwegian Institute at Athens 2. Bergen: Norwegian Institute at Athens.

Vorster, Johannes N. (1995). "Constructing Culture Through the Construction of Person." Paper, London Conference on the Rhetorical Analysis of Scripture, July 1995.

Wagner, Ulrike (1994). *Die Ordnung des "Hauses Gottes." Der Ort von Frauen in der Ekklesiologie und Ethik der Pastoralbriefe*. Wissenschaftliche Untersuchungen zum Neuen Testament, 2. Reihe, 65. Tübingen: J. C. B. Mohr (Paul Siebeck).

Wainwright, Elaine M. (1998). *Shall We Look For Another? A Feminist Rereading of the Matthean Jesus*. Maryknoll, NY: Orbis.

Warne, Randi R. (2000). "Gender." In Willi Braun and Russell T. McCutcheon (eds.), *Guide to the Study of Religion*, 140–154. New York: Cassell.

Williams, Gwyn A. (1960). "The Concept of 'Egemonia' in the Thought of Antonio Gramsci: Some Notes on Interpretation," *Journal of the History of Ideas* 21: 586–599. https://doi.org/10.2307/2708106

Wisse, Frederik (1988). "Flee Femininity: Antifemininity in Gnostic Texts and the Question of Social Milieu." In Karen L. King (ed.), *Images of the Feminine in Gnosticism*, 297–307. Studies in Antiquity and Christianity. Philadelphia, PA: Fortress Press.

Yarbrough, Larry (1990). "Canons from the Council of Gangra." In Vincent L. Wimbush (ed.), *Ascetic Behavior in Greco-Roman Antiquity: A Sourcebook*, 448–455. Studies in Antiquity and Christianity. Minneapolis, MN: Fortress Press.

Žižek, Slavoj (1994). "The Spectre of Ideology." In Slavoj Žižek (ed.), *Mapping Ideology*, 1–33. London: Verso.

10

"Our Religion Compels Us to Make a Distinction": Prolegomena on Meals and Social Formation

> Das Mahl *ist* das Gemeinschaftsleben. [The meal is communal life.]
> —Matthias Klinghardt (1996: 524)

Introduction

Consumptive and commensal practices of social groups have long been recognized as "a highly condensed social fact" (Appadurai 1981: 494)[1] that presupposes a range of socio-economic realities (modes of production, relations of commodity exchange, relative wealth and poverty, and the like) and signifies, usually in a ritual performative manner,[2] essential aspects of social relations (rank, rivalry, status, intimacy, estrangement) and identities. Anthropologists and sociologists interested in collective social identity thus have studied meal practices and food ways as an *entreé* to a specified group's sense of itself within, and in distinction to, a larger cultural matrix and to infer social values and relations within the group. Take the following claim as representative:

> In all societies, both simple and complex, eating is the primary way of initiating and maintaining human relationships ... Once the anthropologist finds out where, when, and with whom the food is eaten, just about everything else can be inferred about the relations among the society's members ... To know what, where, how, when and with whom people eat is to know the character of their society. (Farb and Armelagos 1980: 4)[3]

These social-scientific studies on food as socially symbolic and meals as social structuration performances offer resources for a conceptual framework both for ordering the historical data and for explaining this data in ways that illuminate the dynamics and processes by which early Christian associations attempted to work out their marks of distinction on the Greco-Roman social landscapes.

The density, variety and apparent importance of eating and food-related interests in the early Christian sources is one of their remarkable features. Feeding and feasting stories, alimentary concerns and exchange, food metaphors and symbols, and issues of food preparation pervade the Jesus traditions and narratives. The Pauline epistolary literature indicates that the dining room (place), social dining (ritual), and commensal and consumptive metaphors (myth) were core mechanisms in the self-identifying efforts of early Christian associations in the urban centers of the Roman East. The author of the Acts of the Apostles idealizes the unity of the early church by drawing attention to its common eating and food distribution practices. Much of the later literary sources too indicate that Christians evidently identified themselves socially and religiously by means of "differential equations" (Smith 2004: 230–250) that refer to rules of inclusion and exclusion from table fellowship.

Matthias Klinghardt and Dennis Smith have recently devoted substantial monographs to the proposition, both expanding on and correcting earlier scholarship, that early Christian meal practices were not inventions *ex nihilo* (Klinghardt 1996: 1–19; 2003; Smith 2003a, 2003b).[4] Theoretically this means that Christian meal practices do not have a monogenetic origin in, say, the putatively historical last supper of Jesus or in the Jewish Passover tradition, nor are they to be placed on a simple and unilinear trajectory that stretches from Jesus' last supper to the Christian Eucharist. Methodologically this means, as Klinghardt has suggested, that the relations between Christian meals and non-Christian meals in antiquity are not to be imagined in terms of "the categories of dependence and derivation" but in terms of "participation in a larger and encompassing [meal] tradition" (2003: 3; see also Klinghardt 1996).[5] Both Klinghardt and Smith thus assume, heuristically at least, that there was a single "form"[6] or "ideal type"[7] of meal, a form which Smith simply calls the "Greco-Roman banquet" and Klinghardt identifies as the "symposium," which are not really different forms, only different names for an "ideal type" on which Smith and Klinghardt also concur in general. This form served as the rudimentary phenomenological template for all Greco-Roman communal meal practices. Christian meal practices thus were not categorically different but only different in "accentuation and focus," to use Klinghardt's words (2003: 1).

Let us then take for granted that early Christians invented nothing from nothing in general and, therefore, that their banqueting traditions and practices were formally, procedurally and ideologically convergent or divergent variants of a range of Greco-Roman "matter-of-fact"[8] commensal habits that gravitated around a standard form and a culturally shared semiotic index.[9] That is, the work of Klinghardt and Smith (to which one could add others), has established a proper point of departure for the next wave of research into the commensal practices of early Christians—a point of departure that has enabled both to produce major works of very useful redescriptions of early Christian banquet practices.

Typology of Form or Form of Typology?

Note, however, that both Klinghardt and Smith have produced a typology that consists of a single type. Although I am all in favor of reductionism as a valuable second-order analytic virtue (Sperber 1996: 5–6), our chances of thickly describing and robustly explaining early Christian commensal practices may not be helped by a "single type" typology, if such a thing in fact makes any sense at all in terms of typology making. This leads me to ask if we can, at least should try to, come up with a typology of commensality that is *operationally more useful*, that is, a typology that will take us forward not only in our attempts to describe early Christianity in social terms, but especially, and more so, in our *analytic* efforts.

A first and tentative reply to the question is a basic supposition, roughly one articulated by the anthropologist Eric Wolf, who writes as follows:

> In the rough-and-tumble of social interaction, groups are known to *exploit the ambiguity of inherited forms* [and, I should add, of "matter-of-fact" forms that are widely diffused as the way we do things], to *impart new evaluations or valences on them*, to *borrow forms* [and I should add, to alter forms so as to make them] *more expressive of their interest*, or to *create wholly new forms* to answer to changed circumstances. Furthermore, if we think of such interactions not as causative it its own terms but as *responsive to larger economic and political forces*, the explanation of cultural forms must take account of that larger context, that wider field of force. A "culture" [and, I would add, a discrete cultural practice such as banqueting] is thus *better seen as a series of processes that construct, reconstruct, and dismantle cultural materials [e.g., the ideal type banquet], in response to identifiable determinants.* (Wolf 1982: 287 emphasis; added)

What I take from Wolf's theoretical capsule is a fancy for typing the Greco-Roman banquet in reverse, so to speak. Rather than thinking, that is, about a typology of commensal forms, much less a single form, we might think instead about the form of our typology. I suggest this lest our study of the Christian banquet traditions gets washed into the homogeneous stew of Greco-Roman banquets so as to leave us in the rather unremarkable position of saying that "Christians were simply following a pattern found throughout their world" (Smith 2003a: 279).[10] I suggest this, too, because it would bring into the foreground not so much the "ideal type"—which has, in any case, been described adequately enough already—but what Matthias Klinghardt refers to as the differences in "accentuation and focus."

It is not too difficult to work out various morphologies with respect to early Christian dining performances. We could, for example, fret about "accentuations" and "foci" with a view toward differentiating, describing, and explaining them. We might be able to go about this if we take certain morphological cues from key terms in Wolf's description of "rough-and-tumble social interaction" and the exploitation of inherited or generally diffused social forms in these interactions. Thus, for example, what are the "ambiguities" in the typical form of the Greco-Roman meal? Exactly how, if at all, did various Christian groups "exploit" them? Of what special interests where these exploitations, alterations, or adaptations "expressive"? To what forces in the larger contextual "field of force" were they responsive? Can we identify specific "determinants"?

The general sentiment of these questions may be clarified with a morphology of early Christian (and general Greco-Roman) dinner practices that takes instruction from a recent essay by the French sociologist Claude Grignon (2001).[11] Grignon's work focuses on the evolution of French food habits and semiotics and thus he develops a typology with reference to data that obviously is quite removed from our period. This does not matter, however, for I am interested in his conceptual and methodological moves.[12] Grignon's aim is to "outline a reasoned inventory of commensal types" (2001: 25). Important to note is that his types are not a morphological index of meal structures, but of commensal groups—because, he argues, "commensality is a result and a manifestation of a pre-existing group" (2001: 24). In short, Grignon begins not with the form of the meal itself, but with "the diversity of commensal types," a diversity which "is itself a consequence of the great diversity of ... groups" (2001: 24) that make up society, groups that can be categorized by any of a number of different classificatory regimes: age, gender, status, kinship, lineage, ethnicity, voluntary associations, special purpose groups, and the like. Grignon does not trouble himself with the notion of "group" itself, on how groups are made, what the determinants of groupness are, on why some sustain themselves while others have a short shelf life.[13] He simply notes that society consists of a large diversity of groups, however classified, and that groups avail themselves of existing social forms to signify themselves and distinguish themselves from other groups who are also making use of the same social forms. All this needs to be worked out, and there is no shortage of conceptual and ethnographic help if we are inclined to do so, but here I simply stress that Grignon's starting point re-poses our approach to meals. Rather than asking about the *morphology of meals*, our leading question concerns the *morphology of groups*.[14] Rather than asking what do *meals* do, we might ask what specific *groups* do with meals. Rather than pursuing *commensal forms* we might try to identify *commensal interests*.

This list of "rathers" should not be considered as oppositional pairs, of course, but merely as a way of staking out the angle from which approach the problem of classifying Greco-Roman meals and the marks of "distinction"[15] that we might adduce for Christian meals *qua* Greco-Roman meals.

Grignon proposes three paired types of commensality based on his loosely described "social morphology." The pairs are: domestic, institutional; everyday, exceptional; and segregative, transgressive.[16] Several generalizations on this morphology follow:

First, Grignon's stress on commensal groups and meals as a group instrumentalities brings into acute focus *hierarchies and competitiveness* between and within groups in the social whole and allows us to focus on how commensality procedures and rituals are mechanisms both for generating and reinscribing competitive edge, however measured.[17] The late John D'Arms pointed out some time ago that "our chances of penetrating Roman convivial realities will improve if we discard the notion of equality altogether" (1990: 314). Though he was commenting on Roman élite banquets, over against which one might put Greek table-fellowship and its putative aims of "friend-making" (the friend-making of the table; *Mor.* 612D), as Plutarch puts it, or as a ritual of *isonomia*, the friendly and egalitarian aspects of the Greek tradition of commensality are best not exaggerated.[18] Arguably, the old Greek notion of *isonomia*, symbolized chiefly by the distribution of equal portions in civic banquets, was limited to the civic élite and restricted to citizens for their political purposes in the archaic and classical city (Rundin 1996).[19] In the Hellenistic *polis*, and no doubt in part under the influence of *Romanitas* and its more undisguised hierarchical social values, commensal practices served, in the words of Richard Gordon, "to register and naturalise the inequalities of the social system" (1990: 229), as the Dutch scholar Onno van Nijf has recently demonstrated again in his work on professional associations in the

Roman East (1997: 149–152).[20] When we put into the foreground of our inquisition the hierarchical values of Roman society and the stratifying strategies and tactics that groups therein employed,[21] several topics related to commensality come into view as needing more work, both in terms of researching the evidence and worrying about conceptual precision.

Second, we know that social meals, whether Christian or not, neither cooked nor served themselves. Both were performed generally by what John D'Arms calls "the human props" (1991: 171) in ancient domestic and non-domestic dining venues, i.e., slaves, who by and large continue to remain invisible in scholarship on early Christian meals even though by some estimates there were six million slaves in the Roman empire of the Principate—with who-knows-how-many in Christian households (Scheidel 1997). Especially in light of the work by Jennifer Glancy on the obstacles to slaves' participation in the Corinthian Christian association (Glancy 1998, 2002) we perhaps ought to adduce as much evidence as we have—and there is not much from the early period, I suspect[22]—and see what a focus on the slave allows us to learn (or plausibly imagine) about early Christian banquets.[23] For example, Pedar Foss makes the following summary statement on slaves and banquets: "While slaves were accepted as part of the banquet's course and (sometimes) admired for their entertainment, they were simultaneously segregated from the real camaraderie of the meal. In a sense, they were performing puppets, subject to derision, degradation, abuse and punishment" (Foss 1994: 54).[24] It remains a task still to examine if Christian meals demonstrated a difference in this regard, whether in nuance or in focus.

Third, hierarchy was heavily gendered. Although gender and early Christian commensality has been brought into relation in scholarship, more work remains to be done, both in light of some recent revisionist classical scholarship on women's commensality in the Greco-Roman world[25] and in light of an increasingly clear picture of voluntary associations. It seems to me that when it comes to early Christian meals, as in other topics as well, we have been somewhat too seduced by the metaphorics of egalitarianism and fictive families (imagined too often as happy modern families), metaphorics which, by idealizing, camouflage the social realities, perhaps even deliberately deconspicuate them so as thereby precisely to leave them be and/or reinforce them. I am suggesting that we can do better than we have done on issues of intramural hierarchies in the Christian meal scene and—just as importantly—on clarifying if and how at least some Christian meal practices cut against the grain of the more general Roman meal/food practices as a way of signifying and reinforcing non-egalitarian social regimes.

Fourth, there is the underworked topic of commensality as a stratifying practice in the relatively recent and intriguing argument by John Riggs in his study of food in the *Didache* (1995; cf. 1984). Riggs argues for a trajectory that goes from the "table-sharing of Jesus" to a form of cultic activity (the eucharist) that places food in the custody of the patriarchal control of the bishop. I am not much taken by his trajectory but *do* think that his suggestion of a connection between the development of the mono-episcopate, "the growth of patriarchy" and "power over food" in early Christianities deserves our serious consideration in the form of careful study (1995: 275–283; see also Bobertz (1993).[26] A focus on food, resource management and early Christian alimentary distributive schemes will assist our study of meals to contribute more broadly to the wider effort to (re)describe the early history of Christianity. In addition, it may be in examining Riggs' provocation that we could find a plausible scholarly narrative on the development of the relatively foodless eucharist.

Fifth, when we think of meals it is common both in popular and in scholarly thought to stress the inclusionary aspect of commensality, the bonding effects of meals, meals as instrumental in the formation of *communitas*.[27] Grignon helps us to reposition our imagination with his category of "segregative commensality," which, he argues, is "likely to be found in hierarchised and discontinues societies, those in which hierarchisation is the very principle of structure and social life, and where this hierarchisation goes with social heterogeneity and repulsion, which render the distances between social universes impassable and the very idea of passing across them unthinkable" (Grignon 2001: 29). In such social contexts, commensality tends to "approve and express discontinuities that separate human groups"; and "to meet for eating and drinking is a way to set up or to restore the group by closing it, a way to assert or to strengthen a 'We' by pointing out and rejecting, as symbols of otherness, the 'not We', strangers, rivals, enemies, superiors, or inferiors. From this point of view, to include means first of all to exclude, to invite [means] to avoid" (2001: 28–29). One is reminded here of the Pompeian graffito, "The man with whom I do not dine is a barbarian to me."[28] One could cite many explicit or implied instances of this from the early Christian material. A good example comes from the *Clementine Homilies*:

> [W]e do not live with all indiscriminately; nor do we take our food from the same table as Gentiles, inasmuch as we cannot eat along with them, because they live impurely. But when we have persuaded them to have true thoughts, and to follow a right course of action, and have baptized them with a thrice blessed invocation, then we dwell with them. For not even if it were our father, or mother, or wife, or child, or brother, or any other one having a claim by nature on our affection, can we venture to take our meals with him; for our religion compels us to make a distinction. Do not, therefore, regard it as an insult if your son does not take his food along with you, until you come to have the same opinions and adopt the same course of conduct as he follows. (*Clementine Homilies* 13.4; ANF 8)[29]

Looking at this (and other instances) as an example of segregative commensality may achieve a usefully different regard for the conviviality of social dining (perhaps, what Smith calls "festive joy"), a theme that is usually prominent in studies of early Christian meals. In Grignon's social-theoretical view, however, we should not confuse commensality with conviviality (or joy, for that matter) (2001: 24, 29). They are related, of course, but the latter is the result of the former, and in commensalities that are identifiably driven by segregative motives, the euphoria that comes from eating together may be at least as much the result of the pleasure gained from those who are delectably absent, not invited, than from those who are present:

> The attention attracted by this in-group conviviality (and academic analyses generally do not fail to provide it) must not allow us to forget that the group shows itself so freely to itself only because it is out of sight of strangers—that part of the memorable pleasure that the participants get from the meeting is due to the feeling of the deprivation of "others" (who do not even know "what they are missing"). (Grignon 2001: 29)[30]

And as John F. Donahue has pointed out:

> the segregative model would seem to fit especially well with those meals eaten by the many *collegia* of the Roman world. Comprised of free men and/or slaves and commonly centered around a specific deity or trade, the *collegium* met a strong desire for exclusivity in Roman society among the lower orders ... allowing them to imitate in many ways the social and administrative organization of the larger society. (Donahue 2003: 432–433)

There is not space here to consider all the implications and possibilities this notion of segregative commensality, but it does offer both corrective and constructive potential, if only to highlight not solidarity—which we usually do, and by no means errantly so—but reactive, even aggressive rejection, exclusion and scorn that, paradoxically, enhances the conviviality of the in-group.[31]

Sixth, although segregative commensal practices are typical, perhaps the norm, of strongly hierarchized societies, they also manifest what Grignon calls "transgressive commensalities," by which he means those commensal practices that "temporarily and symbolically" expose the ambivalence of the firm borders that divide groups in a society, but "by transgressing them ... contributes to recognising and maintaining them" (Grignon 2001: 30–31). The Roman *saturnalia* and the famously lavish *cenae* of Domitian are the most spectacular and best known examples of transgressive commensality in antiquity,[32] but I would suggest that we also consider the Greco-Roman so-called "anti-symposia" that we know especially from the satirical literature, a type of banquet that used parody, comedy, obscenity and burlesque to subvert the ideology and deface the coin of the standard élite banquet; it is a type that is exploited at least by Luke where it appears to have all the characteristics of Grignon's model of transgressive commensality.[33]

Summary

Matthias Klinghardt and Dennis Smith have, with their work, brought us to a terminus that should now be our point of departure. Let's grant the point that Christians in the Greco-Roman world knew themselves, and were recognized by others, as practicing a culturally familiar type of commensality. Pointing our classificatory effort at the morphology/structure of the typical Greco-Roman banquet or symposium may thus not require too much scholarly fuss any longer. I suggest, rather, that we devise a typology of commensality that will be more productive for a social history of early Christian associations. Urged by the possibilities suggested by Claude Grignon, I suggest that we pay attention to commensal groups and ask not what they do *at* meals, though that too of course, but what they do *with* meals and food.³⁴ This will lend detail, specificity, and conceptual robustness to the commensal effects that Dennis Smith rightly identifies and allow us to close in on what Klinghardt calls the differences in "nuance" and "focus" of early Christian commensal practices. I, for one, am much more intrigued by difference-making differences than difference-obscuring similarities.

Notes

1. Cf. Dietler (2001: 71): "feasts provide a site and medium for the highly condensed symbolic representation of social relations."
2. On consumptive practices as ritual practices see Dietler (2001: 65, 67, 69–75).
3. See the same point restated with reference to social eating in ancient Roman societies by Donahue (2004: 1–2).
4. A full *tour d'horizon* of scholarship on early Christian meal practices is to be found here.
5. See especially Klinghardt criticizing "monokausal-historisierende Erklärungen" (1996: 2–3).
6. Smith (2003b: 1): "It is my contention that there was *one form* of meal that served as the basic model for all formal meals of significance in the Greco-Roman world. I define this meal model as the Greco-Roman banquet" (my emphasis).
7. Klinghardt (2003: 1–2): "Not numerous single forms, but different representations of a greater, encompassing model"; "there is a common type of meal underlying the uncountable literary descriptions of and epigraphical references to communal meals in the Greco-Roman world"; the ideal type is then presented as the "symposium" in the same paper.
8. The term here refers to an old distinction in anthropology between "matter-of-fact" elements of culture and secondary rationalizations or specifically interested deployments of these elements (elements being either material objects or specific practices). The distinction allows me to introduce some distance between "ideal types" and actual deployments of the types; and it is the latter that interests me much more. The distinction itself appears to have been invented by Robert H. Lowie in the early part of the 20th century; see Wolf (1982: 387–388) and Kate Crehan (2002: 181–184).
9. On the semiology of food and dining see of course the classic article by Mary Douglas (1972); see also Lowell Edmunds (1980). Edmunds focuses on food, but his comparative sketch is instructive also for thinking about the semiotics of commensal forms.
10. As I indicated above, this statement on the "ordinariness" of early Christian dining rectifies studies that proceed on the presumption of the extraordinariness or uniqueness of Christian commensal activities, but I should here perhaps add that Smith's adverbial stroke "simply" is both theoretically and ethnographically infelicitous. It is precisely the nature of the "following" (or "departing") from the cultural everyday that needs attention.
11. Note also the useful mapping of anthropological scholarship on food and commensality by Scholliers (2001).
12. Note that Grignon's typology has now also been adapted by Donahue to generate a morphology of Roman dining (Donahue 2003). See also the types discussed by Dunbabin (2003a: 11–35) and Nenci (1989). A typology that lends itself to cross-cultural comparison of commensal practices see Dietler: "empowering feasts," "patron-role feasts," "diacritical feasts" (2001: 75–93).

"Our Religion Compels Us to Make a Distinction" • 173

13 This is not the place for me to trouble myself with "group," around which a huge social-scientific literature has been piled, of course. My starting inclinations are best articulated by Bourdieu (1982) and by Lincoln (1989: 3-26).
14 Note the relevance of this apart from strictly theoretical considerations. Thus Donahue (2003: 431-432): "it is readily apparent that the Romans preferred to dine in distinct groups, whether priest, senator, plebeian, patrician, or *curia* member." Though note Davidson (1997: 53-61) on the *kapeleia*, popular eateries/taverns that provided a place for the individual diner/drinker and spontaneous commensality of those who happened to be present.
15 See Bourdieu (1987) for theoretical assists on the question of why and how groups within a society/culture differentiate themselves from other groups and/or classes in the same society. Cf. Warde, Martens and Olsen (1999: 106-107): "people ... use consumption behaviour to signify who they are to other people, from whom they hope to gain approval and esteem for their 'style' ... In [a consumptive society] two typical problems occur for groups or classes trying to establish their claims to good taste; firstly, to legitimate the superiority of their own cultural practices and, secondly, to demonstrate in communication with others that they are indeed members of a superior grouping."
16 These pairs are separated by a comma rather than by an oppositional siglum, such as "versus," in order to indicate spectrums and ambiguities in the relationship of the two types in the pair.
17 On commensality in hierarchical societies, see Grignon (2001: 28-31).
18 E.g., Peachin (2001) and the literature cited there; see also Schäfer (1997); instructive evidence and analysis also in Davidson (1997). More generally on the instrumentality of "friendship" for competitive gain see Herman (1987).
19 For instructive analogies on the politics of commensality see Sancisi-Weerdenburg (1995) and Kifleyesus (2002).
20 As van Nijf points out (1997: 152-153), "Roman forms of commensality had a very different tradition. Roman sacrificial banquets (as well as other forms of commensality for which they served as model, including private and public banquets) emphasised the difference between the participants. ... This model was characteristic of all kinds of formal dinner, and of other food-sharing and food-giving rituals in Roman society. Even private dinners had a hierarchical set-up; the size of the portions, the location of the seats and the quality of the food could all be used as stratifying devices, allowing even the subtlest of status distinctions to be recognised." Van Nijf (1997: 153) cites Pliny's well-known sentiment as representative of the Roman view of dinners as stratifying practices: "I mean to congratulate you on the way in which you preserve the distinctions of class and rank; once these are thrown into confusion and destroyed, nothing is more unequal than the resultant equality" (*Ep.* 9.5.3). For additional argument see Garnsey (1999: 113-143) and Corbier (1999).
21 I use the terms "strategy" and "tactic" as defined and differentiated by de Certeau (1984: 34-42).
22 Although the interaction between master and domestic slave in the *domus* is a recurring topos in Greco-Roman literature, it is still the case that "[i]nspite of this [literary] interest we know much too little about the physical details of the cohabitation of slaves and free in the Roman household" (Fitzgerald 2000: 4). Though I am not familiar with what evidence we have for domestics in Christian households, I suspect Fitzgerald's general conclusion applies even more in this particular instance.
23 The literature on slavery in relation to ancient meals and commensal practices is meagre, indicating an underworked topic in relation to ancient meals. On slavery in

general see, e.g., Wood (2002) and literature cited there; on slaves and banquets see especially D'Arms (1990, 1991, 1999); cf. Foss (1994: 45–56). Iconographic evidence in Piccottini (1977); Dunbabin (2003b).

24 Foss continues (1994: 55–56): "Kitchen and Dining Rooms." Foss continues: "Slaves were socially as well as physically dirty. Except for the Saturnalia, they tended not to dine in a well-decorated room with nice furnishings and service of their own; they are pictured instead snacking in the kitchen. Some slaves were allowed only the leftovers of the leftovers of the meal, taking what the guests left behind after filling their own napkins. Slaves on some country estates are shown receiving rations from the bailiff and eating them around a fire. Slaves, the original 'nobodies' and lacking social identity, were not allowed to eat what, how or when they liked. That picture is given by their masters; how true is it? Were slaves scavengers, eating off the plates as they cleaned them, fighting for scraps? Or did slaves have their own place and time for rations during which they could enjoy the social interaction of their peers? Did slaves of differing status within a household eat differently?"

25 Glancy (2002: see n. 31) is most relevant even though she does not focus on female slaves' participation in Christian meals per se; in general see Burton (1998), Roller (2003) and Bookidis (1993).

26 Cf. Braun (1995: 181), where I argue in the context of an analysis of a Lukan banquet that Luke shows an interest in defending "a centralized and authoritarian kind of proto-bishopry."

27 Dietler (2001: 70-71) attributes this to the tendency to think of feasts largely in Durkheimian functionalist terms, that is, feasts as maintaining social solidarity. He demonstrates that this view is "partial and flawed."

28 *At quem non ceno, barbarus ille mihi est* (*CIL* IV, 1880).

29 The early Christian traditions concerning purity in relation to the participation in the common ritual meal are variants of this. See van de Sandt (2002), cf. Hellerman (2003).

30 On the "socially negative" effects of commensality see also Hirschman (1998: 11–32).

31 "Segregative commensality" may be conceptually thickened with the notion of "public mystery": the segregated commensal unit advertises its closedness by publicly announcing its segregation, and the very fact of its public self-obscuration aids in the in-group's self-definition arouses the conviviality of the public-but-hidden in-group. On the notion of "public secrecy" as a strategy for social formation see Jameson (1999) and Taussig (1999); an instructive ethnographic example is in Levy (1990: 335–338).

32 On the *cenae* of Domitian as examples of transgressive commensality see now Donahue (2003: 434-37).

33 Description of and literature on the literary and social "anti-symposia" in Braun (1992) and (1995: 38-39); cf. Bracht (1989). According to Harland (2005: 21): "In virtually all the cases dealt with throughout this paper, the inversion or perversion of the shared meal, along with inherent sacrificial connections, stands out as a symbol of the group's relation to surrounding society, as a sign of an anti-societal threat and the epitome of social and religious disorder." A fascinating analogous ethnographic exemplum and analysis is in Schneider and Schneider (1982). There is much to learn from the Schneiders' effort to explain an odd Western Sicilian feast in which the central ritual is "an obscene and vulgar mass performed by men in women's clothes in mockery of the priesthood, also in mockery of women for their blind allegiance to the Church" (Schneider and Schneider 1982: 431) that is witnessed, however, by clerics and civic officials.

34 Additional warrant for this is urged also by recent studies on the functions of rituals in heterogeneous, competitive social contexts where rituals help to define boundaries around sub-groups and articulate status divisions within groups. See, e.g., Platvoet and Van der Toorn (1995) and Safran (2003).

References

Appadurai, Arjun (1981). "Gastro-Politics in Hindu South Asia," *American Ethnologist* 8: 494–511. https://doi.org/10.1525/ae.1981.8.3.02a00050

Bobertz, C. A. (1993). "The Role of the Patron in the *Cena Dominica* of Hippolytus' *Apostolic Tradition*," *Journal of Theological Studies* 44: 170–184. https://doi.org/10.1093/jts/44.1.170

Bookidis, Nancy (1993). "Ritual Dining at Corinth." Nanno Marinatos and Robin Hägg (eds.), *Greek Sanctuaries: New Approaches*, 45–61. New York: Routledge.

Bourdieu, Pierre (1982). "What Makes a Social Class? On the Theoretical and Practical Existence of Groups," *Berkeley Journal of Sociology* 32: 1–17.

—— (1987). *Distinction: A Social Critique of the Judgment of Taste*. Richard Nice (trans.). Cambridge, MA: Harvard University Press.

Bracht, B. R. (1989). *Unruly Eloquence: Lucian and the Comedy of Traditions*. Cambridge, MA: Harvard University Press.

Braun, Willi (1992). "Symposium or Anti-Symposium? Reflections on Luke 24:1-24." In John S. Kloppenborg and Leif E. Vaage (eds.), *Scriptures and Cultural Conversations: Essays for Heinz Guenther at 65*, *Toronto Journal of Theology* 8(1): 70–84. https://doi.org/10.3138/tjt.8.1.70

—— (1995). *Feasting and Social Rhetoric in Luke 14*. Society for New Testament Studies Monograph Series, 85. Cambridge: Cambridge University Press.

Burton, Joan (1998). "Women's Commensality in the Ancient Greek World," *Greece & Rome* 45: 143–165. https://doi.org/10.1017/S0017383500033659

Corbier, Mireille (1999). "The Broad Bean and the Moray: Social Hierarchies and Food in Rome." In J.L. Flandrin and Massimo Mantanari (eds.), *Food: A Culinary History*, 129–140. New York: Columbia University Press.

Crehan, Kate (2002). *Gramsci, Culture and Anthropology*. Berkeley, CA: University of California Press.

D'Arms, John H. (1990). "The Roman *Convivium* and the Idea of Equality." In Oswyn Murray (ed.), *Sympotica: A Symposium on the Symposion*, 308–320. Oxford: Oxford University Press.

—— (1991). "Slaves at Roman *Convivia*." In W. J. Slater (ed.), *Dining in a Classical Context*, 171–183. Ann Arbor, MI: University of Michigan Press.

—— (1999). "Performing Culture: Roman Spectacle and the Banquets of the Powerful." In Bettina Bergmann and Christine Kondoleon (eds.), *The Art of Ancient Spectacle*, 301–319. New Haven, CT: Yale University Press.

Davidson, James (1997). *Courtesans and Fishcakes: The Consuming Passions of Classical Athens*. London: HarperCollins.

De Certeau, Michel (1984). *The Practices of Everyday Life*. Steven Rendall (trans.). Berkeley, CA: University of California Press.

Dietler, Michael (2001). "Theorizing the Feast: Rituals of Consumption, Commensal Politics, and Power in African Contexts." In Michael Dietler and Brian Hayden (eds.), *Feasts: Archaeological and Ethnographic Perspectives on Food, Politics, and Power*, 65–114. Washington, DC: Smithsonian Institute Press.

Donahue, John F. (2003). "Toward a Typology of Roman Public Feasting," *American Journal of Philology* 124: 423–441. https://doi.org/10.1353/ajp.2003.0043

—— (2004). *The Roman Community at Table During the Principate*. Ann Arbor, MI: University of Michigan Press.

Douglas, Mary (1972). "Deciphering a Meal," *Daedalus* 101: 61–81.

Dunbabin, Katherine M. D. (2003a). *The Roman Banquet: Images of Conviviality*. Cambridge: Cambridge University Press.

—— (2003b). "The Waiting Servant in Later Roman Art," *American Journal of Philology* 124: 443–468. https://doi.org/10.1353/ajp.2003.0044

Edmunds, Lowell (1980). "Ancient Roman and Modern American Food: A Comparative Sketch of Two Semiological Systems," *The Comparative Civilizations Review* 5: 52–69.

Farb, Peter and George Armelagos (1980). *Consuming Passions: The Anthropology of Eating*. Boston, MA: Houghton Mifflin.

Fitzgerald, William (2000). *Slavery and the Roman Literary Imagination*. Cambridge: Cambridge University Press. https://doi.org/10.1017/CBO9780511612541

Foss, Pedar W. (1994). "Kitchens and Dining Rooms at Pompeii: The Spatial and Social Relationship of Cooking to Eating in the Roman Household." Ph.D. dissertation, Ann Arbor, MI: University of Michigan.

Garnsey, Peter (1999). *Food and Society in Classical Antiquity*. Key Themes in Ancient History. Cambridge: Cambridge University Press. https://doi.org/10.1017/CBO9780511612534

Glancy, Jennifer A. (1998). "Obstacles to Slaves' Participation in the Corinthian Church," *Journal of Biblical Literature* 117: 481–501. https://doi.org/10.2307/3266444

—— (2002). *Slavery in Early Christianity*. New York: Oxford University Press.

Gordon, Richard (1990). "The Veil of Power: Emperors, Sacrificers and Benefactors." In Mary Beard and John North (eds.), *Pagan Priests: Religion and Power in the Ancient World*, 201–231. London: Duckworth.

Grignon, Claude (2001). "Commensality and Social Morphology: An Essay of Typology." In Peter Scholliers (ed.), *Food, Drink, and Identity: Cooking, Eating, and Drinking in Europe since the Middle Ages*, 23–33. Oxford: Berg. https://doi.org/10.5040/9781350044845-ch-002

Harland, Philip A. (2005). "Culturally Transgressive Banquets in Greco-Roman Associations: Imagination and Reality." Unpublished paper presented at the Greco-Roman Meals Seminar, Society of Biblical Literature, Philadelphia, PA.

Hellerman, Joseph (2003). "Purity and Nationalism in Second Temple Literature: 1–2 Maccabees and Jubilees," *Journal of the Evangelical Theological Society* 46: 401–421.

Herman, Gabriel (1987). *Ritualized Friendship and the Greek City*. Cambridge: Cambridge University Press.

Hirschman, Albert O. (1998). *Crossing Boundaries: Selected Writings*, 11–32. New York: Zone.

Jameson, Michael H. (1999). "The Spectacular and the Obscure in Athenian Religion." In Simon Goldhill and Robin Osborne (eds.), *Performance-Culture and Athenian Democracy*, 321–340. Cambridge: Cambridge University Press.

Kifleyesus, Abbebe (2002). "Muslims and Meals: The Social and Symbolic Function of Food in Changing Socio-Economic Times," *Africa* 72: 245–276. https://doi.org/10.3366/afr.2002.72.2.245

Klinghardt, Matthias (1996). *Gemeinschaftsmahl und Mahlgemeinschaft: Soziologie und Liturgie frühchristlicher Mahlfeiern*. Texte und Arbeiten zum neutestamentlichen Zeitalter 13. Tübingen: A. Francke Verlag.

—— (2003). "A Typology of the Community Meal." Unpublished paper presented to the SBL Consultation on Meals in the Greco-Roman World, Atlanta, GA.

Levy, Robert I. (1990). *Mesocosm: Hinduism and the Organization of a Traditional Newar City in Nepal.* Berkeley, CA: University of California Press.

Lincoln, Bruce (1989). *Discourse and the Construction of Society: Comparative Studies of Myth, Ritual, and Classification.* New York: Oxford University Press.

Nenci, Giuseppe (1989). "Pratiche alimentari e forme di definizione e distinzione nella Grecia arcaica." In Oddone Longo and Paolo Scarpi (eds.), *Homo edens: Regimi, miti e pratiche dell'alimentazione nella civiltà del Mediterraneo,* 25–30. Milan: Diapress.

Peachin, Michael (2001). "Friendship and Abuse at the Dinner Table." In Michael Peachin (ed.), *Aspects of Friendship in the Graeco-Roman World,* 135–144. Portsmouth: Journal of Roman Archaeology.

Piccottini, Gernot (1977). *Die Dienerinnen- und Dienerreliefs des Stadtgebietes von Virunum.* CSIR Österreich II.3; Vienna: Österreichische Akademie der Wissenschaften.

Platyoet, Jan and Karen Van der Torn (eds.) (1995). *Pluralism and Identity: Studies in Ritual Behaviour.* Leiden: Brill. https://doi.org/10.1163/9789004378896

Riggs, John W. (1984). "From Gracious Table to Sacramental Elements: The Tradition-History of Didache 9 and 10," *SecCent:* 83–101.

—— (1995). "The Sacred Food of *Didache* 9–11 and Second-Century Ecclesiologies." In Clayton N. Jefford (ed.), *The Didache in Context: Essays on its Text, History, and Transmission,* 256–283. NovT Supplements 77; Leiden: Brill.

Roller, Matthew (2003). "Horizontal Women: Posture and Sex in the Roman Convivium," *American Journal of Philology* 124: 377–422. https://doi.org/10.1353/ajp.2003.0052

Rundin, John (1996). "The Politics of Eating: Feasting in Early Greek Society," *American Journal of Philology* 117: 179–215 https://doi.org/10.1353/ajp.1996.0029

Safran, Jaina M. (2003). "Rules of Purity and Confessional Boundaries: Maliki Debates about the Purity of the Christian," *History of Religions* 42: 197–212. https://doi.org/10.1086/375036

Sancisi-Weerdenburg, Heleen (1995). "Persian Food: Stereotypes and Political Identity." In M. J. Dobson, F. D. Harvey and John Wilkins (eds.), *Food in Antiquity,* 286–302. Exeter: Exeter University Press

Schäfer, Alfred (1997). *Unterhaltung beim griechischen Symposion: Darbietungen, Spiele und Wettkämpfe von homerischer bis in spätklassischer Zeit.* Mainz: Zabern.

Scheidel, Walter (1997). "Quantifying the Sources of Slaves in the Early Roman Empire," *Journal for Roman Studies* 87: 156–169. https://doi.org/10.2307/301373

Schneider, Jane and Peter Schneider (1982). "Mafia Burlesque: The Profane Mass as a Peace-Making Ritual," *Sociologisch Tijdschrift* 9: 408–433.

Scholliers, Peter (2001). "Meals, Food Narratives, and Sentiments of Belonging in Past and Present." In Peter Scholliers (ed.), *Food, Drink, and Identity: Cooking, Eating, and Drinking in Europe since the Middle Ages,* 3–22. Oxford: Berg. https://doi.org/10.5040/9781350044845-ch-001

Smith, Dennis E. (2003a). *From Symposium to Eucharist: The Banquet in the Early Christian World.* Minneapolis: Fortress Press.

—— (2003b). "The Greco-Roman Banquet as a Social Institution." Unpublished paper presented to the SBL Consultation on Meals in the Greco-Roman World, Atlanta, GA.

Smith, Jonathan Z. (2004). *Relating Religion: Essays in the Study of Religion.* Chicago, IL: University of Chicago Press.

Sperber, Dan (1996). *Explaining Culture: A Naturalistic Approach.* London: Blackwell.

Taussig, Michael T. (1999). *Defacement: Public Secrecy and the Labor of the Negative.* Stanford, CA: Stanford University Press.

Van de Sandt, Huub (2002). "'Do Not Give What Is Holy to the Dogs' (Did 9:5d and Matt 7:6a): The Eucharistic Food of the Didache in its Jewish Purity Setting," *Vigiliae Christianae* 56: 223–246. https://doi.org/10.1163/157007202760235373

Van Nijf, Onno M. (1997). *The Civic World of Professional Associations in the Roman East*. Dutch Monographs on Ancient History and Archaeology 17. Amsterdam: Gieben,

Warde, Alan, Lydia Martens, and Wendy Olsen (1999). "Consumption and the Problem of Variety: Cultural Omnivorousness, Social Distinction and Dining Out," *Sociology* 33: 105–127. https://doi.org/10.1177/S0038038599000061

Wolf, Eric R. (1982). *Europe and the People Without History*. Berkeley, CA: University of California Press.

Wood, Ellen M. (2002). "Landlords and Peasants, Masters and Slaves: Class Relations in Greek and Roman Antiquity," *Historical Materialism* 10(3): 17–69. https://doi.org/10.1163/15692060260289707

Part III

Afterword

Reification, Religion, and the Relics of the Past

William E. Arnal

> The philosophers have only *interpreted* the world, in various ways; the point, however, is to *change* it.
> —Karl Marx, "Theses on Feuerbach" (1972 [1845]: 109, thesis 11)

Some years ago, I read an interview with Willi Braun that had appeared, I believe, as part of a faculty profile in an internal University of Alberta publication. The interviewer asked a rather inspired question of Willi: if he could go back in time and meet only one past individual, who would it be? Willi's astonishing answer? Ludwig Feuerbach. Of all the possible enigmas of history, including those in his own area—Jesus, Paul, the author of the Gospel of Luke (subject of Willi's dissertation), Irenaeus—Willi selected a relatively obscure nineteenth-century German philosopher, one probably better known incidentally from his much more famous critic (Karl Marx) than for his own work. An odd choice, perhaps, but, I think, also a revealing and important one. The choice is significant, I argue, for making sense of this collection of essays, both in terms of identifying the unifying purpose or methodological thread that makes this a coherent collection, and indeed that makes Willi's scholarly output as a whole a *body of work* rather than a simple accumulation of insights. And the choice of Feuerbach is significant in terms of the relation of these essays to the confused and conflicted field of Christian origins and its future possibilities. With only minor overstatement, Feuerbach may be the secret key, not only to Willi's academic work, but to a consistent and discriminating conception of the field of New Testament/Christian Origins as a whole.

* * *

Feuerbach's 1844 book, *The Essence of Christianity*, articulated—decades before Max Müller or E. B. Tylor came along—a full-throated, modern, and critical theory of religion. According to Feuerbach, human nature is intrinsically *projective*: we experience our capacities, our faculties, our virtues, by casting them onto an external reality, a screen of sorts, and in that objectified form we are able to appreciate, and, in the deepest sense, to *realize* those qualities.[1] When, for example, I observe the activities of a bird through my binoculars, falling into fascination with its behaviors, its courting rituals, its feeding practices, the intellectual thrill I experience in so doing is not—cannot be—a function of or response to what is, after all, just a *bird*; it is rather the thrill of recognition of my own intellect, my astonishing capacity to understand a bird's actions. And that capacity takes my breath away in a fashion no mere bird could ever do. Likewise when I admire a hero—say, Ludwig Feuerbach, or Willi Braun—I am in fact admiring my own self, my capacity, as a human being, to attain to the intellectual clarity and penetration of such thinkers (whether I personally have done so or not—what I am admiring is a human virtue, not a personal one, a matter of *Gattungswesen*). And likewise again, when we fall in love, what we are really in love with is the capacity of love itself, projected onto and admired in the form of the beloved. Religion or, rather, its objects—gods, non-obvious beings, superhuman entities, whatever—is just this. Religion and its gods are *human* creations, fabricated by externalizing human qualities. And so, Feuerbach says, "Such as are a man's thoughts and dispositions, such is his God; so much worth as a man has, so much and no more has his God. Consciousness of God is self-consciousness, knowledge of God is self-knowledge" (Feuerbach 2008: 12).[2] The creation of gods is simply a way of knowing oneself, and so "religion is the first form of self-consciousness" (Feuerbach 2008: 270).

Notwithstanding the appreciative poetic language, and the claim that the gods proceed *naturally* from human nature and indeed reflect that nature, nonetheless, for Feuerbach religion is not unequivocally a positive thing. The projective tendency is potentially misleading, after all, insofar as it tempts us—or even forces us—to imagine the virtues genuinely proper to us exist only outside ourselves. And the problem with this, in turn, is not primarily its *falsity*, but its *harm*. It is "an illusion … which is by no means indifferent, but which, on the contrary, is profoundly injurious in its effect on mankind" (Feuerbach 2008: 274). Since religion denies that its "substance and object" is human (Feuerbach 2008: 270), it denies that substance *to* humans: "in proportion as the divine subject is in reality human, the greater is the apparent difference between God and man; that is, the more, by reflection on religion, by theology, is the identity of the divine and human denied, and the human, considered as such, is depreciated. The reason of this is, that as what is positive in the conception of the divine being can only be human, the conception of man, as an object of consciousness, can only be negative" (Feuerbach 2008: 26). It is as if, gazing into a mirror (and hence projecting and objectivizing my physical appearance in order the better to appreciate it), I concluded that I *must* be ugly, since I could never possibly be as attractive as that charming fellow in the mirror. Religious projection steals from us what is most proper to us, what is quintessentially human.

And this in turn brings us to Marx. Perhaps a little unfairly, Marx famously criticizes Feuerbach for what amounts to idealism: Feuerbach posits a human essence, invariant over time, and focuses his attention on ideas rather than material realities (see especially theses 6–8, Marx 1972 [1845]: 109). But Marx retains from Feuerbach the central notion that human qualities are projected onto an external field—now transferred from the intellectual to the palpably material: social labor, work, commodities, economic value—and that in this projected form come to be seen as alien. Value, instead of something that we actively create, comes to be a mystical thing that stands outside of us:

> The mysterious character of the commodity-form consists therefore simply in the fact that the commodity reflects the social characteristics of men's own labour as objective characteristics of the products of labour themselves, as the socio-natural properties of these things. ... It is nothing but the definite social relation between men themselves which assumes here, for them, the fantastic form of a relation between things. (Marx 1990 [1867])

It is telling that Marx uses precisely religious language to characterize this mystifying tendency of the commodity form: a commodity "is a very strange thing, abounding in metaphysical subtleties and theological niceties" (Marx 1990 [1867]: 163).[3] For Marx, capitalism does to human labor what, for Feuerbach, religion does to human virtue—in essence, it absconds with it, and thereby deprives us of what is properly ours.[4] Among other things, Marx's argument suggests that religion is by no means the only mechanism by which alienation arises. In the end, the critique of both thinkers is levelled at *reification*, that is, thingification, the act of perceiving "things" that are in fact processes—and processes in which our own activities, mental or physical, are thoroughly imbricated—as if they were actually objects, and hence external to ourselves. Whether we are speaking of a deity or a Gucci handbag, something profoundly human is *alienated* from us.

* * *

Feuerbach's notion of projective alienation is, I maintain, the secret essence of Willi's work; indeed, perhaps Feuerbach himself ought to be the new patron saint of the academic study of ancient Christianity, his portrait hung in every office. The central agenda of Willi's work, and what unifies this set of chapters devoted, variously, to religion, to the historical Jesus, the Q document and its tradents, the Gospel of Mark, ancient Christian dining practices, gender in antiquity, and so on, is very straightforwardly an effort at demystification. Nowhere is this clearer than on the first page of Chapter 1 of this volume, entitled "Religion":

> researching the world we live in, including comparatively across time (worlds of past societies) and space (worlds other than our own), is always a complex exercise of selecting, inventing and fiddling with categories in order to render—to force—the natural world and the range of human doings as intelligible, differentiated, ours to respond to, to make and remake.

This is the essence and project of Feuerbach revived for the twenty-first century: to ensure the human intelligibility of practices (and "things") that might, when viewed superficially, be taken as alien and mysterious. And that in turn is a liberative act of reclamation: these things are *ours*, they are proper to us, they must not be alienated from us. Understanding is ultimately harnessed to liberation. In the case of *religion*—just as Feuerbach claimed, some 175 years ago—human intelligibility is threatened by the self-presentation of those activities normally gathered under this rubric as, precisely, transcendent and non-human, as super-human,[5] and so in various ways, *not*-ours, not proper to us, and thus *taken* from us, alienated. Grasping the genuinely human nature of religion, its human points of reference, and its deep intelligibility, its status as a relic of what Marx would call "human sensuous activity" (thesis one, Marx 1972 [1845]: 107) is therefore a reversal of this alienation, a stripping away of the mystique that prevents us from realizing that the image in the mirror is really we ourselves. As Willi argues in "The Irony of Religion" (Chapter 2, this volume), the very concept of religion itself may encode alienation, may be a way of denying the fundamentally human character of the objects of our study, a way of separating them from intelligibility. Regardless, in his work, every intellectual act of translation that demonstrates the fundamentally *ordinary* character of religion and its products, or that presents those products as outcomes of *actions that we can easily imagine ourselves taking part in*, restores to us an alienated element of our essential nature.[6]

In the case of the study of the New Testament or "Christian origins," the more precise focus of Willi's expertise and the focus of the bulk of his work, "religion" is but one element of a triple reification built into the subject-matter itself, or at least into the more usual ways of approaching that subject-matter, especially under their older rubric as "biblical studies." First, as already noted, describing and, more importantly, understanding ancient Christian texts as necessarily and exclusively *religious* documents tends to set them apart from ordinary or quotidian concerns. It suggests that our texts are caught up in lofty matters, universal (as opposed to positional) ethical imperatives, and timeless truths extracted from superhuman sources. By contrast, one sees in most of the essays included in this book a strong tendency to describe NT and other ancient texts not in the language of religion, but in the language of politics and sociology, at times, explicitly so. This should not be understood as the result of some conviction on Willi's part that everything is political, or some sort of axiomatic privileging of the social. Rather, the import of the socio-political language is that this is precisely the terminology we use to describe and understand *ourselves*. Thus the process of translating the ostensibly "religious" ideological claims of the NT and other ancient writings into claims about power, social relations, and the like is precisely a process of making these writings intelligible, and, again, intelligible in the strong sense that the people who produced these documents are acting in ways in which we could imagine ourselves acting, and hence their actions are not alien, and so not somehow lost to us or foreign to us.

A second temptation to reification arises from the idea that we are investigating the *origins* of something (a problem not especially ameliorated by shifting to the language of "beginnings"). These ancient writings are taken from us once again, made into something more-than-human and so not-human by treating them as representative or reflective of a *novum*, some sort of irruption of the genuinely new into human history, and so something fundamentally incomprehensible as an outcome of ordinary political and social forces (that is to say, human forces, at least as we today understand them). Origins are already highly mystified, and, as Tomoko Masuzawa has shown, gain their special standing from a *post hoc* selection which retroactively invests them with a status out of the ordinary (Masuzawa 1993). To speak of our texts as originary (of something) is therefore, once again, to place them in a realm almost-necessarily beyond our own experiences, and to give a quasi-historical imprimatur to theological decisions made some 18 centuries ago. Again, Willi's work runs consistently and deliberately counter to any such tendency—no individual work is especially privileged, later texts are found to be as complex and interesting as earlier ones, extra-canonical as worthy of study as canonical.[7] Part of the antidote to this kind of reification is to focus on processes already in place. Any phenomenon has a prehistory, depending on our approach. If it seems that the ideas in a text, or the format of the text, are absolutely unique, or seem to come out of nowhere, then we have once again abjured comprehension, and are clearly looking in the wrong places: in the history of ideas rather than the history of people, groups, or other ranges of human doing. Put more sharply: the appearance of something new is always in fact a transformation of something already extant. And so on this point, too, the essays in this volume enact the agenda of Feuerbach, and reveal even these "special" writings as human processes and so as *ours*.

The third, final, and perhaps the most insidious of the reifications is that the "origins" in question are imagined to be *Christian* origins. Indeed, the characterization of our texts as Christian provides further warrant for treating them as originary, insofar as they are made explanatory of the "rise" of this apparently *new* ideological system. It also, as with "religion," returns our gaze to the free-floating concept, rather than the active and motivated processes of real people. But worst of all, designating our texts as "Christian" (or even worse, as "biblical") separates them more or less entirely from the cultures in which they were composed. This is because those cultures were clearly not Christian until a much later date, and so the "Christian" dimensions of our texts serve simply to separate them from and render them different from, even militantly opposed to, their actual contexts. Thus does context become "background" and a whole slew of ancient writings come to be understood as *oppositional* to that "background." The effect is emphatically again to make our texts "special"—and special in the peculiar and reified sense of being utterly detached from the range of predictable behaviors of human actors. The documents available to us, and the people behind them, may be *in* their world, but they are not *of* it.[8] Hence we have no real cultural framework for understanding them, apart from the isolated and abstracted ideology within the texts themselves, which then, somehow, auto-interpret. It is by way of liberation of this particular reification that perhaps the most striking, the most consistent, and the most familiar dimension of Willi's scholarly work on antiquity comes into play. Since his doctoral work, one of the most recognizable and persistent features of Willi's scholarship has been a hard-nosed insistence on seeking out Hellenistic and especially Roman-era analogues for the ideas, expressions, and behaviors attested in the ancient literature of the Jesus-people. Does Luke talk about dining practices? Then we'd better look at what ancient symposia texts look like, investigate ancient dining conventions in general, and figure out how these conventions intersect with social stratification and ideological stances (see, for example, Chapter 10, this volume, as well as Braun 1995). Want to understand gender and the role of women in ancient Christian texts? Better look at Greco-Roman theories and values regarding gender and character (see especially Chapters 8 and 9, this volume). Q or Thomas as a school? Better look to scribalism, writing technologies, and social aspects of instruction and learning in the Roman world (see especially Chapter 6, this volume). The reason for this emphasis is clear: the norms, technologies, symbols, ideas, and possibilities of the environment of the first Jesus-people are the ideas and possibilities—really, the only ideas and possibilities—that they themselves had to work with. More than this, a reconstruction of a writing's themes, an effort to explain its authors' motivations, to make sense of the human actors and actions behind it, is only plausible—and hence accurately understood in a non-alienating way—if we can find instances of *other people in similar circumstances doing the same thing*. In short, seeing ancient Christian behaviors and literature as particular instances of what lots of contemporary people were doing is to make them *normal*; and if normal, *human*; and if human, *ours*: in Braun's words (cited above), "ours to respond to, to make and remake."

* * *

All three of these reifying tendencies are consistently and self-consciously resisted in Willi's work, in his tendency to seek the social and political processes behind ancient Christian writings, and to view these writings as thoroughly and genuinely part of, and aspects of, the Greco-Roman world. This methodological rigor is not about fetishizing "theory," or engaging in "methodolatry." It is about explaining human things in human ways, about seeing these reified artifacts as the products of human activities and making sense of them in ways that accord with our understanding of human behaviors. Nor again should the instinct to deprive our texts of their special-ness, to reject theologically-imputed constraints on analysis, a matter of "positivism" or a war against "theology" in the abstract. Nor still is this insistence on the *ordinariness* of religion, or of ancient Christian writings, canonical or otherwise, in any sense an exercise in debunking. The charge, in fact, is doubly culpable: it uncharitably misreads Willi's agenda *and* it misconstrues the importance of the ordinary. It assumes that the ordinary is deficient, is compromised, has been deprived of its excellence, and therefore any effort to describe our data in ordinary terms, as instances of the day-to-day capacities and interests of human beings, must be an active effort to demote them somehow. That assumption embodies the alienated experience of the human as defective. It is all nonsense. The impulse to demystify our texts comes not from any desire to repudiate them but finally and definitively to own them. The effect, as I have argued, is liberative. In reclaiming our absconded property, the literary products of the first Jesus-people become instances of ways of being human, and these strange mystical repositories of what are in fact human activities, once appearing to exist outside and apart from us, and mocking our limitations from that vantage point, can finally return to their proper home.

Notes

1   The Hegelian influence here should be obvious: the subjective comes to self-realization via its imposition upon or entanglement with an other, an object, a not-self.

2   I have preserved the use of "man" from the translation, in part because I think that the conception of *Gattungswesen* that Feuerbach is working with is, indeed, a masculine one. The use of Feuerbach made here is notwithstanding that particularistic masculinization, which is alienating in its own right.
3   He makes the connection explicit a few paragraphs later: "In order, therefore, to find an analogy we must take flight into the misty realms of religion. There the products of the human brain appear as autonomous figures endowed with a life of their own. … So it is in the world of commodities with the products of men's hands" (Marx 1990 [1867]: 165).
4   Again, Marx is explicit at times about the parallel. See, e.g., Marx (1972 [1852]: 50, emphasis original): "Objectification is the practice of alienation. Just as man, so long as he is engrossed in religion, can only objectify his essence by an *alien* and fantastic being; so under the sway of egoistic need, he can only affirm himself and produce objects in practice by subordinating his products and his own activity to the domination of an alien entity, and by attributing to them the significance of an alien entity, namely money."
5   This understanding of religion is also central to Bruce Lincoln's approach (see Lincoln 2006: 5–7).
6   This is not to imply, I must stress, that different and "alien" cultures do not in fact have dimensions that are difficult to understand, including widely divergent symbol-systems. This kind of strangeness is especially true of ancient Christian writings, which because of their currency in cultures of the last 2000 years appear, deceptively, to trade in our conceptions and interests, but in fact come from a culture dramatically distant from ours. In that particular sense, these texts are indeed not ours at all—nor for that matter do they belong to their contemporary theological claimants, for exactly the same reasons). The point here is that the effort to *understand* must bridge the gaps between cultures by invoking shared human realities, and at least be able to apply the same language of analysis that we apply to our own doings. This is precisely the intellectual labour (and art!) involved in approaching ancient materials: finding the lineaments of our own kinds of behavior behind what appear to be—and in some true sense really are—alien forms.
7   For an explicit critique of the discourse of "origins" in our field, see Willi's comments in Chapter 5, and especially Chapter 4, this volume.
8   In some ways, engagement of ancient Christian materials with ancient Jewish culture is used to similar ends: marking out the culture of context for NT and other writings as Jewish serves, on the one hand, to protect those writings from "contamination" by the larger Greco-Roman culture of their composition (the same culture that was also, of course, the context for Judaism), while at the same time, (often) serving as a foil against which to establish Christianity's evident superiority. On this point, see Smith (1990).

References

Braun, Willi (1995). *Feasting and Social Rhetoric in Luke 14.* Society for New Testament Studies Monograph Series. New York: Cambridge University Press. https://doi.org/10.1017/CBO9780511520303

Feuerbach, Ludwig (2008). *The Essence of Christianity.* George Eliot (trans.). New York: Cosimo Classics. https://doi.org/10.1017/CBO9781139136563

Lincoln, Bruce (2006). *Holy Terrors: Thinking About Religion After September 11*. 2nd ed. Chicago, IL: University of Chicago Press.

Marx, Karl (1972) [1845]. "Theses on Feuerbach." In Robert C. Tucker (ed.), *The Marx-Engels Reader*. New York: W. W. Norton & Company.

Marx, Karl (1972) [1852]. "On the Jewish Question." In Robert C. Tucker (ed.), *The Marx-Engels Reader*. New York: W. W. Norton & Company.

Marx, Karl (1990) [1867]. *Capital, Volume 1*. Ben Fowkes (trans.). New York: Penguin Books.

Masuzawa, Tomoko (1993). *In Search of Dreamtime: The Quest for the Origin of Religion*. Chicago, IL: University of Chicago Press.

Smith, Jonathan Z. (1990). *Drudgery Divine: On the Comparison of Early Christianities and the Religions of Late Antiquity*. Chicago, IL: University of Chicago Press.

Index

accentuation, 81, 82, 166, 167
Acts of the Apostles, 59, 62, 165
Acts of Jesus, The, 53
Acts of Paul, The, 145
Acts of Thecla, The, 145 f.
addiction, 45–6
    heroin likened to history, 45–46
agency; see also ideology, hegemony,
        power, self
    agency metaphysics, 157 n. 6
    personhood as autonomous, 155
    and structure continuum, 156
    structural limits, 155
    therapeutic, 153
alienation (deracination), 44, 85, 86, 89,
        183, 186, 187 n. 2
    as objectification, 187 n. 4
    projective, 183
    reversal, 184
alphabetization
    of Europe, 99
alterity, 29
Althusser, Louis, 158 n. 6
Anderson, Hugh, 65
androcentrism, 141, 142, 143, 145, 151–155;
    see also hegemony
    erasure of femaleness, 143
    reinforced by renunciation, 145
androcracy, early Christian, 156
androgyny
    androgyne, 143, 156 n. 3
    as reconstituted masculinity, 143
Anson, John, 148
anthropocentric stance, xi, 27
    in biblical studies, xi
apocalypsis, 63
Apollonius of Tyana, 82, 91, 94, 135 n, 21
Aristotle, 3, 98, 102, 110 n. 9, 123, 147, 148, 149, 150
    Pseudo-Aristotle, 147, 150, 151

Arnal, William E., viii, xii, 21 n. 1, 55, 60, 69 n. 3, 69 n. 6, 76, 81, 86, 92 n. 30, 93 n. 39, 115 n. 38, 143, 156 n. 1
Artemis (Diana), 122, 127
artificiality, 10, 47, 92 n. 27, 133 n. 1
Asad, Talal, 23 n. 11, 146
asceticism, 123, 145, 148, 155; see also gender, monasticism
associations; see also schools
    proletarian, 78
    voluntary, 78, 89 n. 4, 168, 169
Athena (Minerva), 122
Attis, 122, 127, 133 n. 4
Attridge, Harold, 52
Augustine, 65, 71 n. 24, 129, 144
Austin, J. L., 111 n. 16
authenticity, 29, 33, 52, 62, 63, 65, 70 n. 11
author, idea of, 90 n. 12
authority xi, 10, 11, 46, 81, 88, 89, 91 n. 20, 113, 125
autobaptism, 146
autobiography, 47

Barth, Fredrik, 110 n. 8
Bauer, Ferdinand Christian, 66
Beard, Mary, 126
Bedner, John, 105
Benveniste, Émile, 110 n. 5
bible
    Holy Land Experience, 51
    King James version, 50
binary logic, 7
biography, 60, 89 n. 2, 156
Blanton, Ward, xi
Bloch, Maurice, xi
body; see also agency, gender, hegemony, power, self
    and soul, 150
    cultivated, 152
    Greco-Roman theories of gendered bodies, 131

as ideological construct, 151–152
inscribed, 127
politic, 151
reading, 150–151
self-developable, 146
semiotic bodyscape/chart, 147, 150, 152
site of suppression, 145
social, 76, 101, 106, 121
types, spectrum of, 151
Bono, 51
Borg, Marcus, 52
Bourdieu, Pierre, 92 n. 27, 110 n. 6, 134 n. 9, 146, 173 n. 13, 173 n. 15
Boyarin, Daniel, 22 n. 4
Brower, Gary R. 135 n. 21
Brown, Peter, 89 n. 3, 124
Brubaker, Rogers, 67
Burkert, Walter, 135 n. 22
Burrus, Virginia, 146, 152

Cameron, Ronald, 91 n. 25
Canadian Society of Biblical Studies (CSBS), viii
canon, 49, 65, 88, 115 n. 33
biblical or Christian 43, 45, 59
canon-making, 68, 86
cultural canon, 81
logographic technics of argumentation, 105
capitalism, 33, 155, 183
Casadio, Giovanni, 135 n. 20, 136 n. 22
Castelli, Elizabeth, 144–145, 148
castration, 127, 130, 135 n. 21, 135 n. 22; see also eunuchs
in early Christianity, 135 n. 19
outlawed in Rome, 128, 129
ritual 130
as sexual disablement, 129
celibacy, 122 f.; see also virginity
etymology, 122
as making men, 124
in myth and ritual, 123
as self-care, 123
Celsus, 155
Centre for Religious Studies, University of Toronto, vii
Certeau, Michel de, 10, 31, 99, 109 n. 4
arts de faire, 10, 11, 12, 13, 20, 23 n. 13, 31, 154

scriptural economy, 99
strategy v. tactic, 173 n. 21
voice/orality, 110 n. 5
Chidester, David, 7
choice, 6
Christian origins, vii, 59, 184
as conflicted field, 181
redescription of, viii
Cicero, 98
class (economic), 76, 84, 89 n. 2, 91 n. 20, 92 n. 27, 92 n. 30, 93 n. 38, 105, 112 n. 22, 113 n. 26, 173 n. 20
as concept, 9
classification
driven by interests, 8
Clement of Alexandria, 62, 65, 66, 70 n. 14, 71 n. 26, 71 n. 29, 144, 145
Cohen, Shaye, J. D., 156 n. 2
Comaroff, Jean, 158 n. 7
Comaroff, John, 29, 158 n. 7
commensality, 166, 168–171, 172 n. 11, 173 n. 14, 173 n. 17, 173 n. 19, 173 n. 20, 174 n. 30, 174 n. 31, 174 n. 32
segregative, 168, 170–171, 174 n. 31
transgressive, 168, 171, 174 n. 32
comparison, ix
incomparability, 33
metaphoric vs. metonymic, 92 n. 31
Comte, Auguste, 12
concepts
as establishing relations among things, 30
as problems, 3
select theories, 11
self-conscious formation of, 9
councils
of Chalcedon, 42, 43
of Gangra, 149
of Nicea, 42, 43
criticism
feminist, 141
form, 53, 90 n. 8, 90 n. 12
ideology, 142
redaction, 53, 63, 64, 70 n. 9, 78, 79
rhetorical, 98, 106, 109 n. 3
source, 53
Crossan, John Dominic, 52, 54, 70 n. 20, 115 n. 34
Culture Studies, 5

Cybele, 122, 124, 127, 129, 133 n. 4, 134 n. 15
Cynics, 52, 82, 83, 84, 86, 111 n. 11, 123

D'Arms, John 168
Denaides, the, 123
data, vii
DaVinci Code, The, 51
Davies, Stevan, 70 n. 16, 107, 108, 115 n. 37, 115 n. 38, 153
Davis, Charles, 19, 22 n. 8
Dawson, Lorne, 22 n. 8
definition, ix, 3, 77, 127
   as the beginning of wisdom, 3
   of religion, 10, 11
   self-definition, 148, 174 n. 31
   taken for granted, 8
demystification, 34, 103, 186
Derrida, Jacques, 3, 5
description, ix, 18, 27, 31, 36, 84, 87, 88, 111 n. 14, 167
   social description, 76, 78, 79
Détienne, Marcel, 92 n. 29, 93 n. 37
difference, 23 n. 12
   aims vs. achievements, 157
   of degree vs. kind, 83
   disinterest in question of, 93 n. 40
   evoke similarity by drawing attention to, 101
   making, 172
   markers of, 33
   obscuring, 172
   relations of difference need attention, 107
   ritual incantations of, 19
   as theoretical challenge, 86
   untranslatable, 33
displacement, 61, 68, 69 n. 6, 85, 90 n. 8, 135 n. 22
   of ritual into writing, 93 n. 35
   of sacrifice into speech, 93 n. 35
Donahue, John F., 171
Doniger, Wendy, 22 n. 9
Doran, Robert, 148
Douglas, Mary, 22 n. 8, 151, 172 n. 9
Durkheim, Émile, 12, 69, 71 n. 22. 127
   definition of religion, 22 n. 5

Edmunds, Lowell, 172 n. 9
Ehrman, Bart, 59

Eliade, Mircea, 4, 18, 19, 69
   homo religiosus, 19
enlightenment, Greek, 110 n. 10
emic/etic, 29, 45
Epicureans, 33, 86, 93 n. 40
Eros, 104, 112 n. 23
essentialism, 157 n. 6
   rejected, 33
ethnicity, 45, 60, 68, 132, 149, 168
ethnography, 13, 29, 174 n. 33
Eucharist, 166
eunuchs; see also castration
   as dangerous, 130
   disdained in Rome, 130, 135 n. 18
   held in esteem, 130
   as impure, 135 n. 22
   new category of person, 129
   perception of, 128
   priest, 121, 122, 124, 127, 128, 133
   coming from slave class, 135 n. 15
   social position of, 135 n. 15
   whether celibate, 129
Eusebius, 65, 66, 71 n. 26
experience, 3, 4, 82, 108, 110 n. 8
   alienated, 89, 186
   of displacement, 85
   Holy Land Experience, 51
   and projection, 181
   social, 83
explanation, ix, 11, 18, 27

family; see also gender, hegemony, hierarchy
   fictive, 169
   household management codes, 142
   idea of in antiquity, 121
   leaving, 145
   normalized structure, 133
   patrilineal, 125
   relations to ancient city and state, 131, 152
   renounced, 145
   Roman, 122
   as strategy, 121
   structure, 133
   values, 121, 133
Feuerbach, Ludwig, 12, 181–183, 185, 187
fictioning (*fingere*), 45, 47
Fitzgerald, Timothy, 23 n. 15

Five Gospels, The, 52, 53
First Century, CE
  as product of the second, 68
Fish, Stanley, 70 n. 19, 114 n. 31
food
  banquets, 166, 167
    redescribed, 166
      slaves role in, 169, 173 n. 22, 173 n. 23, 174 n. 24, 174 n. 24, 174 n. 25
    structure of, 171
  meals as structured performance, 165
  morphology of meals, 168, 172 n. 12
  patriarchal control of, 169
  as ritual, 172 n. 2, 174 n. 29, 174 n. 33
  semiology of, 172 n. 9
  as socially symbolic, 165 f.
  symposium as ideal type, 166
Foss, Pedar, 169, 174 n. 24
Foucault, Michel, 48, 90 n. 13, 121
Frazer, James G., 12, 69, 101
Freud, Sigmund, 12, 69
Friedman, Kinky, 51
Frischer, Bernard, 86
Fuchs, Stephan, 156, 157 n. 6
functionalism, 135 n. 22, 174 n. 27, 175 n. 34
Funk, Robert, 50, 52, 53, 55

Geertz, Clifford, 30, 77, 100
  counting cats in Zanzibar, 77
Gellner, Ernst, 19, 33, 35
gender; see also body, hegemony, hierarchy
  andreia (manliness), 132, 143, 154, 155
  as classification problem, 128
  coding, 132
  cross-dressing, 149
  dimorphism, 131, 142, 144, 149
  femaleness, 130, 131, 132, 144, 145, 150–154
    deficient personhood, 154
    female manliness, 154
    as incomplete man, 149
    lacked dryness, as per Hippocratic theories, 150
    pathologized, 153
    subsumed/erased, 143
  ideology, 130, 131, 149, 150, 153, 154, 155; see also Thecla

  Greco-Roman, 131
  maleness, 130, 131, 145, 148, 150–151, 154
  masculinization, 142, 143–144, 145, 146, 148, 149, 187 n. 2
    of piety, 144, 145, 153, 156
  sexual disguise, 148
  transvestism, 148
  unification, 143
generalization, 32
Giddens, Anthony, 87, 92 n. 26
  recursive reproduction, 92 n. 26
Girard, René, 127
given, myth of, 35
Glancy, Jennifer, 169, 174 n. 25
Gnosticism, 30, 86, 115 n. 39, 144
Goffman, Irving, 114 n. 30
Goldhill, Simon, 113 n. 26, 114 n. 30
Gordon, Richard, 168
Gorgias of Leontini, 100 f., 110 n. 9, 111 n. 11, 111 n. 14, 111 n. 17, 112 n. 23
  quasi-scientific, 101, 111 n. 14
Gospel
  of John, 64
  of Luke, vii, 59, 61, 62, 64, 171, 185
    as feminist gospel, 142
  of Mark, 42, 43, 59 f., 183
    canonical, 61, 65–6, 67–8
    as mythistory, 42
    as Pauline ἀναγραφή, 66
    origins in Peter, 65
    secret, 62–63, 70 n. 8, 70 n. 9, 70 n. 11
  of Matthew, 62, 64, 129, 142
  Q (Sayings), 44, 54, 61, 63–64, 76, 185
    formation of, 79 f.
    literary history, 90 n. 11
    source among itinerant radicals, 83
  of Thomas, 44, 54, 62, 64, 70 n. 16, 86, 91 n. 22, 93 n. 40, 107, 108, 115 n. 37, 115 n. 38, 115 n. 39, 142, 143, 185
  two source theory, 65
Gramsci, Antonio, 136 n. 25, 157 n. 4, 157 n. 5
Gregory of Nazianzus, 144
Gregory of Nyssa, 144
Griggs, Wilfred, 70 n. 14
Grignon, Claude, 167, 170, 171, 172 n. 12
Guide to the Study of Religion, 5 f., 30
  totalizing desire, 30

Habermas, Jurgen, 114 n. 31
habitus, 146
Hagevi, Magnus, 51
hagiography, 149, 156
Hanson, Norwood R., 9
Harris, Marvin, 5, 29
hauntology, 5
Hegel, G. W. F, 26, 69, 186 n. 1
hegemony; see also ideology, power
    of andreia (manliness), 121, 155
    of androcentrism, 153 f., 153
    defined, 157 n. 4
    of empire, 121, 133
    vs. ideology, 136 n. 25, 158 n. 7
    of patriarchy, 141, 145
    transgressed, 136 n. 25
    as universal lexicon and grammar, 157 n. 4
Helen of Sparta/Troy, 100, 102, 104, 111 n. 14
hermeneutics, see interpretation
    hermeneutic of suspicion, 141
Herodotus, 42, 123
Hesk, John, 113 n. 25
Hester, David, 129, 135 n. 18, 136 n. 24
Hestia (Vesta), 122 124; see also Vestal Virgins
hierarchy, 92 n. 32, 129
    gendered, 169, 143, 150
    master/slave, 173 n. 22
history
    amnesia in historical production, 49
    compared to heroin, 45–46
    je me souviens, 46
    made in hindsight, 46
    moments of loss in historical production, 47–49
    as raw material for nationalism, 45
    as self-serving rhetoric, 153
    strategic tinkering with the past, 82
Hobsbawm, Eric, 45–46, 82, 91 n. 18, 92 n. 25
hubris, 29, 30, 103, 104
human nature, 128, 182, 183
    as projective, 181
human sciences, 5, 26, 115 n. 32
Hume, David, 12, 69

I Ching, 115 n. 36
ideal type, 166, 167, 172 n. 7
    distinguished from actual, 172 n. 8

idealism, 28
    as effects of practices, 28
    hyper-idealism, 28
identity, vii
    collective, 165
ideogram, 145, 152
ideology; see also hegemony, power
    formation, 46
Inanna, 127
incongruity, 61, 67
indigeneity, 29, 33
intellectuals, 83, 84, 86, 105, 113 n. 25
    as strategic, 90 n. 7
    as ritual, 108, 115 n. 37
    role in social formation, 78
interpretation, xi, 18, 43, 108
    as preservationist, xi
    as ritual, 115 n. 37
    theological motives, 109 n. 3
interpolation, 158 n. 7
invention, 81
    of tradition, 82; see also mythmaking
Irenaeus, 65
Ishtar, 137

Jagger, Mick, 51
Jameson, Frederic, 33
Jefferson, Thomas, 50, 53
Jerome, 144, 149
Jesus
    American fascination with, 50, 51, 54
    as apocalyptic visionary, 53
    as bastard messiah. 53
    Christ hymn, 42
    Christology, 42, 43
    as cynic, 53, 84
    of discourse, 55
    family, 67, 71 n. 29
    Galilean, 43
    groups, 44
    as hero of Mark, 43
    historical,
        does not matter, 55
        excess of, 41
        as substitute myth of origins, 55
        turned to dust, 55
    as Jewish stand-up comic 53
    lives of, 42
    of Mark, 63

194 • *Jesus and Addiction to Origins*

    Pauline Christ, 108
    as peasant, 53
    as moral philosopher, 44, 54
    production of, 49
    as sage, 50, 53, 54
    sayings, 107
    as shaman/healer, 108
    as shepherd, 44
    as social gadfly, 53
    as source of Q, 83
    as wonder-worker, 44
    WWJD, 51
Jesus Nation, 51
Jesus School, 61
Jesus Seminar, 52 f.
    voting rules, 52–53
John of Chrysostom, 144
John the Baptist, 81
Journal for the Study of the Historical Jesus, 52
Joyce, Janet, xii
Judge, E. A., 78, 90 n. 8
Jung, Carl G., 12

Kant, Immanuel, 100, 110 n. 7
Kaster, Robert A, 84, 92 n. 31, 92 n. 32, 92 n. 33
Kautsky, Karl, 78
King, Karen, 52
kinship, 147, 168
Klinghardt, Matthias, 166, 167, 171, 172 n. 5, 172 n. 7
Kloppenborg, John, 52, 79, 80, 82, 83, 91 n. 14, 92 n. 30, 93 n. 39, 93 n. 40

La Barre, Weston, 11
Lawson, Sierra, xii
Laqueur, Thomas, 131, 149
Leuba, James, 4
Lévi-Strauss, Claude, 103, 112 n. 18
Lieu, Judith, 143
Lightstone, Jack, 87–89, 93 n. 41
liminality, 93 n. 40
    of eunuchs, 130, 132, 135 n. 17
    of Vestal Virgins, 127
Lincoln, Bruce, xi, 10, 11, 69, 82, 87, 91 n. 20, 103, 112 n. 21, 157 n. 4, 173 n. 13, 178 n. 5
    sentiments (of affinity and estrangement), 68, 89, 93 n. 42, 103, 104, 112 n. 21

    as sociogravitational forces, 112 n. 22
Lowie, Robert H., 172 n. 8
Lucius Apuleius, 128
    Monty Pythonesque excesses, 128
Lycinus, 128

MacDonald, Dennis, 143, 152
Mack, Burton, 42, 59, 64, 77, 87, 90 n. 13, 91 n. 18, 91 n. 25
mythmaking and social formation, 89 n. 1
magic
    contagious, 101
    Greek Magical Papyri, 86, 93 n. 35, 115 n. 38
    vs. miracles, 31
Malina, Bruce, 93 n. 40
Marcus, Joel, 66, 67, 71 n. 27, 71 n. 29
Martin, Luther H., 106, 115 n. 34
Martyr, Justin, 65
martyrdom, 145; see also gender
    martyrologies, 147, 156
Marx, Karl, 12, 48, 158 n. 6, 181, 182, 183, 187 n. 3, 187 n. 4
Masuzawa, Tomoko, 18, 21 n. 2, 22 n. 7, 46, 69, 184
Mauss, Marcel, 151
McCutcheon, Russell T., xii
McNeil, William H., 42
Meaning, 34
Meeks, Wayne, 143
Melania the Elder, 144
Mellencamp, John, 4
method, 30
Method & Theory in the Study of Religion, vii
metis (cunning intelligence), 86, 92 n. 29, 93 n. 37
metonymy, 121, 132, 133
Meyer, Marvin, 52
Mishnah, 88, 93 n. 41
Mithraism, 105, 106, 113 n. 28
Momigliano, Arnaldo, 60
monasticism, 144, 145; see also celibacy
    female tonsure, 149
morality, 14
Morrison, Toni, 35
moulding, 111 n. 13
Müller, F. Max, 69, 181
Murphy, Tim, 36
Muses, 111 n. 14

myth
    Christian, 59
    Ifa, 115 n. 36
    mythmaking, 43, 67, 68, 76, 78, 83, 87, 92 n. 26, 121; see also social formation
    as rationalization, 67
    as socio-mythic activity/invention, 76, 89 n. 1
    of origins, 59
    prototypes, 123
Myth of Innocence, A, 59–60

nationalism, 46, 68
naturalization, 168
Nietzsche, Friedrich, 48
Nijf, Onno von, 168, 173 n. 20
Noble, David, 141, 153
Nock, Arthur Darby, 127, 129, 135 n. 20
North American Association for the Study of Religion (NAASR), viii, xii

obscurantism, 5
ontology, 5
Origen, 65
origins, 14, 33, 41, 55, 59, 67, 68, 69, 78
    vs. beginnings, 72 n. 32, 184
    discredited category, 127, 187 n. 7
    golden age, 141
    as imagined, 185
Orye, Lieve, 22 n. 8
Otto, Rudolf, 4, 8, 19

Paden, William E. 70 n. 22
Palladius, 144
Pandora, 26, 27, 34
Parker, Holt, 127
Passover, 166
Patristic period, 65
patron-client relations, 54
Paul, 42, 55, 63, 67, 68, 71 n. 27, 71 n. 29, 71 n. 30, 91 n. 22, 113 n. 25, 143, 145, 146, 148, 181
    and the Christian myth, 59
    Christology, 42, 43, 66, 108
    on gender unification, 143, 156 n. 2
    letters of, 165
    post-Pauline Christianity, 92 n. 26, 143
    pre-Pauline creed, 42
Penner, Hans, 27, 123

performance, 11, 49, 50, 98, 103, 106, 113 n. 25, 113 n. 26, 114 n. 30, 114 n. 31, 114 n. 32, 165
    improvisation, 105
    meals as, 165, 167
persuasion, 14, 101–103
    patterns of, 99
phenomenology of religion, 29
Plato, 106, 111 n. 11, 123, 157 n. 3
pluralism, 31, 34, 36
Plutarch, 125, 126, 134 n. 9, 168
poetry, 4, 101
Polemo of Valens, 147, 150–151, 153, 154
Pope, Alexander, 27
positionality, 105, 106
positivism, 47, 109, 185
post-colonialism, 29
postmodernism, 18, 33, 34
power, 14, 31, 35, 48, 49, 81, 82, 85, 91 n. 20, 93 n. 39, 101–105, 111 n. 14, 111 n. 16, 112 n. 20, 114 n. 28, 114 n. 29, 125, 129, 131, 134 n. 11, 151, 153, 155, 156; see also agency, hegemony, ideology, hegemony
    agentive and non-agentive (structural), 158 n. 7
    as productive network, 121
presuppositions, 31, 32
Priestly, Joseph, 50
Printing press
    and scribal discourse, 110 n. 6
    spreading religion, 110 n. 7
Prowse, K. R., 134 n. 11
purity, see also origin, discredited category
    and chastity, 129
    Christian traditions of, 174 n. 29
    in Greek religion, 135 n. 20
    methodological, 22
    ritual, 129, 132
Pygmalion, 133 n. 1
Pythagoreans, 86, 123
Pythia, 122, 133 n. 5

Quntilian, 98

Rabbinism, 88–9
    redescription of, 89
rationalization, 6, 67, 100, 103, 172 n. 8
reason
    exercise of, 100

logographic/logo-textured, 99, 101, 102
public use, 110 n. 7
textualized, 99
universal, 33
rectification 12, 32, 68
redescription, 31, 48, 59, 77, 79, 86, 89, 108, 109
of ancient banquets, 166; see also food
reductionism, 22 n. 6, 31
reification, 49, 77, 181 f.
Reimarus, Hermann Samuel, 43
religion
and the problem of excess, 4
as caretaking, 22 n. 9
colonial frontier, 7
as concept, 6 f.
as culturally induced mental representation, 4
as Experience-near category, 3–4
as floating or empty signifier, 4, 8
as human performance, xi, 17, 19, 182
as kind of human talk, 10
as marker of difference, 8
as modern political category, 21 n. 4
and self-consciousness, 182
as specter, 3
vs superstition, 7
Religionswissenschaft, 6, 12, 31, 33
vs. Glaubenslehre, 7
Religious Studies
anthropological beginnings, 12
as bewildering jungle, 5
as comparative religion, 7
as humanistic, 17
as social scientific, 17
classes in, 20, 21
disciplinarity of, 13, 21 n. 2
irony of, 17 f.
vs. theology, 17 f.
defined by its theological content, 17 f.
representation, 12, 34, 50, 78, 87, 92 n. 32, 158 n. 7
self-representation, 33, 78
Reuther, Rosemary Radford, 152
rhetoric, xi, 35; see also criticism, rhetorical
adversarial, 60
ambiguated, 100, 105

of anti-rhetoric, 113 n. 25
art of, 98
apocalyptic, 86
biblical, 104
of dissent, 82
and fictive narrative, 47
ideological, 103
liberationist, 141, 156
of marginality, 86
metonymic, 101
as mobilizing, 78
as performance, 113 n. 30
as product of ideas, 100
religious, 98
restricted, 113 n. 27
rhetoricality, 105, 106, 113 n. 28, 114 n. 32
rhetorolect, 106
technicalization of, 100
theorized, 105
Riggs, John, 169, 170
ritual, xi, 19, 45, 82, 85, 87, 93 n. 35, 108, 115 n. 37, 115 n. 39, 123, 126, 127, 129, 134 n. 11, 134 n. 12, 135 n. 22, 168
as performance, 165
rites of passage, 126
theory, 32
speech, 101, 111 n. 16
specialists, 136 n. 26
Robbins, Vernon, 52, 106, 109 n. 3, 142
Robinson, James M. 52, 80
Rowlandson, Mary, 69 n. 6

Sabean, David Warren, 113 n. 28
sacred, as super-value, 34
Sahlins, Marshall, 68
Said, Edward, 72 n. 32
salvation
becoming male, 143
Schiappa, Edward, 100, 112 n. 19
schools, ancient 77 f., 89 n. 4, 99; see also associations
analogies, 85
defined, 77
displaced, 90 n. 8
Schüssler Fiorenza, Elizabeth, 141
Schweitzer, Albert, 42, 52
self; see also agency
self-authorization, 11

autonomous, 155
body/self, 151
gendered, 147, 151, 152
individualism, 86
knowledge, 182
laceration, 148
modern assertion, 32
mutilation, 129
myth of, 100
obscuration, 174
ontic selfhood, 10
and other/not-self, 186 n. 1
presentation, 183
realization, 186 n. 1
social precondition, 158 n. 6
transformation of, 148
Sellars, Wilfred, 35
Sheldon, Charles, 51
Sherwood, Yvonne, xi
Simon, Paul, 4
simulacrum, 48
Sissa, Giulia, 123, 133 n. 5
Smith, Dennis, 166, 171, 172, 172 n. 6
Smith, Wilfred Cantwell, 5, 71 n. 31
Smith, Jonathan Z., viii, ix, 4, 9, 21, 22 n. 4, 26, 30, 31 f., 36, 61, 68, 70 n. 11, 71 n. 31, 86, 92 n. 31, 93 n. 35, 106, 115 n. 34, 115 n. 37
    exaggeration in the direction of truth, 145
    riding hell-bent for leather, 32
    there is no data for religion, 9, 21
Smith, W. Robertson, 12
Snyder, Graydon, 44, 106
social formation, 46, 60, 64, 76, 77, 78, 85, 87, 88, 89, 89 n. 1, 90 n. 13, 91 n. 25, 104, 112 n. 20, 112 n. 21, 112 n. 22, 165 f., 174 n. 31; see also mythmaking
    emergent, 91 n. 25
    exploit ambiguity of inherited forms, 167
    as experimentation, 67
    group-making, 67, 173 n. 13
    organized power networks, 81
    role of intellectuals, 78
social sciences, 5, 6, 30, 32, 36
Society of Biblical Literature (SBL), xi
Staples, Ariadne, 126, 134 n. 8

status
    Greco-Roman women's, 145
    egalitarianism, 141, 169
    ritual status, 134 n. 10
    social, 83, 84, 89, 91 n. 17, 113 n. 26, 114 n. 30, 126, 168
    status quo, 111 n. 15
    subtle distinctions in, 173 n. 20
    of undisputed facts, 65
Stoddard, Brad, xii
Stoics, 111 n. 11, 123, 149
Stowers, Stan, 28, 69 n. 7
Streisand, Barbra, 148
structuration, 12, 90 n. 7, 92 n. 26, 165

tarot, 115 n. 36
Tertullian, 65, 144
textual practice
    defined, 109 n. 4
Thecla, 145 f., 153 f.
    alternate personhood, 152
    body as locus of conversion, 148
    as example of women's liberation, 152
    as hero (unwomanish heroism), 152–153, 156
    liberationist readings as structural symptom of gender ideology, 153
    premarital, virgin status, 146
    as role model, 152
Theissen, Gerd, 92 n. 29
theology
    determinism, 106
theory, vii, 30
    cognitive science, 33
    exchange, 32
    monomaniacal, 31 f.
    rational choice, 32
    of religion, 29, 36
    ritual, 32
    social, 13, 79, 103, 109 n. 3
Thessalos of Tralle, 86, 93 n. 36
Thompson, E. P., 76, 87, 112 n. 22
Torah, 66, 88, 93 n. 39
tradition, 82, 91 n. 18
transcendence, claims of, 18
translation, 31, 184, 187 n. 2
Trouilloit, Michel-Rolph, 47, 87, 92 n. 28
Turner, Victor, 93 n. 40

Tylor, E. B., 12, 181
Tyson, Joseph, 67

unique, 33

Vaage, Leif, 83, 92 n. 29
Valentinian, 134 n. 6
    Christianity, 115 n. 39
Valerius Maximus, 133 n. 2
Vernant, Jean-Pierre, 92 n. 29, 93 n. 37, 122
Vestal Virgins, 121–122, 124–127, 133, 133 n. 2, 134 n. 8, 134 n. 10, 134 n. 11
    as ambiguous figures, 126
    cult of Vesta, 134 n. 6
    eligibility, 134 n. 8
    freed of men, 127
    genealogy of, 124
    live burial for transgressions, 134 n. 11
    representational value, 127
    as totem of Roman, 127
    Temple of Vesta, 125, 126, 134 n. 11
Veyne, Paul, 46
virginity; see also celibacy
    ambiguous, 133 n. 5
    virgin birth, 133
    virgin of God, 145

Volkmar, Gustav, 66
Vorster, Johannes, 152

Weber, Max, 12, 91 n. 25
Wellbery, David, 105
Whaling, Frank, 5
Whitehouse, Harvey, 100, 106, 107, 115 n. 37
    doctrinal mode, 98, 102, 106, 107, 108, 109
    imagistic mode, 102, 107, 108, 115 n. 37
Wiebe, Donald, 21, 22 n. 3, 22 n. 8, 23 n. 14
Wilken, Robert, 22 n. 9
Williams, Raymond, 103
wisdom genres, 63
    myth of Wisdom, 82
Wissenschaft, 11
Wolf, Eric R., 103, 112 n. 20, 125, 167
    mentifacts, 112 n. 20
Wolfart, Johannes C., 33, 114 n. 28
words
    data-loaded vs. theory-loaded, 9
world
    as represented vs. as lived, 155
world religions, discourse on, 18
Wrede, William, 42
Wright, Eric Olin, 9, 89 n. 2

www.ingramcontent.com/pod-product-compliance
Lightning Source LLC
Chambersburg PA
CBHW062028220426
43662CB00010B/1518